D1738052

A Hard Country and a Lonely Place

The Fred W. Morrison
Series in Southern Studies

The University of
North Carolina Press

Chapel Hill and London

A Hard Country and a Lonely Place

William A. Link

Schooling, Society,
and Reform in Rural
Virginia, 1870–1920

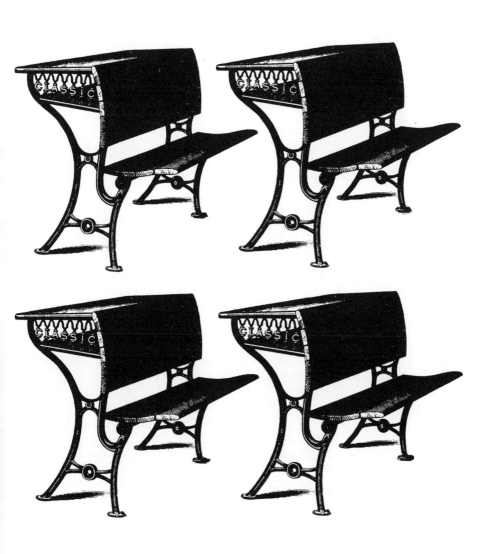

Manufactured in the United States of America

Library of Congress Cataloging-in-Publication Data

Link, William A.

A hard country and a lonely place.

(The Fred W. Morrison series in Southern studies)
Includes index.

1. Rural schools—Virginia—History—19th century.
2. Virginia—Rural conditions. 3. Community and school
—Virginia—History—19th century. 4. Education, Rural
—Virginia—History—19th century. 5. Rural schools—
Virginia—History—20th century. 6. Community and
school—Virginia—History—20th century. 7. Education,
Rural—Virginia—History—20th century. I. Title.
II. Series.

LB1567.L56   1986   370.19'346'09755   86-1412
ISBN 0-8078-1706-6

To Susannah

Contents

Illustrations

Preface

Few of the changes during the past century are more readily apparent or carry such profound consequences as the transformation of rural America. In the past two decades, our understanding of this transformation has been vastly enriched by studies from the perspective of urbanization—that is, from the point of view of the "victor" in this historical process, the American city. In contrast, the social environment of the losers—the sprawling and loosely organized world of pre-World War I rural America—has been, for the most part, forgotten. There are at least two reasons for this neglect. First, geographical diversity makes study of the rural world an imposing subject, full of obstacles to understanding collective pasts; decentralization and regional distinctions make the rural experience considerably more difficult to understand than the urban experience. Second, the sources of rural history, unlike those of urban history, are scattered, largely oral and unwritten, often unpreserved and lost in the oblivion of the past.

My main purpose in this book is to understand the rural past through a study of its schools. Across rural America, schools were a clear window on their social surroundings. Although the quality and extent of mass education in the United States differed by region, nineteenth-century country schools—unlike urban schools—were dominated by local communities. Thus, in the way that they organized their educational systems, rural Americans revealed how they reached decisions, experienced and regarded their surroundings, and valued work, life, and leisure. It should come as little surprise that the characteristics of rural education differed fundamentally from the urban model that dominates our own, late twentieth-century conception of schooling. Nor should it be surprising that the schools of rural America—and the communities that created them—eventually would confront irresistible forces to conform and alter this locally controlled, nonbureaucratic mode of education.

The rural communities of Virginia in the late nineteenth and early twentieth centuries in some respects adhered to, and in others differed from, national trends. But their schools were distinctly southern in at least three respects. Late nineteenth-century rural Virginians lived with the legacy of the Civil War; Reconstruction decisively affected the form and organization of mass education in all of the former Confederate states after 1870. Regional underdevelopment and poverty, another hallmark of the South's historical experience, affected the ability of communities to sustain schools and meant that the South remained the least educated region of any in the United States. Finally, unlike other Americans, the attitudes of Virginians toward education—in a variety of ways —were shaped by race and, in particular, the dilemma of racial coexistence in the postemancipation South.

If in organizing schools Virginians were southern, they were also representative of rural America. As an overarching theme of the development of rural education—and as a curiously unifying national characteristic—I have stressed the role of localism, by which I mean identification with local communities—usually defined by geographical proximity and reinforced by ties of wealth, kin, church, and race—as the primary mode of social organization in the decentralized world of nineteenth-century rural America. At different times, localism and the power of the community declined because of impersonal or personal change; in the process schools were transformed from community-dominated institutions to ones strongly influenced, even controlled, by outsiders. Yet in rural Virginia and elsewhere, there was little that was inevitable about this transformation. Even despite the eventual victory of centralizing reformers—who viewed education from a distinctly alien perspective— localism and the ability of black and white communities to control their schools continued to shape the character of rural public education.

In the research, conceptualization, writing, and rewriting of this book, I have received the help of scholars, teachers, friends, and family. From the earliest discussions about the importance of, and our general ignorance about, American country schools to later urgings to rethink, recast, and reconceptualize, I have always profited from the keen editorial skills and crisp, dispassionate thinking of William H. Harbaugh, who first supervised this study as a dissertation and then, in its transformation into a book, contributed a combination of criticism, counsel, and friendship. Joseph F. Kett provided two critical readings of this manuscript. Each one helped me to improve, clarify, and strive toward making the obscure significant. Louis R. Harlan also read the manuscript twice and made suggestions that have substantially improved its clarity and elegance. Other scholars and colleagues have helped, including Edward L. Ayers, Robert M. Calhoon, John T. Kneebone, Ann P. Saab, Karl A. Schleunes, and Jennings Wagoner. Several students at the University of North Carolina at Greensboro, Jo Gainey, Douglas S. John, Gary Parks, and Philip A. Walker, Jr., contributed invaluable assistance. The patience and wise counsel of the director of the University of North Carolina Press, Matthew Hodgson, and of editors Lewis Bateman, Gwen Duffey, and Trudie Calvert were indispensable.

I am also indebted to those archivists and librarians, past and present, who preserved the record of the Virginia rural school and made it accessible. The following persons helped to guide me toward archival sources: Edmund Berkeley, Jr., Jerrold Brooks, Cynthia Chapman, Margaret Cook, Lucious Edwards, J. William Hess, Fritz Malval, Emilie Mills, Michael Plunkett, James Rogerson, and Thomas Rosenbaum. A travel grant from the Rockefeller Archive Center, North Tarrytown, New York, made possible a trip to that superb collection in the summer of 1980. Marianna L. Durst of the records center of the Prince William County, Virginia School Board, guided me through a particularly rich trove of materials and went to extraordinary lengths to make them available. Similarly helpful on short notice were Glenn McMullen and the staff of the Special Collections Department, Virginia Polytechnic and State University, Blacksburg, Virginia.

The institutional and personal support of the University of North Carolina at Greensboro was also very helpful. I am grateful for the collegial atmosphere and support of the History Department, particularly its heads, Ann P. Saab and Allen W. Trelease. A University Summer Excellence Grant, along with subsequent support from the University Research Council, sponsored needed travel and additional time to write. Tim Barkley and Mary C. Cooper helped to reproduce and identify many of the illustrations. I must also thank the University Academic Computer Center, whose excellent staff shepherded me through the mysteries and changing technologies of mainframe computing. Particularly helpful was Marlene Pratto, who endured countless conversations but patiently explained, or solved, a variety of problems.

I am finally in the debt of my family, who provided support at all times, sympathy at others, and prodding at still others. My parents, Margaret Douglas Link and Arthur S. Link, read the manuscript and suggested numerous stylistic and substantive improvements. Percy allowed me in cramped quarters to share work space with nursery space and, on frequent occasions, added the fresh perspective of a toddler; Maggie, at a late stage, added the zest of new life. Susannah H. Jones turned her incomparable editorial eye toward the manuscript several times, caught numerous flaws and infelicities, and, on more than one occasion, supplied a bracing critique of individual chapters of a kind that can be given and received only inside the state of matrimony. Her support and good humor about rural schools and about everything else, and her love for a distracted spouse, motivated the completion of this book.

Part One
Localism and the Rural School

Chapter One
The Local World of Public Education

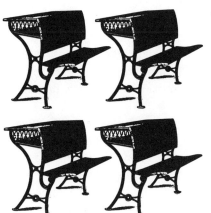

For most Americans in the generation after the Civil War, formal education began and ended in schools established and sustained by local communities. Even urban centers that pioneered in educational expansion and organization operated in a decentralized educational polity. Rural Americans were schooled in defiance of outside attempts to control public education or to incorporate it into a centralized hierarchy. The strength of localism carries important implications for the origins and subsequent development of American public education. It means that, in seeking to comprehend the historical experience of schooling, we must look beyond well-traversed topics such as common school reform and the building of state educational systems. Rather, we must understand the local world of public education and discover how the great majority of Americans outside of cities organized their schools and experienced learning.

Localism and the Rise of Public Education

A consistent organizational and developmental pattern—the dominance of localism—distinguished the rise of mass education in the United States, cutting across regional boundaries and making American schooling unique in the Western world. In contrast, education in western Europe was a direct extension of the state and served announced social and political objectives. After the Napoleonic Wars, Prussian leaders began mass education to create the common bonds of German nationality. French state-directed schools, established later in the nineteenth century, were designed to draw diverse language and regional groups together into an integrated nationality and to inculcate students with secular, republican values. From the early nineteenth century onward, European educators considered centralized control necessary for the achievement of these objectives. For Europeans, whose experience with schooling was rooted in the power of private and church education and whose traditions of law, governance, and administration ran from top to bottom, state control went hand in hand with secular, publicly financed schools.[1]

In the United States, public education not only depended on the pleasure of the local community but derived its expansive power from the grass roots. Despite scattered and ineffectual efforts to establish a national educational policy, American schools developed from below and most commonly were established with only minimal involvement by state governments. Whereas centralization and a rationalized system characterized the European pattern of mass education, schools in the United States were founded and then survived only because of local favor, largesse, participation, and approval.

Localism meant that the spread of American public education was unique in the Western world. In the half century after 1790, urban communities consciously broke with a tradition of private and denominational control over education and established the first "common" schools based on community participation, tax support, the partial elimination of tuition and fees, and the end of any overt church involvement.[2] Subsequently, following the model of Prussian administration and organization, these urban schools first began to build an articulated bureaucratic administrative structure in the middle of the nineteenth century. Out of these early attempts came further leadership and support for strong central control at the state level.[3]

Nineteenth-century school reform brought tangible results. Urged on by such educators as James G. Carter and Horace Mann of Massachusetts, Calvin Stowe of Ohio, and John Pierce of Michigan, by the 1880s all of the nation's state legislatures required the establishment of district schools, allowed local tax support, and created a core of state and local school officials.[4] These legislative accomplishments prompted early historians of education—and even recent scholars—to focus on state administrative structures and reform campaigns. These accomplishments have also led historians of American education to concentrate attention on nineteenth-century urban school systems in the search for the roots of modern public education.[5]

Such an emphasis, however, misses the dynamic quality of the relentless expansion of American schools. In a misplaced focus, this view regards reform, system building, and educational expansion as sequential, related phenomena in which schools came into existence and enrollments rose after the establishment of state common schools. Actually, scholars have demonstrated that the reverse was frequently the case. Especially in the antebellum North, a surge of enrollments preceded, rather than followed, the establishment of state control. And although outwardly confident, advocates of centralized education never completely succeeded except in towns and cities. Elsewhere, they faced potent and widespread political opposition to innovation. Reformers encountered bitter resistance even in New England and the Middle West, where opponents of school centralization united around an ideology of localism. Nor were these sentiments unique; hostility to centralized public and private institutions was a steady current running throughout nineteenth-century American public affairs without regard to region.

Opponents of school centralization rallied popular opposition around two issues: cultural policy and the extent of public tax support. In states with a mixture of ethnic and language groups, cultural conflict translated into Protestant-Catholic conflict, and it underlay the degree of support for or opposition to centralization. Although nondenominational and under secular public control, common schools were dominated by native Protestants and taught their values; state power over schools also meant Protestant control. A diverse ethnic mixture in the Upper Mississippi Valley created problems for reformers, as German and Irish Catholics opposed Protestant-oriented schools, and other foreign-language groups, such as the Scandinavians, resisted instruction in English. Elsewhere in the North, centralization became mired in the quicksand of cultural politics.

Although crucial to the reform program, public tax support for schools ran against a long tradition of private control over educational purse strings. It suggested an opening wedge toward complete state dominance and posed the possibility of future tax increases. Nowhere, therefore, did reformers easily establish tax support for public education. In some states, as in Pennsylvania and Connecticut before the 1850s, reformers managed only to persuade legislatures to enact local-option taxation; elsewhere, their attempts to establish regular state financing encountered local opposition and the hostility of ethnic minorities who feared the absorption of their schools. Not until well after the Civil War did state school systems in the Northeast and Middle West finally settle this troublesome question.[6]

The clear defeat of these mid-nineteenth-century attempts to centralize educational administration meant that most public schools developed without central control. State superintendents and their small staffs typically provided support and guidance but were not able to coerce. On the national level, the United States commissioner of education enjoyed broad prestige and influence and articulated a vision of a nationalized system of schools, but he also searched vainly for ways to influence a community-based system of education. Local communities did not always oppose central direction and often received a limited amount of state money. But the fundamental reality was that governmental control could expand only after a compromise was reached between the objectives of the centralizers and the desires of local communities. This compromise meant a limited toleration of cultural diversity in Catholic and foreign-language schools, an issue reformers deferred until the 1880s. It also meant that most state officials awarded local boards of education and parents wide latitude in the day-to-day operation of schools.

Local power over education was most apparent in rural schools, which, between the mid-nineteenth century and World War I, flourished in isolation from their urban counterparts. Rural enrollments were frequently higher than urban enrollments, but rural attendance was not only usually lower but also erratic, irregular, and more attuned to the fluctuations of the seasons and to the demand for child labor than to the needs of the school. Because school districts were usually poor, they typically provided makeshift facilities and paid low salaries to teachers. Urban students, on the average, spent considerably more time in school; in 1910, for example, urban students attended their schools about 28 percent longer than did their rural counterparts and were about three times more likely to be literate than were rural Americans.[7]

Permanent facilities, regimented and standardized curricula, and, above all, centralized administrative control—all typical characteristics of urban schools—were rarely present in rural schools. Instead, these schools were closely integrated into their environment. They existed only at local pleasure: parents, rather than school officials, made important decisions about school affairs; and education consumed only as much time of the rural young as the community wanted or could afford. In all aspects of the educational experience, control over education emanated from below.[8]

The Rural South and the Tradition of Localism

Nowhere was the strength of localism more evident than in the rural South, where its effects were mixed. One measure, rural enrollments, suggests that community enthusiasm and support in the South compared favorably with that of the rest of the nation. Yet localism combined with grinding poverty to make southerners the most undereducated people in the country. By every measure of educational quality, southern rural schools suffered in national comparisons. In per capita tax support for rural schools, South Atlantic states in 1910 spent on the average only a third as much as did North Atlantic states; in another crucial area, length of school term, the disparity was about three-quarters.

Southern rural schools offered an enlarged portrait of many of the deep defects of the American rural school experience. Neither better nor worse than the society surrounding them, they were the product of an array of factors, the most influential of which were economic. In 1900, the rural South was clearly the nation's poorest region. In that year, the value of South Atlantic farms was the lowest in the United States, about 44 percent below those in the North Atlantic states and 36 percent below those in the North Central region. Inevitably, rural poverty affected the quality of schools. With a low level of tax support, rural southern schools were characterized by the most ill-equipped facilities, the lowest teachers' salaries, and the shortest terms in the nation.[9]

Yet the forces responsible for undereducation were rooted just as much in attitudes toward learning, which were products of past political and social experiences. In the early nineteenth century, rather than joining in the national rush to build and support public schools, white southerners developed a common hostility toward mass education. A native generation of centralizing reformers, among whom Henry Ruffner of Virginia and Calvin Wiley of North Carolina are the best known, were frustrated by strong traditions of community control combined with vigorous political and ideological hostility toward governmental intrusion. Southerners, as well as easterners and midwesterners, equated state-directed common schools with higher taxes. And in a region that more than any other valued individualism, familial identity, and personal honor among white males, hostility toward public control of youth socialization was a virtual certainty. In the antebellum southern belief system, education remained a matter of private choice and an area in which central, outside government had no place.[10]

The region's evolving class and racial relationships gave these social and political factors added urgency. Just as schools were at the center of ethnic and religious differences in the immigrant society of the North, education touched a raw nerve in the slave society of the South. Especially during the thirty years before secession, southern fears of slave rebellion and abolitionism translated into a growing, general indictment of slave literacy and the free expression of ideas which public education appeared to encourage. Based on inequality, slave society bred a paternalism that proscribed black education and an elitism that discouraged the schooling of lower-class whites. Common schools, observed one antebellum southerner who opposed them, unnecessarily raised expectations because even a rudimentary education for a "plain farmer, or mechanic . . . [was] of no manner of use."[11]

Consequently, advocates of publicly run schools enjoyed little political support before 1860, and the region retained a half-private, half-public collection of neighborhood and denominational schools.[12] Nonetheless, the Civil War and Reconstruction stimulated experimentation and innovation in educational policy, in which two groups outside the mainstream of antebellum life—blacks and northern evangelicals—initiated changes culminating in the establishment of a common school system. To both groups, the elevation of schools was crucial. Because antebellum prohibitions against slave literacy and education represented, as Frederick Douglass wrote, the "white man's power to enslave the black man," freedmen across the South crowded into whatever school facilities were made available.[13] Their allies, southern Republicans and northern evangelicals, believed that black education and literacy and ultimately a northern-style common school system would guarantee black rights, challenge elitism, and promote the reintegration of the South into the nation. Together, these two groups sponsored and maintained schools operated by northern missionary organizations and the Freedmen's Bureau.[14]

The spread of private and public efforts to educate freedmen soon mushroomed into a regionwide effort to include public education as part of the new state constitutions of the Reconstruction era. Congressional pressure and the influence of southern white Republicans and black leaders in state constitutional conventions virtually guaranteed that universal education would become a prerequisite to readmission to the Union. The act readmitting Virginia in 1869, for instance, stipulated that its constitution "shall never be so amended or changed as to deprive any citizen or class of citizens of the United States" of their "school rights and privileges."[15] Although these constitutional safeguards, along with subsequent enabling legislation, strengthened public schools in some states, in others, Republican advocacy of schools caused bitter partisan conflict, and the schools became symbols of northern interference. Where partisan conflict was most intense, the anti-Reconstruction Conservative coalition, once in power, reduced both revenues and the number of school officials.[16]

Although Reconstruction clearly did not bring common schools along the lines envisioned by their earliest northern and southern advocates, undeniable discontinuities existed between antebellum and postbellum education. In a wrenching break with past tradition, white southerners after 1880 accepted a limited responsibility to educate blacks. New state systems absorbed the northern-run black schools in towns and cities; at the same time, whites tolerated a small but significant growth in black rural schools. In a departure from antebellum practice, state subsidies for nonpublic education ended, and private and denominational schools never recovered their prewar status. Two essentials of common school education became part of southern schooling: direct tax support and a small educational bureaucracy.

Post-Reconstruction southern schools followed national patterns of growth and development. Better-equipped facilities and higher pay for teachers were the rule in the urban South, where educators also began to identify with the national "one best system." In New South cities and boom towns, school officials built high schools, established an age-graded system, and systematized curricula and instruction. The experience of Richmond, Virginia, was typical. In 1860 it boasted a system of charity-school education; during and after Reconstruction—an era of restricted state financing—the city inaugurated an ambitious school expansion program made possible by generous local tax support.

Drawing upon a national urban model of educational expansion, within a generation Richmond school officials introduced a common curriculum, established regular teacher supervision, and imposed a system of pupil classification and promotion. Bureaucratic control brought rapid growth in facilities. Between 1870, the first year of the state system, and 1900, the number of schools in Richmond increased by 259 percent, attendance by 235 percent, and the value of school property by 533 percent.[17]

The story of Richmond, typical of the expanding southern urban school systems, contrasted with the experience in rural areas. In both enrollments and number of schools, southern rural education expanded rapidly following Reconstruction, but in a very different way than in towns and cities. Urban schools possessed ample local financial support; rural schools were impoverished and usually impermanent entities. Urban bureaucrats gained more control over school administration; rural schools were noncompulsory and functioned without state intervention. In urban schools, power and decision making flowed from top to bottom; in rural schools parents participated in, and often dominated, school governance.

The decentralized growth of common schools in the post-Reconstruction rural South requires a special understanding of primarily local institutions, rooted in local society. Most Americans lived in the countryside, in villages and on farms, and it was there that they organized schools and educated their children. It is possible to generalize about this experience from the very different scenes of American rural life. But in the local world of public education, the lens of historical inquiry finds clearer focus in the locale of a single state, at once both unique and representative of a region and the nation.

A Rural Setting: Post-Reconstruction Virginia

Virginia, the oldest state in the Union and the seat of the Confederacy, possessed the social and political characteristics of a rural southern state. Despite the impact of the Civil War and emancipation, the plantation and cash-crop agriculture remained the principal means of organizing land and labor and of generating wealth. Like most of the South, politics and governance in nineteenth-century Virginia largely concerned unresolved issues surrounding black freedom in a white-dominated society. And as in most of the region, a self-conscious network of families controlled the state's wealth and provided a united political leadership.[18]

In the rapid economic growth typical of the New South, Virginia was a society in flux. In southern Piedmont towns such as Danville and Martinsville, scenes of spawning cotton textile factories and new industrial lifestyles were common; in southern Appalachia, rich coal lodes were opened after the mid-1880s; in the ports and major cities, regional transportation centers were emerging. Economic growth brought urban expansion: steady population increases in small and large incorporated communities, the physical sprawl of large urban areas in Richmond and Norfolk, and—less spectacular but nonetheless significant—the quick, almost magical, rise of large towns out of cow pastures and cornfields.

One example of urban growth was the town of Martinsville, county seat of Henry County, located on a strategic railroad site on the southwestern rim of the tobacco district. By the latter two decades of the nineteenth century it had grown into a regional center of tobacco and cotton textile production. Although not quite a city, it was certainly a large town, boasting a population of almost twenty-four hundred in 1900. To one observer, describing the town's growth in the mid-1880s, the rapid pace of change was evident everywhere—in the large, new residences expressing an unprecedented prosperity, even opulence; in the construction of impressive brick stores; in the establishment of tobacco warehouses and factories; in the opening of a bank and other services such as livery stables, brickyards, and sawmills. Another observer of urban growth in the Virginia Piedmont was equally astonished. "New buildings and other improvements greet the eye in every direction," and townspeople gained "new life and vigor." This urban vitality brought a step more "elastic," a language more "brief and prompt," and a dress more "business-like." The "hum of industry" superseded "idleness"; progress and prosperity succeeded "inactivity and adversity."[19]

Urbanization and economic change nonetheless belied another reality: the persistence, abetted by geographical diversity and isolation, of old patterns of life. For every Virginian lured to a modern new town, four or five stayed in dusty villages and forgotten communities. Those late nineteenth-century observers who left New South cities and ventured beyond railroad lines into Virginia's hinterlands encountered stagnation and provinciality. This was the "real" Virginia, wrote a native, a land of back roads, where time moved in slow motion and the populace was "indifferent to public opinion—at least, of all public opinion outside of Virginia itself."[20] Visiting the state in the early 1880s, the English historian Edward Augustus Freeman discovered "a civilization of two hundred and fifty years standing," which was "not altogether wiped out." Rural Virginia's isolation and stagnation were what most impressed Freeman, who described the absence of social contacts and the pervasive monotony.[21]

The contrast between traditional, rural society and dynamic, urban communities presented but one example of the clashing hues of late nineteenth-century Virginia. Dominated by tobacco, it was also a land of lush wheat and truck vegetable farms. Burdened by tenancy, sharecropping, and the crop lien, it was also home to yeoman farmers and agricultural independence. Blacks furnished most unskilled cheap labor and constituted a majority, or near majority, of the population in a third of its counties, but in another third, they were a distinct minority. Geographical diversity, above all, lay behind the state's socioeconomic diversity. Visitors frequently noted the varied landscape of its five major regions, each of which was distinctive. Eastern Virginia's Tidewater, site of the state's colonial wealth and home to its leading families, was defined by the state's major rivers and distinguished by its unique topography of low-lying, sandy ridges descending into the Chesapeake Bay. Although it was Virginia's most densely populated region at the turn of the twentieth century, it had long lost its economic preeminence. About half of its population was black, the highest percentage in the state.[22]

Today, as a century ago, the scene changes rapidly as one moves into the Piedmont. The most obvious change is in landscape: the rivers become more rapid, rocky, and less navigable, and the soil acquires a reddish tint. In the nineteenth century, the Southside, the area south of the James River and west of the Tidewater, was known for its tobacco culture and large black population. In 1900, it was also abjectly poor, with the state's lowest value of land, next-to-lowest value of crop, and highest rates of tenancy and sharecropping. North of the James, the condition of agriculture improved only slightly. Northern Piedmont farmers raised less tobacco and more dairy products, fruits, and vegetables for urban markets. Although land values were double those in the Southside, the northern Piedmont also suffered from problems endemic to eastern Virginia: a large, poor black population; tenancy and sharecropping on about a quarter of all farms; and farm products worth only slightly more than in the Southside.

West of the Blue Ridge lay a starkly different environment. The Shenandoah Valley, a lush region settled by Palatinate Germans and Scotch-Irish in the eighteenth century, never adopted plantation agriculture. Antebellum Valley farmers consequently made little use of slave labor, and by the early twentieth century blacks composed only about a tenth of the region's population. By far the richest region in Virginia, the Valley produced the most valuable yields in every crop except tobacco, and its land was worth more than three times that of the Southside. Affluent and generally white, Valley farmers more than those elsewhere in the state tended to own their farms. Encircling the Valley to the east, west, and south, Appalachia had long been cut off from the outside world. The most sparsely populated region in the state in 1900, it was also poor in agricultural produce, its yield the lowest in the state.

Despite the state's diversity, the large majority of Virginians lived in a similar, local world. In 1870, the ten largest communities in the state accounted for only about 9 percent of its total population; and although that proportion had increased by 1900, even then almost 77 percent of Virginians lived in communities of less than five hundred people.[23] These rural Virginians inhabited a distinctly different world, which, in its basic characteristics, was similar across the American countryside. An expanding railroad network drew much of the state into the market economy and exposed country people to outside influences, but they still depended on uncertain water and overland transport. The state was blessed with numerous natural waterways, but overland transportation tended to be inefficient and expensive. Not unusual in the nineteenth century was the lament of a Virginian who observed that, in one typical rural community, the roads were always "out of order" and the wagons breaking down. A fact of life for most rural people was "delay, delay, in all matters of transportation."[24]

Isolation affected life in the Virginia countryside as decisively as it did elsewhere in rural America. It made rural life often monotonous, unattractive, and stagnant. For rural Americans, life was hard—a struggle against the vicissitudes of nature to scratch out a subsistence—and usually meant constant work, with few rewards or opportunities for human contact beyond a restricted geographical area. Neighborhoods became self-sufficient cocoons, insular in attitudes and suspicious of any intrusions by outsiders. The rural Virginia described in Ellen Glasgow's *Barren Ground* (1925) was an environment of "brooding loneliness" and solitude in which human contact and communication were dictated by the land. Men and women worked from dawn until dusk, and the few hours before bed were spent in prayer or silence, for "conversation was as alien to them as music." Numbed by monotonous isolation and exhausted by constant work, the rural Virginians of *Barren Ground* were imprisoned by the "relentless tyranny of the soil."[25]

Isolation pervaded life in rural America, but with varying consequences. In the Middle West and West, it was mitigated by almost constant movement of American, Canadian, and European immigrants, whose presence created an ethnocultural mix and dynamism at least partly absent from the South. Whereas in New England and, to a lesser extent, in the Middle Atlantic states, rural depopulation was prevalent, quite different forces were at work in the South. Here geographical isolation combined with comparatively little emigration to produce stagnation and inertia, often described by early twentieth-century observers as "idleness." "Idlers" dominated rural Virginia, commented one reformer: farmers and laborers lacked a sense of thrift, had little desire to improve

Virginia and Its Regions

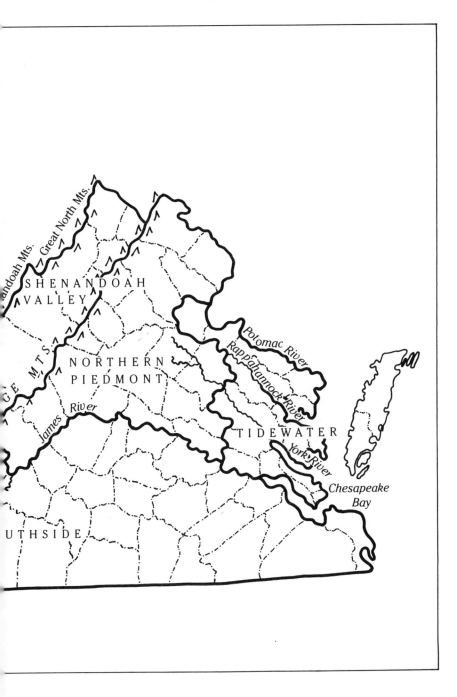

their environment, and, worse still, were content to stagnate. Even affluent Virginians lacked the dynamism that contact with the outside world
brought; they made little more than "a living for the family," and in many
cases, barely that.[26]

To most Virginians, the locality—perhaps the county but more often the neighborhood—was an exclusive world. Most persons stayed
"closely at home," a Southside planter commented in 1874, and were
aware of "but little," and cared less, about outside events.[27] The Virginia
novelist and future ambassador to Italy, Thomas Nelson Page, remembered the pervasive isolation when he wrote in 1908 of the "sequested"
and "self-contained" life in his boyhood neighborhood. He described
the existence throughout Virginia of "similar neighborhoods," each of
which constituted "a sort of separate world all to itself." Rural life in
Virginia was unchanging, as though it was "caught in an eddy," and "old
customs of speech and of life survived for generations almost without
change."[28]

When public schools entered the scene after 1870, they thus faced an
environment seemingly hostile to formal government and public institutions. Rural Virginia society was based on the locality, knitted together
by the diverse strands of kinship, denomination, and race, with little
place for formal education and the exercise of centralized governance.
This society was described by a European visitor as peopled by "careless, quiet, and secure" denizens who had "no business with any man"
and "no magistrate to put them to shame in anything."[29] It was a social
environment at once both rural American and southern yet also composed, as W. J. Cash observed, of patriots supremely loyal to "their com-
munes and to their various states."[30]

The Adaptation of Public Education

In an atmosphere of deeply rooted and pervasive hostility to public education, schools developed in rural Virginia only by adapting to local
institutions, mores, and values. Common schools became rooted and
then grew primarily in a political process in which leadership and advocacy played a crucial role. Seldom do social institutions like public
schools develop through the work of a single person. More frequently,
their character is determined by a complex mixture of social, cultural,
economic, and political factors, the full effect of which usually is un-
clear within the span of a single generation. Yet schools came to Vir-

ginia through a political phenomenon, Reconstruction; their future was
shaped by the actions of policy makers during the 1870s, among the
most important of whom was William Henry Ruffner, canonized by a
later generation as the "Horace Mann of Virginia" or, more generously,
as the "Horace Mann of the South."[31]

When he was elected Virginia's first state superintendent of public
instruction in 1870, it seemed unlikely that Ruffner would ever emerge
as an assertive educational statesman. A year earlier, in 1869, voters had
elected a Conservative government under the Reconstruction constitution, and to the restored rulers, Ruffner, though without experience in
education, had superior qualifications. After graduation from Washington College (now Washington and Lee University), he had pursued a
brief career as a Presbyterian minister in Philadelphia and in the Shenandoah Valley during the 1850s and 1860s. Most important, he had
strong political connections. During the autumn of 1869, he secured the
endorsement of leading educators, including the new president of Washington College, Robert E. Lee, as well as the Virginia Educational Association, a group of private school educators with powerful associations
with the Conservatives. Few of the people in power in 1870 viewed
Ruffner as a threat. Most instead regarded him, according to one contemporary, as a "good, easy sort of half-way enemy to the common
school system, who would be content to draw his salary and not trouble
himself about putting the schools in operation."[32]

But the new state superintendent soon surprised these observers. Required by the constitution to draft a new school law, at the end of April
1870 he presented to the legislature what he described to his wife as the
"best and most finished school law in America."[33] The statute, approved
in July, resembled the school laws of New Jersey and Pennsylvania and
created, at least on paper, a structure of public education that departed
significantly from antebellum practice. The state assumed responsibility
for black education, but segregated schools were specifically mandated.
The law also established a statewide agency of public education—the
Department of Public Instruction—composed of a state superintendent,
a state board of education, and local officials. Equally significant, the
state government as well as the cities and counties could now contribute tax revenues.[34]

The new public school system was established in fact only after a
crucial period of adaptation and testing. For most of the 1870s, it
seemed likely that the same political and ideological forces that had
prevented a serious attempt at mass education before the Civil War

would reassert themselves in the post-Reconstruction era. Elitism and paternalism did not end with Appomattox, and upper-income whites tended to oppose mass education and to refuse to enroll their children because of a social stigma against public schools. Because schools violated southern taboos by their very existence, they also encountered widespread popular opposition. By delegating at least theoretical authority over schools to state officials in Richmond, the post-Reconstruction system violated a tradition of local exercise of power. Most white Virginians probably believed that outsiders had imposed the new school system, and it was considered a symbol of the tyranny of Reconstruction. Even more seriously, by incorporating black education as a state responsibility, the new system had to answer the charge of racial leveling.[35]

In this atmosphere of hostility, Ruffner spent much of his time as state superintendent defending the new system. After he presented his school law to the legislature in 1870, an anonymous writer in the *Educational Journal of Virginia* claimed that the new schools were but a copy of those found in the "regions of Yankeedom." Three years later, only strenuous effort by his supporters prevented a group from unseating him as state superintendent. No sooner had the legislature reelected him to another four-year term in 1874 than he faced a more serious crisis involving the diversion of funds from school administration to the financing of the state's mammoth antebellum debt.[36]

Some of the state's religious leaders mounted an equally serious assault. Beginning in the winter of 1875, Bennett Puryear, a Baptist educator at Richmond College, published a series of blistering attacks in the state Baptist journal, the *Religious Herald*. Then, during the next year, Robert Lewis Dabney, formerly Stonewall Jackson's chaplain and professor at the (Presbyterian) Union Theological Seminary, published an extended denunciation of public education in the *Southern Planter and Farmer*.[37]

Although very different in tone and emphasis, both of these denominational attacks on public education reasserted antebellum views on the proper roles of state, church, and individual in schooling. To Puryear, the state government had no right to intervene in education. Free schools were a foreign invention, a product of "Yankee civilization," which eliminated social distinctions and imposed an artificial uniformity. Education could not, nor should not, reshape the social order. By God's ordinance, children should inherit the physical, moral, and intellectual characteristics of their parents, and, when that parentage was bad, so was the offspring. Active intervention in the social hierarchy through public education overstepped the natural bounds of government because it violated the traditional shape of society. Puryear had no objection to education of paupers as a function of public charity, but a "charity enforced is no charity at all."

Puryear's strongest objection to public schools was that they threatened parental authority. Should Virginians accept common schools in the 1870s, he warned, compulsory education would inevitably result. Within fifty years, if the system became an "accepted and fixed part of our educational policy," compulsory education would become law. And it was compulsory education, rather than common school education, that Puryear feared most. It meant the end of familial authority over children; it upset the "reciprocal relations and duties of parent and child" and denied God's authority. Compulsory education meant that the child would become public property and would learn such subjects as the state determined. "His manners, his health, his politics, his morals, even his religion" would be subject to state control.

For slightly different reasons, the new common schools also troubled Dabney. Secular schools usurped the functions of church and family and thus violated God's law. "True" education was necessarily moral, yet there was no morality without Christianity; and because public schools were secular, they were a "degrading, brute" influence. Dabney, like Puryear, had a clear notion of what kind of schools should exist—those that respected social rank and the moral authority of the church. But Dabney differed significantly in the manner in which he denounced, in a flood of embittered prose, the leveling influences of public education. This "Yankee heresy" was "corrupting" and "debauching" the independence of free people. Worse still, not only did state-controlled education threaten parental authority, it also elevated blacks. Public schools were ill suited to emancipated slaves, whom the Presbyterian divine described as indolent workers who needed strict and constant supervision, not coddling. Unlimited access to free schools only raised black expectations falsely. "The free schools," he wrote, produced not educated citizens but "discontent with, and unfitness for, the free negro's inevitable . . . destiny—manual labor."

The public schools were able to survive this furious assault for several reasons. Most Virginians believed, probably correctly, that any attempt to reverse the gains of Reconstruction would invite northern intervention. But a more subtle reason was that the public school system was reshaped and adapted. It was an adaptation by compromise. By the end of the 1870s, in part as a result of Ruffner's leadership, the fiscal crisis had ended and public schools were entrenched as permanent governmental agencies. He fended off his critics by reassuring them that public schools would not alter the established social and racial order. In lengthy responses to Puryear and Dabney, Ruffner argued that public schools would preserve rather than challenge the basic aspects of Virginia life. He stressed the need to separate religious instruction—the duty of parents—from other types of education, which were more properly the duty of the schoolteacher. And because denominational and private schools were not possible for most Virginians, public schools would provide more effective training anyway. Rather than encourage social leveling, they made workers more industrious and productive and attracted hardworking immigrants and investment from northern and European capitalists. Rather than posing a threat to the racial order, schools buttressed social segregation. Black education presented no possibility of racial mixture, for it encouraged "a purifying and stimulating power" and a "pride of race" that would "gradually overcome that contemptible ambition to associate with white people." Schools were, if anything, a bastion of segregation: "We find Negroes in our churches, our court houses, our halls of legislature, but there is one place where no Negro enters in Virginia, and that is a white school house."[38]

Ruffner further shaped the system by restricting the extent of state control and accepting local control as a key part of the system. In 1873, he persuaded the legislature to transfer the selection of trustees of local schools from the State Board of Education to localities; two years later, he loosened the rules for the selection of textbooks so as to allow considerable local power of choice.[39] Guiding this transformation was a combination of ideology and practical politics. As Ruffner argued in 1871, schools were voluntary institutions, available to but not required of children. Rather than an obligation, schools were a privilege no more requiring all the people to use them "than a provision of a public hydrant." State-controlled schools in this setting would not compel or coerce but defer to local custom. The proper function of the state was to "create among the people a universal appetite for knowledge," because effective public education was "self-acting" and the government's role should be that of "organizer" rather than of "ruler."[40]

The Dynamics of Growth

When Ruffner retired from the state superintendency in 1882, he left behind a system of schools permanently adapted to the realities of society and politics. His most important response to a primarily political challenge was to decentralize common schools and thus not only to ensure their survival but also to make possible rapid expansion during the last three decades of the nineteenth century. Measured by growth, Ruffner's system was a success; the numbers of both black and white schools, teachers, and enrolled and attending pupils tripled between 1870 and 1900.[41] Once tenuous and vulnerable, schools had become a familiar part of southern rural life by 1900.

The record of school expansion, striking though it is, calls attention to the state as a whole and thereby masks a fundamental reality: the system's success or failure—and the active force of educational growth—ultimately depended on local conditions. The presence of state officials and state funds, rather than corresponding with school expansion, had little effect.[42] Whether schools succeeded depended instead on the extent of two primary forms of community support—enrollments and taxes—which reflected different degrees of local educational enthusiasm. Enrollments were a community referendum, a vote of confidence about the current state of public education; if high, they indicated local approval and a pledge, though certainly not a firm promise, of future support through good attendance. Highest outside of towns and cities, enrollments were an important measure of success in rural America.[43] In Virginia, the more sparsely populated western counties recorded the highest enrollments in 1900; those in the eastern counties were below the state average.[44]

Several factors influenced parents' decisions about enrolling their children. The rise or fall of land tenure and agricultural wealth had no clear relationship to enrollments of either race.[45] Type of crop, literacy, population density, and race were important, yet their impact was complex and sometimes contradictory. The impact of cash crops differed, as tobacco counties tended to have lower white enrollments and peanut counties higher black enrollments. Statewide, black literacy corresponded with higher enrollment, yet had a conflicting impact in the state's regions. Population density associated with higher enrollment, but a higher proportion of blacks corresponded with lower enrollments among both races.[46]

Similarly, community tax support for public education and the length of the school term varied by localities. Although the state government provided a large pool of funds to pay teachers' salaries, the most important sources of funds for school facilities were property taxes assessed by state, county, and district officials. County superintendents distributed state property levies, which the legislature established by dividing them equally based on school population. On the county and district levels, however, revenues were also distributed on a per capita basis, and regional differentials in property values meant that the amount of money available for schools varied locally.[47]

Significant intrastate differences were an obvious result of this system. In 1900, Virginia school districts spent a mean of about 19 cents per capita on public schools, a figure that disguises wide differences. The taxpayers of urban Alexandria County spent $1.36 per capita, the highest in the state, but Appalachian Grayson County spent less than 4 cents per capita, the lowest in the state. Levels of community tax support also diverged on the regional level. The Southside thus spent the lowest amount of any region in the state, only about a quarter of urban school revenues and about half of Valley revenues.[48]

Regional differences in tax support brought qualitative disparities. The state as a whole recorded an average school term of 110 days in 1900, but length of school sessions varied across the state. Longer school terms, and in general, better school facilities, were most available in the counties that surrounded large urban centers. The longest school term in the state in 1900, 167 days, was in Henrico County, adjacent to the city of Richmond, but five urban counties held sessions lasting an average of 147 days. Outside of urban counties, school terms were much shorter—the shortest in the state, 72 days, in Appalachian Craig County. Among the five regions, mountain counties, which had the highest enrollments, had the shortest term, about 95 days, and the other four regions managed no more than 116 days.[49]

The willingness of rural communities to sustain longer school terms and better facilities through generous school revenues hinged on a number of factors. The community's ability to pay for better schools and facilities weighed heavily. Statewide, the higher the county's wealth and the heavier its population density, the more literate its white population, and the larger its proportion of blacks, the longer its school sessions and the more generous its district funding. The only variable corresponding to shorter terms and lower district expenditures, in contrast, was white landownership—a statistical relationship that reflected the traditional resistance of yeoman farmers to property tax increases supporting public schools.[50] Even so, there was considerable regional variation in the interplay between social and economic variables and school session and district funding.[51]

Whatever the reasons for its expansion, rural education in post-Reconstruction Virginia, far from being a static process, exhibited a dynamism in which growing numbers of schools, teachers, and pupils participated in public schools. This generation witnessed basic attitudinal changes toward schools and education, from popular opposition to widespread toleration and perhaps even approval. Yet the way in which common schools finally took root in Virginia would surely have disappointed the Reconstruction reformers who originally brought them to the state and who regarded them as central agencies in the remaking of southern folkways. Instead of transforming institutions, schools themselves were transformed. School expansion depended on local enthusiasm and support, and rural education increasingly integrated itself into its environment, expressing community conditions and values and serving as clear windows on southern rural society. Housed in makeshift buildings—often barns, churches, and homes—nineteenth-century schoolhouses did not project the primacy of state power but blended into the topography. Indeed, schools embodied central features of their social surroundings. In an isolated, rural society, they were intensely local; in a culture that valued family above all, they were family-dominated; in a society based on strict racial and class rankings, they reflected widespread social inequality; and in an impoverished agricultural economy, they were poor and makeshift.

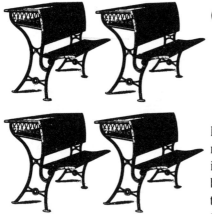

Chapter Two
Governance

Localism shaped every aspect of nineteenth-century rural education in the United States. It made possible popular support and even enthusiasm for schools and spurred the establishment of mass elementary education. Dominating educational expansion, localism ensured that country schools would become distinctive and embody the characteristics and attitudes of the communities creating them. Frequently, the symbiotic relationship between schools and their social environment fostered qualitative differences evident statewide and regionally. Yet in Virginia and elsewhere, localism also united rural schools under a similar system of governance, in which educational policy and decision making were formed, managed, and executed. Democratic and responsive to the community, but by no means efficient and streamlined, this system loosely managed public education. Rarely challenging local power, school officials relinquished educational authority to communities and disclaimed coercive administrative power. Exercising what Richard L. McCormick terms "distributive" governance, officials supervised the sharing of power among public and private interests; they attempted to satisfy individuals and groups by dispersing favors instead of by intervening or exerting central authority.[1]

The Apparatus

The Reconstruction constitution of Virginia created a state educational bureaucracy with considerable theoretical powers. At the top of the system was the State Board of Education. In mandating school by-laws, it performed legislative functions; in appointing superintendents, it exercised executive power; and in hearing appeals from school officials, it served as the supreme judicial board in the system. But a significant gap existed between the legal and actual powers of the school bureaucracy. Governors of post-Reconstruction schools followed an all-important imperative: they dispersed, rather than exercised, authority and responsibility. The state government did not provide leadership through either the state superintendent or the State Board of Education.[2]

Nor did the local representative of the state, the county superintendent, possess much real power. Serving as the only paid local official and as the chief executive officer of the county school system, he convened and led the local school boards, arbitrated local disputes, apportioned state monies, and paid teachers' salaries. Like state superintendents, county superintendents usually lacked professional training and worked in an official capacity an average of only 140 days of the year. One reason why county superintendents worked part-time was that they could not survive on their salaries. Soon after the Presbyterian educator Benjamin Mosby Smith was appointed as the first county superintendent for Prince Edward County, he complained that even with two incomes his finances were "very much embar[r]assed."[3] Smith's financial problems were not unusual. A decade later, a county superintendent in Appalachian Virginia supported his family by surveying on the side; as his wife observed, his salary "w'd scarce keep a man—much less his wife and daughter."[4] Most county superintendents considered education only a secondary vocation. When a school reformer investigated the qualifications of Virginia's county superintendents in 1903, he described only twelve as full-time and "well qualified." Seventeen were either "earnest" or interested but had no special training, and the remaining seventy-one had little to recommend them.[5]

Far more important to most Virginians than professional qualifications were personality and political skills. Ideal county superintendents, advised one contemporary, were "intelligent, fair, calm, deliberate, [and] cautious" and commanded the "respect and confidence" of their "countrymen." A symbol of unity in the county, they avoided divisive decision making and exhibited proper political views, if any at all. "Of course I am a Democrat," one applicant for a superintendency wrote, "otherwise I would not apply for the place." Successful superintendents satisfied diverse political, denominational, and sectional interests; fatherly figures, they stood above the fray and enjoyed, as one Virginian put it, the "entire confidence" of the county. Superintendents maintained a neutrality among the churches and avoided embroiling the schools in denominational rivalries and controversies. Mindful of the dangerous potential in a community-controlled school system, they carefully refrained from identifying with any section of the county. One patron, who claimed that his county superintendent showed sectional favoritism, demanded that his locality rightfully deserved "one appointment and that one is Supt. of schools, whether it be myself or some one else."[6]

In such circumstances, county superintendents rarely intervened in local disputes. Although most made an effort to visit local schools, their tours tended to be brief, and they rarely made a second visit.[7] One teacher saw nothing of the superintendent until the last day of school, when, in a whirlwind appearance, he shook hands with the teacher, told him that the patrons of the school "were pleased with him, and would be glad to have him return[,] and bade him good-bye."[8] As part-time officials with almost no coercive power, county superintendents frequently improvised and made up rules that satisfied local interests.[9] In effect, state officials governed by abdicating responsibility for policy making to parents and trustees. When confronted with the necessity of a decision, the superintendent of Shenandoah County schools told local trustees to make it themselves. "Settle it without my presence," he wrote, adding later that he would "stand to" the trustees unless they committed a "fatal mistake."[10]

Much of this abdicated power devolved to trustees. In each magisterial district (a judicial subdivision of the county), three trustees served as the local governing body—the district board—of the public school system. They were carefully chosen and wielded considerable power, and, together with other trustees, made up the county school board, which, unlike the district boards, met infrequently, had few responsibilities, and exerted little actual power. The office of school trustee reflected local social hierarchies. In Virginia, county electoral boards, which were appointed by the legislature and dominated by local elites, appointed rural trustees. These electoral boards ensured that most of the trustees were white men with proper (in most cases, Democratic) political affiliations.[11] Because the position brought no salary, trustees usually possessed some, though not necessarily great, wealth. Southside trustees were "*farmers*," recounted a contemporary, and this was "true of the majority of Counties in the State, as landholders are usually selected." Trustees' loyalties were frequently divided. Often torn between running their farms and fulfilling the obligations of public office, they were at least as accountable to their communities as they were to state officials.[12]

More than any other public school officials, district trustees kept themselves informed about parental, or "patron," opinion. Successful trustees valued the good favor and approval of parents. Unless they supported the schools, parents would not enroll their children, see that they attended them regularly, or provide nontax support that was essential to the schools' survival. If they found trustees unresponsive, patrons had the unlimited right to petition either the district board or the superintendent—a drastic procedure that they frequently exercised. Districts with dissatisfied patrons soon came to the attention of state officials.

As in other aspects of school governance, the absence of state power decisively affected financial support for education. A lack of clear fiscal authority infused every stage of public education, from the payment of property taxes to day-to-day expenses. Empowered to collect all state, county, and district taxes, the county treasurer worked part-time and, instead of a salary, received a commission on collected taxes that ranged from the highest legal rate of 5 percent to a much higher actual rate.[13] Tax collection and the commissions depended on the discretion of the treasurer. One Southside treasurer demanded a 10 percent commission on the county tax and 8 percent on the district tax because collection of these taxes, as he explained to the local county superintendent of schools, would "take at least four months," and "the most important part of the Year for farming will have elapsed, in consequence of which I should fail to make a crop."[14]

The irregular collection of public school revenues consequently hinged on the dubious abilities and honesty of treasurers. In 1900, for example, fifty-eight out of one hundred county treasurers applied to the Virginia legislature for relief because they could not pay the full amount of taxes.[15] A general shortage of hard currency in rural Virginia, which prevented many propertyholders from making tax payments promptly, admittedly caused many problems. Because they possessed a valuable resource of cash reserves for at least several months a year, moreover, some treasurers exploited an opportunity to turn a profit by lending public funds and receiving interest on them.[16]

With tax collections often in arrears, school officials endemically lacked cash and paid their bills in scrip or by barter. In turn, trustees sometimes issued scrip in anticipation of future cash, but, in the process, overextended themselves. In the Southside, after a local trustee issued scrip to buy wood for a schoolhouse, the county sheriff served a summons on the county superintendent to answer a "comeplaint" that the "monny" had not been paid. The financial affairs of a Shenandoah

Valley district board proved no more solvent. A trustee was advised to consolidate his board's accumulated debt and to eliminate "the an[noy]-ance of having so many men to contend with & satisfy." Because the district finances were in confusion, the trustees were ignorant about how much or to whom they owed and suffered the "unpleasantry" of their scrip "being hawked around and every body talking about it."[17]

The isolated public schools of rural Virginia, in short, shared an important characteristic: they were closely adapted to their social and political environment. They were nonbureaucratic in a society in which governance involved little active state intervention; they were intensely local institutions, established only at the pleasure of the community, without whose support and participation they could not survive. Even so, public education in this setting involved frequent exercises of power: power to finance, or not to finance, education; power to establish schools and to determine their location; power to select teachers; and power to assert control in the classroom. In each of these areas, rural school governance, at its best, produced compromise and consensus; at its worst, conflict and dissension.

The Compromise of Governance

Running a school, both today and in the nineteenth century, requires constant decision making. In the environment of rural education after Reconstruction, decisions were reached consensually. A vital decision requiring such assent was the location of the school, which trustees reached only after considering patron opinion carefully through conversations or formal petitions. Following a time-honored procedure, Pittsylvania County patrons petitioned their district board to locate a school in their neighborhood. The group scrupulously listed the number of parents and "schoolable" children in the area and claimed that "at least 30 other Schollars" could be added to the list. The same procedure was followed in Prince William County, where black patrons requested a public school by presenting a list of sixty children, twenty-five of whom lacked access to "proper school facilities."[18]

Once agreed on a location, the trustees were responsible for establishment of the school. During the decade after Reconstruction schools often met in whatever facilities were available, but by the 1880s, district school boards held title to an increasing number of schoolhouses. The further details of establishing a school required an active partnership between patrons and trustees. Parents "help us build if we help them," observed a trustee. He obtained promises of labor and supplies if the trustees would "furnish the Hardware, which is generally a cash outlay." Northern Piedmont trustees agreed to support a school only if the community constructed the building and then deeded it to the board. The trustees further promised to supply furniture but to pay only half of the teacher's salary; the community would pay the other half "untill this board feels justified in assuming the paying of the whole salary."[19] Patrons often contributed noncash resources. When the roof and floor of a Valley schoolhouse needed repair, the district board agreed to provide timber and nails if the patrons supplied the labor. In a Southside school patrons supplied not only labor but also dippers, brooms, water buckets, crayons, and matches.[20]

Governance by compromise and consensus also affected the selection of teachers, whose hiring rarely followed any clearly delineated set of standards. Certification remained in the hands of the county superintendents, without any standardization or supervision. Before the turn of the twentieth century, there were as many standards as there were superintendents, and examinations varied widely from county to county.[21] Most superintendents enjoyed almost complete discretion in determining criteria for certification. A superintendent in southeastern Virginia once conducted an examination during the late 1870s by inviting the applicant to dinner, during which he asked the teacher in passing to spell "license" and another word. After dinner, he informed the applicant that she had passed the examination. Decentralized teacher certification provided ample opportunity for abuses. One superintendent granted certification to teachers who attended his private school for at least three months. The superintendent magnanimously offered to postpone payment of tuition and board "till the teacher could make it by teaching in the public schools of the county."[22]

Following certification by the county superintendent, teachers presented themselves to the local school boards. Candidates came prepared with recommendations. "If you want a Lady—well educated to take charge of a white school, [and] there is a nice family on which she can board not too far from the school house," reads one such letter, "I can send you a very nice one." With or without influential recommendations, local candidates usually were hired. Numerous accounts affirm the observation of one county superintendent that localities should get their "own people if they can be had." A Piedmont county school board thus resolved that its schools should, if possible, hire applicants who were "residents of this county." As an afterthought, the board added that this stipulation should not "be so construed as to sanction the employment of incompetent or of inferior in lieu of good teachers." The preference for local candidates persisted into the twentieth century. In 1902, one observer declared that schools were a "neighborhood affair" that should be "given to a neighborhood boy or girl"; another trustee in the eastern part of the state wrote ten years later that "home girls" should receive "some prefferences."[23]

If officials and patrons agreed on a teacher, their decision was sealed in the teacher's contract, which embodied a communal consensus about the school's most important details. It stipulated a salary, usually determined by teaching proficiency, number of students, and local cost of living. The contract also specified the opening date and the length of the school session, both of which were subject to negotiation between trustees and parents.[24] Aside from the requirement of a minimum school session of three months, neither state nor county officials intervened in this decision, and district trustees adapted the opening of schools to local necessities. "We have our school affairs settled," wrote a black teacher, commenting that school would soon open. "We would have begun sooner," he explained, "but the farmers have been having such a very dry time with their crops that they could not afford to spare their children to go to school."[25]

The opening date and length of the school session were among the clearest expressions of the impact of localism on rural education. Not surprisingly, school sessions specified in contracts were geared around planting and harvest seasons and followed no regular schedule. Most communities preferred to conduct sessions during slack periods, and this was usually, although not always, the pattern. In one unusual instance in Southside Virginia, a patron requested that the school session begin in July, "owing to our children's being small and girls mostly." Generally, the length of the session depended on the financial resources of the community. Rural communities frequently extended school sessions either through higher district property taxes or through voluntary donations that paid teachers' salaries beyond the conclusion of the contract.[26]

The agreement over school location, teacher, and the timing and length of the session embedded in the teacher's contract sealed the compromise between the various groups, governmental and nongovernmental, that operated the rural schools. Parents often visited the teacher and then indicated their approval, or disapproval, informally to the trustees; trustees kept themselves closely informed of the progress of the school and especially how parents regarded it. In a vivid demonstration of the importance of communal assent, a black teacher, after receiving a contract, met with parents and children. Those present gathered around him, and he described his plans for the school. According to the teacher, the parents indicated their approval and "gave their children to me as a father."[27]

Teacher Selection and the Dynamics of Governance

Highly responsive to the local community, rural schools were run under a distributive system of governance that was participatory and voluntary. When policy making alienated no one, schools operated in an atmosphere of consensual bliss, blending public authority with local voluntary support. But the practical application of governance was not always harmonious, and school officials frequently confronted dissension and conflict. Teacher selection was a vital and usually controversial decision in school governance. Schoolmen and local Virginians often differed over criteria. The official standard, as expressed by Ruffner, was that school officials were "duty bound" to reject incompetents; parents "ought to be thankful" for such protectors of their children.[28] School officials' desire for qualified teachers, however, played a small part in teacher selection. Without a system of teacher training and certification, the competence of candidates was indeterminable, and, of all criteria, approval of patrons was probably the most compelling.

In most instances, officials employed teachers with the full cooperation and agreement of the community. Although not always the case statewide, in some communities trustees sometimes summoned parents to meetings to elect teachers. A northern Piedmont board, following this practice, thus advertised "special notice" by which it provided "patrons a voice in the selection of a teacher," and it held carefully conducted elections before each school session. Into the 1890s, these elections became regular affairs in which parents chose teachers either by personal appearance at special trustees' meetings or by proxy. In communities without provision for teacher selection, at the least patrons usually expressed their preferences to trustees by petition. A group in Southside Virginia requested the appointment of one James Murdock because they knew him "well" and could vouch for his "capacity[,] morals and general fitness." In a Valley district, a parent explained that, although he usually avoided having "aneye thing to do with Selecting teachers," he supported rehiring a teacher because his children had "done better" with him than "aneye one I ever sent to" and because he was the "most compitent of aneye one that we have had for years."[29]

Even if patrons did not express their opinions directly, trustees, or the candidates themselves, ordinarily sounded out the community. A teacher reported to the district trustees that he had visited the "princi-ple" patrons of a local school and found them "*perfectly* willing"; by the teacher's account, they were "anxious for the school to start." When asked if this approval would "settle the matter," the board responded by hiring the teacher. Patron approval was so important that some candi-dates competed for their favor. In one instance, a disappointed candi-date complained that a competitor was hired because he "knew the im-portance of seeing all the patrons."[30]

Objections from patrons would doom the candidacy of a prospective teacher. In the Valley, a majority of parents supported hiring a teacher, but because a minority expressed opposition, the board ruled that "good reasons" existed for choosing another candidate who was "not in an[y] way connected with the troubles which had existed at [the] above place." A teacher discovered similar consequences of patron disap-proval in another part of Virginia, where trustees "condemned and sen-tenced" him without bothering to hear his point of view. To the trustees, the important reality was that a portion—if only a portion—of the neigh-borhood did not want the teacher to return, and it promptly transferred him to another school.[31]

More often than not, the employment and subsequent fate of teachers depended on community approval. Because of "neighborhood little-ness," wrote one observer, some parents deliberately kept their children away from school to punish unpopular teachers. These parents ex-pressed "no objection specially" to a teacher. Nonetheless, by boycott-ing the school because they supported another candidate for the job, they deliberately sabotaged the incumbent's prospects. In another dis-trict, although patrons claimed that a teacher possessed insufficient qualifications, competency was not their real concern. Like "some other places," wrote a trustee, these patrons were indifferent about qualifica-tions, "provided they get their man," and if they happened "to get an-other man, they are very particular."[32]

The strength of localism in teacher selection transcended race; rural blacks also resented outside intrusions. When a Piedmont district board chose a woman from another county over a local candidate, a group of patrons and pupils requested "Justice" from the county superintendent, charging that they had not been "treated right." They further warned that they would not "recognize & will not Patronize" the teacher. The trustees and superintendent held firm, but the dissident patrons tried to prevent the teacher from holding school by withdrawing their patronage and by influencing other parents. Although the denouement of this struggle is unknown, the episode illustrates the tense dynamic between localism and public authority at work in rural school governance.[33]

Another crucial factor among both races was "influence"—the pervasive force of family, class, and denomination. A black teacher at the turn of the twentieth century complained that teacher selection in his community was "worse" than it had been a decade earlier. Whereas trustees had earlier exerted the exclusive privilege of choosing teachers, parents now "injudiciously and thoughtlessly" interfered, and men of influence led their "weaker fellows . . . for the sake of some individual benefit or favor." Influence assumed different forms. Trustees or other school officials sometimes exploited their office, and the charge that many trustees used the office to provide jobs for relatives and friends, "regardless of fitness," was not uncommon.[34]

The extent of nepotism practiced by trustees in teacher selection is impossible to determine. The state government recognized the existence of the practice in 1878, when it banned the employment of any teacher who was "related by blood or marriage" to a trustee or the superintendent. Yet the law sanctioned hiring relatives if the trustees unanimously agreed to make an exception.[35] But turn-of-the-century reformers probably exaggerated both the importance and the frequency of overt nepotism in rural schools. Although family ties were influential, nepotism was practiced subtly by school officials. A man of standing might write recommending a candidate; or, if prospective teachers came from well-connected families, their name alone would carry considerable weight. When Ruffner informed a county superintendent about a friend of "honorable ancestry" whose son was an applicant for a teaching job, that phrase was a strong recommendation. In other instances, the influence of family ties was more obvious. In 1891, the superintendent of schools in Nelson County wrote another superintendent in a neighboring county about hiring his cousin. "I do not like to undertake to put a relation in—in my own County," he explained. He felt no such compunction, however, about exerting pressure to get her a job in an adjoining county.[36]

Patrons were less squeamish about invoking family ties. When the decision was left to the patrons, commented one parent, they not infrequently chose "the most poorly qualified and inexperienced teacher among the applicants" because he or she had "more relations and intimate friends than any other of the applicants." In one school, nearly all of a teacher's advocates were related to him in some way. In still another instance, a teacher was fired in one community and then replaced by a candidate who had a "large relationship in the County." One observer reported that the new teacher was "very undesirable" to the majority of the patrons, who were not his relatives.[37]

Denominational affiliation was also often decisive, and prospective teachers openly exploited church identifications. A Southside applicant informed the county superintendent, a Baptist, that the superintendent in his county was Episcopalian, and "we think him not partial to baptist families." The teacher then promised that, if hired, he would perform valuable missionary work in black schools. A black teacher wrote about a different effect of denominationalism in another part of the state. There were two black churches in this neighborhood—one Baptist, one Methodist—and educators maintained a cautious impartiality. The teacher wrote that he had not incurred the "displeasure of either party," but added that patrons usually evaluated teachers on the basis of church affiliation.[38]

The Authority of the Teacher

The struggle for control and authority, waged not only by governmental and nongovernmental participants in rural education, was also fought inside the schoolroom. Rarely in contact with school officials, teachers occupied an uncertain position, carefully watched by inquisitive, searching, and frequently hostile parents. As Carl F. Kaestle has suggested, discipline in the nineteenth-century schoolroom displayed the tensions and ambiguities of common school education.[39] In a system without authority, teachers had to impose their control, and the resulting conflict—frequently physical—often determined the length of their tenure.

It was essential that teachers establish such control early in the school session. Because the one-room school contained pupils of different ages, discipline was a substantial challenge. A black teacher recalled in his autobiography that he boxed to establish his authority over his older and larger students. Students frequently challenged new teachers, and a favorite way was "turning out" or "passing out." Although the teacher's contract specified the length of the school session, no provision was made for holidays, which were given at the teacher's discretion. If a teacher refused to give a holiday at Christmas or New Year's, the bigger students sometimes physically prevented him from holding school. Edward Eggleston, in *The Hoosier School-Master*, described a rural school in Indiana in which the hero, Ralph Harstook, refused to grant a Christmas vacation and the pupils then plotted to "turn out" the teacher. In the culmination of the struggle, students blockaded themselves inside the school only to have Harstook outwit them by stuffing paper down the chimney and smoking them out. "Turning out," according to one teacher's autobiography, was also practiced in Virginia. Unable to fulfill his promise of a week's holiday at Christmas time, the teacher discovered that a group had locked him out of the school. He then battered the door down with an ax, and the students, properly humbled, never "passed out" another teacher.[40]

The struggle for control was usually less dramatic than these episodes would suggest. Most nineteenth-century educators agreed that good teachers exerted strict discipline not in sudden, dramatic incidents but in steady, unrelenting fashion. As Ruffner maintained, school discipline was a "leading feature" of education. "Unless the school can be managed," he noted, "it cannot be taught; and unless the pupil is brought under control his knowledge will probably only give power to his wickedness."[41] School officials were not alone in their concern that teachers control the classroom; most parents in the nineteenth century considered teachers unqualified unless they employed strong discipline *in loco parentis*. Thus a group of Valley patrons protested that a teacher had not had "good discipline" and was hence unqualified. According to a black teacher, parents in his locality also expected strong discipline. The "principal instruction" that he had received from parents was to rule through harsh discipline—to "whip, whip, whip" the pupils. These parents considered that teachers were "not teaching" if they were "not whipping." A white teacher similarly recalled the importance of discipline. When he taught in rural schools, he was never certain "which created the more noise in that schoolhouse, the whistle of the wind as it came through the logs or the whirl of the switch as I belabored the bad boys."[42]

Parents considered ability to control larger boys a crucial test of the teacher's effectiveness, and on this issue alone they might withdraw the boys from school or demand a new teacher. A group of petitioners described a teacher as unable to "give satisfaction" because he could not "govern boys from 14 to 18 years of age and over." Following the same rationale, a Piedmont school board hesitated to hire a fourteen-year-old black teacher. The candidate had recently been a pupil in the school, and the board wondered whether she could maintain order among her former classmates. In still another instance, the father of a nineteen-year-old who could not be controlled told the board that he would not allow the boy to attend "upon any conditions." The board subsequently decided to dismiss the teacher.[43]

Yet teachers found that establishing control in the schoolroom was not simply a matter of exerting harsh discipline. In fact, they trod a treacherous path. If they exercised too much control, they risked alienating parents; although parents demanded good discipline, they were reluctant to relinquish total control over punishment.[44] According to one observer, when teachers "held the children up to the bit, and flogged them sometimes," parents might respond by withdrawing their children from school. A black teacher who exerted strong discipline in a rural school near Richmond faced vigorous opposition from one parent, who appeared at the school and challenged her "with a long stick, taller than she." In yet another case, a teacher who had whipped a student who had apparently stolen her gloves soon faced the community's united opposition.[45]

Closely intertwined with the issue of control were any indications of sexual attraction between pupils and teachers. Not only did such misconduct violate strict taboos in rural Victorian society, it also suggested larger issues about parental control over their children. In eastern Virginia, an early twentieth-century superintendent received a complaint about a teacher which was apparently "brought by some *Little frisky girl who also wanted to flirt with him*." When another teacher began, she first boarded with a local woman but then switched to another home because it was closer to her school. According to the teacher's account, the woman then incited her children to "disobedience" and began rumors about sexual improprieties on the part of the teacher. Soon the teacher resigned from the school because of the controversy. "While there may not be any thing wrong with Mrs. Davis," commented a trustee, "I don[']t think she has acted altogether prudent for a teacher and there is a good deal of talk about her."[46]

School Location

Next to the choice of a teacher, the location of a school most often provoked conflict in school governance. Not only was it an important decision, but, because schools often closed, it was also a subject school boards were frequently forced to consider. In the absence of good transportation, the location of a school was crucial because it made education more accessible to one community at the expense of another. And population diffusion rendered isolated schools difficult to reach, and sometimes inaccessible, for a significant portion of the population. In remote areas, school-age children never had a school in their neighborhood because, as one superintendent in a mountainous county claimed, "rich centres got the first schools, the best houses, and best teachers; while the poor people on the outskirts were told to 'hold on awhile.' "[47]

Remote areas lacked schools primarily because sparse population and nearly complete isolation made it difficult to support a sufficient level of attendance. These areas were not necessarily unique to any region of the state. Even in the densely populated Southside, one superintendent reported that "a small minority," either "without children or without schools," "cavil and condemn" public schools because of their "peculiar location." But instead of recommending more schools, the superintendent advised greater flexibility about attendance requirements; he warned that "otherwise some of the largest taxpayers are so located that they will not in a generation desire any benefit from Pub[lic] schools."[48]

The location of the nineteenth-century school was usually a compromise, but because of the loose and decentralized structure of governance, a decision was rarely final. Here again, the official standards of the school system sharply diverged from the reality of school politics. State officials, believing that efficient use of school funds was the main criterion, considered the geographical center of population as the ideal location. But this was a generally meaningless standard. Not only was it impossible to measure the center of population precisely, but without concrete boundary lines for schools it also often shifted. When a Valley parent complained about a badly located school, his trustee responded by contending that it lay as close to the "centre of population" as could be determined. Some parents had "a little far to send to school," he admitted, but never more than two miles.[49]

As with teacher selection, patrons played a major role in deciding school location. A crucial determinant was whether the trustees found a piece of land and a building. Patrons exploited the school district's poverty ruthlessly. Soon after the post-Reconstruction schools began in their community, John Brill and his wife, Elizabeth, gave a parcel of land to a local school board on the condition that a school be built on it and that their gift would be "null and void" without a school. Similarly, another rural Virginian donated land provided the trustees locate a "comfortable School House thereon"; if no school was constructed, the land was to be returned to the donor.[50]

Yet few schools were located without careful consideration of community opinion. Frequently, this meant formal and informal polling of parents and taxpayers. After the board requested a vote among black parents on the location of a Southside school, only three of the patrons voted to retain the site and twenty-three voted to change it. In a Valley district, trustees, equally willing to consider patron opinion, heard a petition from a group who complained that their school was uninhabitable without extensive repairs and who objected to the location of the school. The board promised to find a new site. Trustees were wary of alienating patrons over school sites. Disgruntled patrons had a right to appeal any decision, and they, along with trustees, fully realized the local officials' precarious position. A group of petitioners thus gave force to their complaint to a school board about the location of a school by threatening to "refer the matter to higher authority." In another community, a trustee, worried about the repercussions of building a new school in the district, suggested that the board meet to determine the best location. Above all, he wrote, he did not want the burden of a decision on his shoulders: he did not "feel inclined to take responsibility" because it was "very difficult" to "suit all parties."[51]

Even when consulted, however, patrons often disagreed. School location was always a "bone of contention," recalled a county superintendent. "No matter whether officers wanted to do right or not, no matter where the houses were put, the people would not be satisfied, because every man wanted the house 'put at his own door.'" A Valley parent who was "put out" about a school site visited a school trustee; supported by the "great majority of the patrons," the parent proposed a new location that would be "convenient for all to reach." A similar situation confronted trustees when a group in the western part of their Piedmont county complained that a school was located "in an extreme end" of the neighborhood and caused "great trouble and inconvenience on account

of two mountain ridges." The group requested that the county superintendent appoint a special appeal board to solve the dispute.[52]

The impact of localism was clear in the issue of school location. Over
time, the desire of communities to have schools led to a scattering of
schools, which reinforced rather than transcended sectional divisions in
counties and school districts. Differences over location only aggravated
these sectional conflicts. Increasingly, the story of one northern Piedmont school district became the rule instead of the exception. There,
the question of locating a school to satisfy two communities was resolved only after trustees agreed that it was impossible to find a satisfactory compromise location. Instead, the board decided upon a course of
action reached by countless boards across the state: it promised, on the
condition that patrons "would subscribe sufficiently," eventually to establish schools in both communities.[53]

Race and the Rural School

A pervasive and potentially divisive factor in school governance in Virginia, as elsewhere, was race. Although blacks played a major role in
the establishment of a state system of public schools during Reconstruction, schooling reflected the racial attitudes and hierarchies of rural society. Racial segregation in public education brought obvious inequalities because black schools were unquestionably inferior in funding,
duration of attendance, level of enrollment, and quality of instruction.
These were all basic realities of the segregated system of education
forged during the late nineteenth century.

From the inauguration of the public school system, black and white
children attended separate schools.[54] State, county, and district funds
were apportioned according to school population, and, in theory, superintendents and district boards were chosen without regard to race. Not
only did Ruffner contend that black and white applicants for trustees
"stand upon precisely the same footing," but he also insisted that the
State Board of Education wanted "the best men in each school district
best suited to the position, and when colored men are found fulfilling
the requisite conditions, it will, I am sure, give the Board pleasure to
appoint them." Ruffner's assurances rang hollow, however, throughout
most of the nineteenth and twentieth centuries. District boards were
composed exclusively of white males, usually landowners, and because

of the localization of the school system, these men had complete discretion over both races in most areas of school governance.[55]

White control meant that black schools received disproportionately smaller tax support. According to one estimate, about twice as much money in Virginia was spent, per child, at the turn of the twentieth century for white schools as for black schools.[56] Less money meant inferior facilities and shorter terms for black schools. Not untypical was the admission of a district board that resolved in 1892 that "the School term for colored schools . . . shall be six months, for white, six and a half." Even more obvious inequities existed in teachers' salaries. An early twentieth-century educator noted that black teachers were paid between 20 and 50 percent less than whites. "Strange as it may seem," he added sardonically, no separate statistics existed on this subject, even though "on all other subjects" the facts and figures were "kept apart scrupulously."[57] In an age when Reconstruction was still a clear memory, school officials carefully avoided any suggestion of discrimination. They did not record the areas in which the most obvious disparities existed, most especially teachers' salaries. Indeed, between 1870 and 1910, only six issues of the reports of the state superintendent—1883, 1884, 1885, 1905, 1907, and 1909—included separate data on salaries of black and white teachers. These data confirm a pattern of inequality. In 1906, black male teachers earned about 32 percent as much as white males and black females about 73 percent as much as white females.

District boards rationalized paying black teachers poorer salaries on the ground that they possessed lower qualifications. Undeniably, black teachers were, in general, less qualified. In 1909, for example, about 33 percent of all black teachers were granted "emergency" certificates and received, on the average, $110.76 in annual salary. Yet white teachers who were also granted emergency certificates during the same year were paid a substantially higher salary—on the average, $147.76 per year—than blacks.[58] Black teachers throughout this period suspected, and these figures appear to support their suspicions, that blacks received lower certification because school officials wanted to pay them less.[59]

District trustees also possessed discretionary powers in the allocation of revenues for the construction of black schoolhouses. Although comparative data on expenditures for the races are not available, there is little doubt that substantially more money was spent for white schoolhouses. Many whites accepted the inequitable distribution of funds implicitly because they assumed that blacks were inferior and therefore needed less formal education. Because schoolhouses were largely

Tatum School, Orange County, Virginia, 1914
(courtesy of the U.S. Department of Education)

funded by property taxes, other whites considered it only fair that these revenues be distributed in favor of white schools because whites owned most of the land and paid most of the taxes. A few blacks challenged inequitable funding. In 1904, one black—described by a white as "one of our best and most intelligent colored citizens"—complained of "unjust discrimination." The white trustees of his district, he charged, were "biassed," "contracted, narrow, and hostile" toward black education. But the vast majority of blacks lacked the powers of articulation or the economic independence to defy or challenge the white majority.[60] Most had no choice but to accept white supremacy in the school system.

Outside the well-defined areas of white control, however, black parents exerted some influence in the operation of schools, for school administrators depended on them for financial support, enrollment, and attendance. County superintendents and trustees thus often granted blacks many of the same privileges white patrons enjoyed. Black patrons had an active voice in the two most important decisions of the nineteenth-century school: selection of a teacher and location of a school. As a group of black patrons expressed it in a petition in the 1870s, a "process of time" had expired so that competent black teachers should teach black children: "We respectfully claim that if our children must be in seperate schools, known and designated as Colored schools, then they should have colored teachers. If the comingling, and educational intercourse of colored and white pupils is contaminating, then why is not such with colored pupils and white teachers contaminating?"[61] By the 1880s, the vast majority of black schools had black teachers.[62] As one graduate of Hampton Institute, a black teacher, observed, blacks were replacing poorly qualified white teachers, even though they were constantly before the school officials, "begging them for employment in our schools as their only chance of support."[63]

The loose structure of the governance of rural schooling allowed considerable autonomy for black schools. Blacks found that white officials expected them to be self-sufficient. "Down in this part of the State," wrote one black, "teachers meet with very little encouragement from any one. The superintendent examines you; the school board will tell you at what place they want you to teach, and many times you will have to look out for the schoolroom, benches, and everything else that is necessary." Like whites, blacks were expected to contribute a substantial portion of the costs of construction and maintenance of schoolhouses. In one instance, a young black graduate of Hampton Institute opened a log-cabin school in an isolated area of the state. The school began with twenty-five students, but within a month it had one hundred pupils and was bursting at the seams. When the teacher and patrons asked trustees for help to build a larger schoolhouse and were refused, they successfully solicited money and other help from patrons, who donated $275 to construct a two-story building. Some of them gave not only money but also time; others even brought "corn and potatoes to the store to help pay for nails, etc." Instances of black self-help were common. A white visitor to a rural school in the Tidewater found that two of the local black schools had been erected entirely by blacks on land they owned. As one black explained, "I ain't got no chil'en, but I thought as how 'twas the best thing I could do for the colored folks." The same visitor found this spirit of self-help in a nearby community, where "most of the cost" of a new schoolhouse for blacks "had been borne by the parents of the children."[64]

The lack of state authority, combined with a policy of neglect, meant that blacks exercised considerable control over the day-to-day operation of their schools. In Gloucester County, a black teacher overcame the

Mount Calvary School, Orange County, Virginia, 1914
(courtesy of the U.S. Department of Education)

opposition of trustees and was able to open a school in which whites had formerly studied. The trustees were afraid that the black children might damage the property, but they eventually consented. But the school had no stove, and students began to leave once winter set in; when the county superintendent paid a visit, he found only seven attending students. The school was reduced to meeting outside, in a little ravine, where the teachers and pupils huddled around a fire protected by a large elm. Perhaps in response to this hardship, the trustees relented and, soon after Christmas, installed a new stove.[65]

In some respects, both blacks and whites felt the consequences of localism in the diffusion of rural school governance. Although glaring racial inequities were common to nineteenth-century public education, in rural schools both races operated within similar parameters. Both attended schools that were little affected by outside administration and were governed by parents and unpaid officials. In a system that functioned from the bottom up, decision making, for blacks and whites, was often not easy, and though the school was an example of rural democracy at work, it also incited deep-seated underlying tensions. But rural school governance was by no means the entire story of the nineteenth-century rural school, for there were other threads that led from noncompulsory schooling, the most interesting of which was its impact inside the schoolroom.

Chapter Three
Experiences

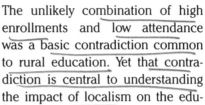

The unlikely combination of high enrollments and low attendance was a basic contradiction common to rural education. Yet that contradiction is central to understanding the impact of localism on the educational experiences of teachers and pupils. The simultaneous expression of community enthusiasm and indifference demonstrates an essential characteristic: schools reflected community desires and achieved popularity only by playing a small, unobtrusive role in rural society. Rural Americans regarded schools as local institutions best run by communities, but they also considered education a part-time, peripheral experience. Because schools and the process of learning were so attuned to local needs, rural Virginians produced a record of regular attendance only when it did not compete with other, more pressing, demands.

A Free Market of Education

Although rural school governance was democratic and highly participatory, it was also keenly sensitive to local realities, often reflecting less "democracy" than powerful centrifugal forces. Without a strong state role in governance, public schools functioned in a free market of education, and they furiously competed among themselves, with private education, and with other forms of socialization for survival. Whatever position public schools assumed in rural society depended on local realities and parental desires; in the absence of compulsory education or bureaucratic school governance, parents exerted considerable power as consumers in this marketplace.

In late twentieth-century usage, a "school" usually denotes a building—or the physical site—in which students receive formal education.

The physical surroundings and the institution of education assume greater importance than the temporary presence of students and teachers. During the nineteenth century, the phrase—and the concept of education—had a different meaning. Rather than a building or physical structure, the school was the interaction between teachers and pupils. By definition, that interaction was not only more important than the physical site but was also a transitory experience, adapted to the needs of parents rather than to those of the institution. The key to understanding this important distinction is that rural schools, leading a capricious existence, were impermanent entities that existed only by adapting to community desires.

Crucial to a school's survival was its success in attracting and keeping students. To receive state funds for teachers' salaries, schools were required to meet a minimum level of attendance. Teachers recorded attendance and, at the end of each month, calculated the average daily attendance, which they then sent on to the county superintendent. If this figure dropped below fifteen by the end of the month, public support ceased, unless, as Ruffner noted, "*good* evidence" indicated that "the deficiency will not exist in the future."[1] Trustees exercised this power broadly. Unable to make the required average attendance during the first month of the school session, a northern Piedmont schoolteacher appeared before the district board. Acknowledging that unusual circumstances caused the declining attendance, the board granted a reprieve "for the present" and directed the teacher to "report the number of scholars for month no. 2." In another instance, the same board promised support for a black school whose attendance was below the state standard after the patrons provided an assurance that attendance would increase in the future. The exceptions to this rule were frequent enough to suggest that attendance requirements were generally unenforced. As the *Educational Journal of Virginia* pointed out, many trustees and superintendents openly ignored the rule, viewed it as "merely nominal," and "winked at its open violation."[2]

Because the noncompulsory school existed by its ability to attract students, school officials attempted to maximize attendance and enrollment. Trustees scheduled school sessions only after polling patrons and ensuring their cooperation. They allowed local schools considerable discretion in scheduling the opening date according to the varying needs of the community. In one district, schools thus began, according to the board's resolution, "on Monday the 22d day of September"—"or as soon thereafter as practicable." Trustees were acutely aware that a

One-room school, Orange County, Virginia, 1914
(courtesy of the U.S. Department of Education)

school's location could determine its success. Because of parental influence, however, finding the best location required political skill and careful consideration of local geography.[3] A process of trial and error en-
sued: schools that attracted students survived, and those whose attendance fell below the minimum closed. Clearly, a school within walking
distance of the greatest number of pupils had an immediate advantage.
Schools located "without much regard" for the convenience of the
neighborhood, wrote one official, generally did not survive very long.[4]

   In the free market of education, locating a school called for a delicate
balancing act. School officials were especially concerned not to encourage competition among public schools. As Ruffner warned, trustees
should carefully position schools so that they were not "too near, or too
distant" from other public schools. School officials, however, were often
unable to balance local interests. Attempts on the district level to distribute pupils according to some rational plan usually met with failure
because of geographical impediments and decentralized governance;
and in many instances schools competed for the same clientele. In such
cases, trustees often made an attempt to impose boundary lines. An

episode in a Valley district is illustrative. A trustee suggested a boundary between two schools located in communities known as Buck Hill and Chapel. "None of the parties will have over 1¼ miles [to walk]," he noted, and "the school at the Chapel is too large anyway and the parties we wish to take to Buck Hill will not have it any farther and some will have it nearer to Buck Hill." But conflicts over boundaries persisted near the Buck Hill school when a group of patrons, who had established a school nearby in Craig, later complained that "certain persons" had withdrawn their children and were sending them to Buck Hill. Attendance consequently languished at Craig, and the petitioners requested that the district board intervene and prevent pupils from attending at Buck Hill. The board rejected this drastic solution and compromised by giving the Craig school another chance to recruit the requisite average attendance.[5]

Attempts to establish regular school boundaries, as these examples suggest, frequently ended in failure. The directives of trustees carried little force, and many parents ignored them and sent their children wherever they pleased. And although district boards usually required such students to pay tuition, this rule was enforced only with great difficulty. When pupils from one district attended a school in an adjacent district because their parents had helped to build the school, a trustee acknowledged that it would be "difficult to stop them." Similarly, a northern Piedmont teacher who pointed out that a large portion of her students were from an adjoining district complained that her school was "too large" to provide "proper attention to the scholars in attendance." Patrons and pupils from another part of rural Virginia freely attended schools regardless of boundaries. Some children thus "deserted" schools nearby in favor of ones farther away for no apparent reason; one school was "weak," the other "overrun." In some instances, an entire family who began a session in one school transferred to another in the middle of the term.[6]

The need to attain a sufficient average attendance forced schools to adapt themselves to other local desires. As we have already seen, it meant that the teacher had to be popular because patrons tended to boycott unpopular teachers. Scheduling the school session at the community's convenience also encouraged attendance. Even with a good location, advised the *Educational Journal of Virginia*, a school might not make the average if the "convenience and rights of the patrons" were not respected concerning a "proper time to open the school." A teacher, the writer continued, "is assigned to a school, and enters into contract to

Wilderness School, Orange County, Virginia, 1914
(courtesy of the U.S. Department of Education)

teach it for six months—it suits *his convenience* to commence, we will say, in September, he opens at that time, and a few who are able to dispense with the services of their children send them. The first day, perhaps he enrolls ten."[7]

The Topography of Rural Education

The physical structures containing schools were no better built than the farms and homes around them, and public education blended into an environment of poverty, isolation, and inertia. A typical school, commented a writer at the turn of the century, was quartered in a makeshift and isolated building "more unsightly often than the corn houses or the tobacco barns" and "frequently situated in some remote or out-of-the-way place, where somebody gave a half acre of land to have the school near him." Another contemporary, a public health reformer, wrote that most of the rural schools in a Piedmont county were "located in the midst of woods or on bleak, windswept hillsides, remote from the dwellings." A black teacher complained about a bleak school lonely enough "to make any man drink." Another teacher, reaching a similar conclusion, told of a school set in "a hard country and a lonely place."[8]

The harsh topography of rural education—its poverty and isolation—could not help but affect the process of education. Teachers were constantly reminded of their isolation. A black teacher lamented that he was about eight miles from either a railroad or telegraphic communications; worse still, the patrons spoke "a language or dialect almost as difficult to understand as Greek or Latin." Isolation, bad communications, and erratic transportation all meant that pupils and teachers were, to an extraordinary extent, at the mercy of weather and environmental conditions. "Roads determine very largely what the social life, school conditions, and church interests are likely to be," wrote a twelve-year-old girl in the early twentieth century. In bad weather, people remained at home "unless compelled to go for the doctor, to the store or post office." Heavy rain or snow quickly rendered most roads in Virginia, even those considered good, impassable. One woman teacher, discovering the power of nature in Southside Virginia the hard way, explained that she had missed a test because of "high water." In another county, a superintendent remembered that in the winter months, roads were so "wretched" that they prevented regular attendance.[9]

The rural school was usually as primitive as its surroundings. Most of the schools of the 1870s and 1880s, according to one contemporary, were "built of rough logs," and "there were but few frame buildings"—and those were unpainted. Inside the schoolhouse, the surroundings were bare. A black teacher related how, in a log-hut school with a chimney "laid upon boards which rested on the rafters," when a board caught fire, the clay and logs fell out and left "holes large enough for a dog to get through." From Prince Edward County another black teacher reported that his log school had large gaps in the floor through which the wind did "not find it hard to creep." A schoolhouse described in 1882 was typical:

It is about twelve feet square, and seven feet high, made of unbarked logs, and daubed with red earth. The floor is of outside plank, flat side up. The chimney is about six feet high, and almost as large as the house. . . . Most of the light comes through the cracks between the boards on the roof, for there is only one window, or rather [a] hole in the wall, which was meant for a window.[10]

Frame schoolhouses increasingly replaced log buildings during the nineteenth century. But even the frame schoolhouse was, by modern standards, rugged and primitive. A reformer was mortified when she discovered that a school had no window shades, no lock on the door, unpainted walls, and a "much used" bucket and dipper. Whether log or frame, the rural school was spartan. Glass windows were a luxury, and the air in the schoolroom was often stifling. A stove, or more commonly, a large open fireplace, heated the room, and invariably the furnishings were sparse. As one teacher observed, her schoolhouse had "neither tables, chairs, blackboard, chart register, water bucket or axe. There are but two windows and . . . small light in all so that the business of the school can with difficulty be carried out in bad weather."[11]

Pupils sat on rough and usually uncomfortable benches of uniform height, often made of slab planks with no backs. An early twentieth-century city superintendent who attended rural schools in southwestern Virginia recalled that he and his schoolmates sat on long benches that were split in the middle, had bark left underneath them, and were smoothed on top with a drawer knife. These benches had no back- or footrests, and "if your legs were too short to reach the puncheon floor you prayed, if you had reached that spiritual stage, for recess or playtime to come so that you could rest tired muscles by exercising them." Older or larger pupils had difficulty keeping their legs in a comfortable position.[12]

Conditions in black schools were almost uniformly worse than those in white schools. A common problem was overcrowding. Although trustees ordered a black teacher not to enroll any more students because of overcrowded conditions, after pleas from patrons as well as from the teacher the board relented and allowed larger enrollments.[13] A white reformer in the early twentieth century noticed on a visit to a black one-room school in southeastern Virginia that 150 to 200 pupils were within walking distance of a school that held only 40 pupils and had an enrollment of 91. During the last thirty years of the nineteenth century, the disparity between black and white schools—at least in overcrowding—declined slightly. In this period, the proportion of enrolled students per

Tibbstown School, Orange County, Virginia, 1914
(courtesy of the U.S. Department of Education)

black school declined by 36 percent and that in white schools increased by about 7 percent. But even in 1900 the average black school had 37 percent more pupils than the average white school.[14]

Attendance and Nonattendance

Because schools adapted themselves closely to rural society, education reflected its needs. Although some communities perceived education as a central and regular component of youth and growing up, for the average rural Virginian school took second priority; it was only part of everyday life. Even had they wanted public education to become a full-time experience, parents would have found schools open less than half a year. Because full-time schools were not available and participation not compulsory, rural youth either attended a public-financed or private school—or did not attend at all. Only once, in 1890, did state officials actually measure this choice, and these data provide a revealing statement on the status of education in rural Virginia. About two-thirds of all school-age children attended a public school some time during the year, although not necessarily with any regularity. Another small elite, 5 percent, attended private schools. At the same time, a large proportion—a fifth of all whites and two-fifths of all blacks—chose not to attend any school.

In spite of the overall rise in attendance and enrollments between 1870 and 1900, attendance remained at low levels. In 1890, for example, close to two-fifths of the total white school population and about a quarter of the blacks attended regularly. There was some regional variation, with the western third of the state reporting slightly higher attendance.[15] Yet this variation was not especially significant. The northern Piedmont reported the lowest white and black attendance of any region in 1900, but both were only about 12 percent below the state averages. Because these data suggest only general trends, they disguise another reality: attendance was not only low, it was also extremely erratic. As a black teacher put it, many patrons tended to send their children only "one or two days in the week"; they expected the teacher to instruct "those scholars as much as he does one that goes every day in the week." Contemporaries and historians alike have concluded that erratic school participation, by no means unique to the rural South, was a trademark of country schools across the United States.[16]

Irregular attendance was most likely the result of a combination of complex, and frequently conflicting, causes and motivations. Most pupils were unable to attend regularly because of the unpredictability of the elements and the unreliability of transportation.[17] Rural Americans did not value regularity as either important or essential, and a disciplined attitude toward time and work—especially the regularized attitudes that have become the rule in the twentieth century—was alien to rural Virginians. Rural schoolchildren attended erratically "out of sheer indifference," complained one school official; he estimated that most students attended only one out of four days. An educator in the Shenandoah Valley was more generous. He wrote that about two-thirds of enrolled students attended regularly; even so, he considered nonattendance a serious problem with a complex array of causes. Some truants were "really sick, some feign sickness," he commented, "a few are helping their parents, some are hunting the rabbit, some have become disgruntled at the teacher, some have stumped a toe, and sometimes the flying squirrel appears from his den, menacing home and friends, and must be dispatched."[18]

Attendance was irregular for another essential reason: children constituted a large part of the rural work force. Although some families could dispense with their labor and, at times, their income, others could not afford to permit their children to attend regularly. Rural poverty, especially among blacks, was a particularly prominent factor. When a black teacher in Piedmont Virginia first arrived at her school, the patrons informed her that "they could not stop their children from their work to go to school." According to another black, poor students tended to be "in one day and out two." The harsh truth, reported one county superintendent, was that "parents (chiefly of the poorest class) must have the services of some of their children or starve."[19]

Perhaps the greatest demand for child labor originated in the rural home. Subsistence and commercial farmers alike depended upon children to perform a variety of duties. "From the time each of the boys would become old enough to do any kind . . . of work," remembered one Virginian, "we had to help do anything that we could to aid in farm duties." On most farms, work "could always be found to employ the time and labor of even very small children." Demand for labor in staple-crop and commercial agriculture also tended to depress attendance. Child labor, especially of older boys, was in greatest demand in rural communities during the fall harvest. A black teacher told how he opened a rural school in Virginia at the beginning of October and noticed that most of the faces in the classroom were young. "The older ones," he explained, "cannot come until the fall work is finished (gathering corn &c.) and then I shall be overrun." Another black educator reported that boys over the age of twelve remained at work and did not enter school, if at all, until Christmas. Recent studies of school-leaving age confirm these contemporary observations. By age fifteen, close to half of all rural children were no longer attending school in nineteenth-century America.[20]

Under the prevailing pattern, most students attended during the winter months, when labor needs at home had slackened. But by spring, these priorities had changed and many pupils were compelled to drop out. Numerous instances confirm that spring planting and fall harvest claimed the time of rural young. A Southside teacher explained declining attendance by citing the labor demand during tobacco season and wheat harvest; another cited the oats harvest as a cause of nonattendance. In a fruit- and vegetable-growing area in southeastern Virginia, an observer explained the effect of labor demands upon attendance. It reached a peak during winter, but after May declined steadily. One teacher, who recorded an enrollment of eighty and an attendance of fifty, faced a crisis by late May, when a sudden call for strawberry pickers went out. Because "the fields gain[ed] forty or forty-four" of the attending students, the school was forced to close for want of pupils.[21]

These accounts suggest that not only the child-labor economy but also poverty, sharecropping, and tenancy depressed rural attendance and that wealth and landowning increased it. Actually, the relationship between economic structure and attendance was far more complex. One way to address this question is to isolate those counties where landlord-tenant relationships might affect attendance. The combined rate of black tenancy and sharecropping was over 50 percent in twenty-three counties in 1900; among whites, a similar percentage appeared in only four counties. In some of these counties—especially in the tobacco- and cotton-producing districts of eastern Virginia—low attendance accompanied black tenancy and sharecropping. Brunswick County, on the southeastern rim of the tobacco district, reported 57 percent black share tenancy and 16 percent black attendance; 59 percent of the black farmers of urbanized and truck farming Norfolk County were either tenants or sharecroppers, and only 13 percent of the county's black children attended school. Yet the pattern in these counties was not necessarily typical, even in low landowning areas. Taken together, the twenty-three highest black share tenancy counties reported an average black attendance rate of 26 percent, as compared with a statewide average of 25 percent. And the examples of staple-producing counties simultaneously exhibiting high share tenancy and high attendance are too numerous to ignore. In the heart of Southside tobacco culture, Mecklenburg County reported 64 percent black share tenancy and 31 percent black attendance, whereas in a Tidewater cotton district, Southampton County recorded 78 percent black share tenancy and an astonishing 46 percent black attendance. Nearby, in peanut-producing Sussex County, with a black share tenancy rate of 51 percent, black attendance stood at 54 percent—the highest in the state. This pattern was no different among whites, with the four counties with rates of white share tenancy above 50 percent reporting attendance either equal to or above the state average.[22]

Whether schools were well or ill attended expressed a swirl of sometimes conflicting factors. The only factor that associated similarly with white and black attendance statewide was race, which tended to corre-

Repression

spond with lower attendance.[23] Otherwise, the relationship between attendance and social and economic variables differed by region. Although wealth was an insignificant variable statewide and in most regions, it correlated positively with white attendance in the Tidewater and with black attendance in Appalachia. A higher rate of landownership among whites associated with higher white attendance in the Valley and urban counties; black landownership corresponded with lower black attendance in the Southside and Tidewater. In still another economic category, type of crop, only peanut production figured significantly, correlating positively with black attendance statewide and in the Southside.[24] Population density and literacy were important, but their impact varied from region to region.[25]

Either by isolating districts with high share tenancy or by examining the question at the regional level, the conclusion is inescapable that a patchwork pattern of factors lay behind attendance and nonattendance. By viewing the problem in still another way—isolating counties with low and high attendance—the same localized pattern emerges. Among both races, low attendance was a statewide problem. It appeared most frequently in eastern Virginia; a majority of counties with high attendance lay west of the Blue Ridge. In some respects, counties with low attendance possessed characteristics similar to the rest of the state. Their rates of landownership and literacy were roughly equivalent to the state average. In other respects, however, some general tendencies were present for both races. For both whites and blacks, low attendance was accompanied by poverty; agricultural wealth in counties with low black attendance thus averaged about 88 percent of the statewide mean. At the same time, such counties were also on the average more sparsely populated and had a higher black population.

Yet the inferences emerging from these data, if true generally, contain plenty of exceptions. Although sparse population and geographical obstacles discouraged attendance in one area, in another these factors made little difference. In some communities higher black population—and black participation in public education—tainted the schools and depressed white attendance, but in other parts the effect was opposite. And although greater wealth and a higher rate of propertyholding might have encouraged parents to send children to school in some areas, in others it made them unwilling to relinquish their children's income. As Lee Soltow and Edward Stevens and others have concluded for rural schools in the Northeast and Middle West, the labor demands of the farm economy had mixed effects on school attendance. Commercial agriculture tended to generate a higher demand for labor, in particular inexpensive child labor, thus depressing school attendance. Yet new opportunities and wealth also stimulated attendance because of higher family income.[26]

If the reasons why some Virginians attended but others did not lie in the local world of rural society, the phenomenon of attendance demonstrates a truism about community-controlled education: for most students, schooling was only an occasional experience. A significant portion of school-age children remained outside the reach of the schoolroom in the nineteenth century. Even for counties with high attendance the rate was significantly below enrollment levels. For the state as a whole, moreover, during an average year a third of school-age children never stepped inside a schoolhouse. For those in school, formal education was an irregular experience; only about half of the enrolled students attended regularly. Geared to the irregular and seasonal rhythms of rural society, schooling for students was only a part-time investment, and their loyalties lay elsewhere.

Inside the Schoolhouse: The Teacher

The irregular pace of rural education decisively affected the experience of teachers. Although rapid educational growth created a growing demand for teachers in the late nineteenth century, they were under the grip of a peculiarly geared system. The new public schools of rural Virginia were sporadic and constantly fluctuating, and as a result, rural teachers were transitory, seasonal laborers whose occupations hung on the vicissitudes of laissez-faire schooling. Further, because the system depended upon local enthusiasm, these laborers, most of whom increasingly were women, toiled in a vocation that appeared to offer little future.

One characteristic of American education that distinguished it from European mass education was the earlier and more rapid increase of female teachers. A flood of women into teaching followed the establishment of common school systems in the Northeast and Middle West by the Civil War. In Massachusetts, where feminization occurred earliest, about 78 percent of all teachers in 1860 were women. Public schools elsewhere followed this pattern, and by 1920, 86 percent of American schoolteachers were female. Feminization of teaching—almost exclusively in common (or later elementary) schools—accompanied educational expansion. But feminization of southern teachers took place somewhat later than elsewhere in the United States; in Virginia, women did not constitute a majority of teachers until the late 1880s.[27]

The entrance of women into teaching progressed at an even slower pace among blacks. While the absolute number of white male teachers declined by about 12 percent during the 1880s, for example, the number of black male teachers increased by about 75 percent. Black males continued to become teachers for several reasons. Demand for black teachers was high because of the transition from white-taught to black-taught schools that occurred during the last twenty years of the nineteenth century. Teaching became an attractive vocation for black males because it was, along with the ministry, a professional option that remained open throughout the late nineteenth and early twentieth centuries. Although black males could enter professions like the law, medicine, and engineering only if they possessed the wherewithal to leave the South, the presence of southern state normal facilities made entry into teaching easier.

A dominant tendency among both races and nationally by 1900, feminization also made teaching less acceptable as a male vocation. School officials encouraged the hiring of women, moreover, because it augmented a hierarchy of public education in which women held subordinate positions and men held more prestigious jobs as school officials, superintendents, and high school teachers. This hierarchy implied that public education could be made cost-efficient by hiring female teachers at low salaries, and educators openly promoted sexual inequalities in teachers' salaries. One district board, surprised to discover that males and females were earning similar salaries, questioned the "right of this Board to ignore the old custom" by placing both genders "upon the same footing as to the am[oun]t of salary."[28]

Because localities had complete control over salary levels, they varied considerably. In Giles School District, in the Piedmont's Amelia County, for example, black female schoolteachers earned on the average $30 per month in 1890; in an adjacent county, they earned only $18.[29] This variation in teachers' salaries followed the pattern of localization in Virginia rural education. Wealthier, more literate, and more densely populated counties tended to pay higher salaries, but these factors were more important in eastern Virginia.[30] Although there was little difference regionally in salaries, there was considerable difference in the impact of socio-economic forces. In western Virginia a high rate of propertyownership associated with depressed salaries, but type of crop appeared to play a minor role. Moreover, the presence of better schools (as measured by greater tax support and longer school term) also associated with higher salaries.[31]

Two censuses of teachers, in 1885 and 1889, suggest that their status resembled that of other American workers in the late nineteenth century. Rural teachers worked in a hierarchy in which gender and age were important. The average teacher was not only female but young. In some schools, indeed, teachers were younger than their older pupils; in an exceptional instance, one male began teaching in the Shenandoah Valley at the age of fourteen.[32] The youngest teachers were among the lowest paid group, black females, and the oldest were among the highest paid, white males. Especially among the bulk of the work force—women—schoolteachers were not only young but also single. About 87 percent of white females were unmarried in 1889; for black females, the rate was 81 percent. In contrast, about 44 percent of white male teachers and 40 percent of black male teachers were married.[33]

Late nineteenth-century teachers had little, and in some cases hardly any, formal education. As one teacher observed, Virginia schools paid such paltry wages and their terms were so short in duration that for those who spent their "time and money in acquiring a classical education," teaching was hardly worthwhile. In 1885, only 27 percent of all teachers held either a high school or higher diploma, and only about 6 percent had received a college degree.[34] Undereducation of teachers was a feature of rural schools that persisted well past the turn of the century. One survey conducted in the early twentieth century revealed that in spite of expanded normal facilities, about four-fifths of the Virginia teaching force had no training beyond high school and about a third had no education past elementary school. During the nineteenth century, most teachers in rural Virginia were undereducated out of necessity, simply because facilities, or access to them, did not exist. Instead, most during this period became teachers through a system of apprenticeship, in which district boards hired teachers' assistants, usually older pupils, many of whom eventually became teachers.[35]

Possessing little bargaining power, teachers were usually at the mercy of their employers. Because school sessions were irregular, prospective teachers looked for work throughout the school year. When a young black teacher was graduated from Hampton Institute, he set out to look for a job in a Piedmont county. A week later he had a school. In another part of the state, a candidate wrote to a county superintendent in search of a job beginning in early March. "I shall be out of any employment at that time," he wrote, and would be willing "to teach at any point in your Co. providing you give me a school." Still another teacher in search of work in the Shenandoah Valley announced his willingness to "teach very cheap to suit the hard time &c" but told a local trustee that he preferred to have a school "through the Spring and Summer mos."[36]

The search for work often took prospective teachers over substantial distances. After departing from Hampton Institute, a black teacher looked for work in nearby Princess Anne County, near Norfolk. The candidate hitched a ride with a cattle driver for twenty miles and then walked two more miles to the house of the county superintendent. To his great disappointment, he discovered that the superintendent was away for a week. More often, the shifting demands of the market and generally bad conditions meant that a teacher rarely remained in the same school for more than a few years. Transiency was a "depressing fact" for rural teachers, wrote an educator, and without "permanency" in education, pupils and teachers were "strangers," for "by the time they get acquainted, they part."[37]

Although its extent varied, teacher transiency was typical. In one Southside school district, only one teacher taught in all the sessions from 1871 to 1874, and none taught in the same school more than once. According to the teacher census of 1889, white teachers taught an average of about three years at a single school, and blacks taught about two and a half consecutive years. Thirty years later, the situation had hardly changed. Investigators from the Virginia Education Commission found that one-third of white teachers and one-fifth of black teachers in one-room schools had never taught before; on the average, whites remained at those schools only one year and blacks only three years. The "normal condition of the teaching force of Virginia," they wrote, was "one of great instability."[38]

Most teachers were transient out of necessity. When a Piedmont teacher decided to take a school for a single session, he explained that although the salary was a "mere pittance," it "would be better than doing nothing." Enterprising teachers augmented their income by teaching as many sessions as possible during the year. After completing four months of a school session in one district, a teacher adjourned school and left to teach in an adjacent school district. But the teacher promised, with the consent of the school board, to return to the first school several months later and teach one more month. Another black teacher subsisting on a paltry salary improvised by teaching school Saturdays and holidays and was thus able to conclude a five-month term in four months.[39]

Transiency was also related to a high attrition rate. The low incidence of married female teachers—both black and white—suggests that like their counterparts elsewhere in Victorian America, women usually left teaching upon marriage.[40] If teachers remained in the profession in their thirties, many of them found the salaries unattractive. A black male graduate of Hampton taught for several years and then gave it up because he "often went hungry" and "had rough times." Another Hampton graduate began a successful retail grocery business in Roanoke after teaching for three years.[41] Working in other occupations—widely practiced among teachers of both races—was openly encouraged by school officials as a way to keep teachers in the profession. Teachers were nothing more than an "irregular jobber," advised Ruffner, unless they had another occupation; only those with "two trades may thrive." It was thus not uncommon for teachers, especially black ones, to have other, often better-paying, occupations. Most often, probably, they doubled as farmers.[42] But among blacks, leading members of the community, especially ministers, frequently served as teachers. As one recounted, he was "preaching and teaching" in four churches and in one school. Every Sunday, he walked from eight to fifteen miles, returning very early Monday morning, sometimes through the "cold, snow, wet, rain and mud" to teach school.[43]

The Rural Schoolteacher: The Challenge of Survival

The harsh environment common to rural America not only made teaching unattractive, it made professional survival a challenge. The experience of one female teacher was not unusual. On arrival at the home of a trustee in a remote section of the state, she felt that she had "left the world altogether" and faced the "unpleasant life of a perfect 'hermitress.'" Acknowledging that some parts of the locality "must be pleasant," she noted that she "unfortunately did not have a home in that portion."[44]

A telling reminder of this isolation was the teachers' housing, which usually depended on local custom and availability. In some communities, patrons considered it their responsibility to furnish room and board free of charge; in others, they simply supplemented the teacher's salary.[45] Almost certainly, such housing was spartan. A black teacher who lodged in what apparently was "the best place" available within three miles of the school slept in an upstairs room with no windows, except for cracks in the slab cover so large that he could put his hand through them. On rainy nights, drops on his face awakened him; when it snowed, flakes "sifting" in his ears did the same. Towns and villages usually had boardinghouses in which teachers could reside, but outlying areas often had no such facilities. They consequently often boarded far from school and began the school day only after a long walk. Not unusual was the complaint of a black teacher whose lodgings five miles from the school necessitated crossing a swamp often "swollen high by incessant rains" that made travel "impassible."[46]

Survival in rural schools, in short, was a challenge. Teachers were under constant pressure to sustain and even to increase attendance. Insufficient attendance would close the schools, of course, but some communities provided other incentives. In Prince William County, a district board contracted with a teacher for a five-month term at a salary of twenty-five dollars a month, "provided the School averages twenty or more in daily attendance throughout the term." If attendance did not reach that number, "a corresponding reduction of his Salary will be made." Another teacher was contracted by the same board for twenty dollars a month, with a promise of a five-dollar raise if her school attracted an attendance of more than twenty.[47]

These pressures frequently induced teachers to solicit students actively to sustain attendance. A black teacher who visited a school with twice her attendance "returned home with the determination that I would have my school filled the next week." She visited parents that next Sunday and even attended a wedding dinner to promote her school. The search for students and for a livelihood drove other teachers to desperate lengths. One whose attendance had declined to the dangerous level of twelve pupils scoured the neighborhood in search of students, soon meeting five little boys. When the children heard the teacher stumble on a large stone in the road, they "lifted their heads," gazed at the teacher, and then darted through the woods like "wild turkeys."[48]

Survival also meant overcoming a haphazard system of financing. Any day-to-day expenses incurred by teachers were only rarely reimbursed. When a northern Piedmont teacher asked district trustees to pay for a school clock costing three dollars, the board refused on the grounds that "if a clock be furnished [in] one school" it would establish an expensive precedent.[49] Rural teachers were responsible for extracting salaries from the school system. Each month of the school session, the county superintendent gave teachers a receipt when the monthly school report arrived. The teacher sent this receipt on to the clerk of the district board, who issued a warrant for the monthly salary, which the teacher took to the county treasurer for, in theory, immediate payment.[50]

In practice, delays occurred at each stage of this process. "I would be very much pleased," complained one teacher, "if you would send my *warrants*, for my money,—as soon as possible,—as I am rally [*sic*] in great need of money." The teacher owed board and warned that "the people are pressing upon me . . . for it." These delays resulted from a series of bottlenecks. Teachers frequently traveled considerable distances to collect their salaries, and, even then, school officials and county treasurers did not consider it essential to pay them. Delay was not unusual. Although one teacher's contract specified a monthly salary of twenty-five dollars "as we have funds on hand," only rarely were funds actually available. A black teacher living twelve miles from the treasurer received only thirty-five dollars for teaching seven months. She depended "entirely upon sending by some one who chances to be going to court any fourth Monday in a month, as that is court day and he is mostly prepared to pay some then." Even teachers taking the trouble to locate the treasurer often found him unable to pay them. Treasurers were frequently either behind in their collections or lacked the available cash. In one county, cash was so short that the treasurer paid off salaries in bonds. Some treasurers even seemed oblivious to the hardships their delinquency caused teachers.[51]

Teachers often went without pay for months and sometimes even years. One teacher whose county reportedly had "one of the best Treasurers in the state of Virginia" told of receiving salaries two years late; "what is due for last year we may get summer after next." Some of his warrants were four years old. Those who needed money quickly were forced to sell their warrants at a substantial discount. A teacher discovered that his monthly salary of twenty-five dollars "when discounted for cash comes to very much less which indeed is a small sum for teaching between 50 & 60 scholars." Elsewhere in the state, a black teacher charged that he had not received "one single cent"; his alternatives were to wait eighteen months for his salary or to discount the warrant at 30 to

40 percent below its face value. Another unpaid teacher wondered whether money would be forthcoming unless the warrant was discounted by about 25 percent.[52]

The Agenda of Rural Education

As community-controlled institutions, Virginia rural schools followed no regular, standardized curriculum. Soon after the establishment of the school system, legislation specified a basic outline of instruction in orthography, reading, arithmetic, and geography; the legislature also ordered the state superintendent to establish uniform textbooks in these subjects.[53] Until the end of the century, however, state superintendents found enforcing uniformity in the school curriculum nearly impossible, and they modified or ignored the law to adjust to local custom. In 1872, a year after Ruffner prepared a list of texts from which county school boards could choose, he announced that "uniformity" should be determined at the local level. "If the central power dictates books and methods for all schools," he warned, "it may well choose teachers, build school houses, and buy furniture and apparatus—a plan which might do in Russia, but does not suit in America." Subsequent state superintendents did little more than Ruffner to centralize control over textbooks. Although the State Board of Education claimed "absolute uniformity" in textbooks and even published a list of appropriate books in 1886, it immediately qualified its new policy by including only new texts and leaving the decision to the county and city school boards.[54]

Textbook publishing was a centralized industry by the 1870s, and it possessed a sophisticated marketing structure that was adapted to the diverse needs of American common schools. It was, without a doubt, furiously competitive.[55] The most successful textbook publishers were located in New York City because its unparalleled financial resources were essential for such a capital-intensive industry. Access to transportation facilities was also important, as was the existence of an efficient marketing network to sell textbooks to local school boards. Because most decisions about book adoptions took place on the local level, agents concentrated their efforts there rather than at the state capital.[56]

Intense competition meant that publishers attempted to satisfy customers in different localities and, at the same time, retain a national system of marketing and production. As Ruffner observed in 1877, school boards generally adopted texts that were appropriate "to the circumstances of particular cases" and "the different styles of teachers and schools."[57] Publishers received information about sales and learned about local preferences from their book agents. According to one successful late nineteenth-century publisher, this atmosphere of "free and constant competition" meant that the most successful texts were those "best suited to the wants of each community."[58]

Because they appealed to the values of Victorian culture, successful schoolbooks are good indicators of the common denominators of rural life.[59] Their success can be judged with some precision because, for the years 1871 and 1885, the state superintendent published adoption lists by county. The most popular textbook was William Holmes McGuffey's *The McGuffey Reader*, which was adopted in sixty-eight of one hundred counties in 1885. Because of its simple language and abundant references to the superiority of rural living, the reader sold extremely well in the South and West, and its publishers concentrated their marketing efforts in those two areas. Next to *The McGuffey Reader* in popularity was *The Holmes Reader*, compiled by George Frederick Holmes, a professor of history and literature at the University of Virginia, and first published in 1870. Textbooks by other Virginians, such as those by Matthew Fontaine Maury in geography and Charles S. Venable in arithmetic, were also among the favorites in Virginia public schools.[60]

These texts were written within a rural frame of reference. Time was expressed in agricultural cycles rather than progressive intervals. The overwhelming considerations of the elements of nature were also ever-present. All of the popular textbooks assumed that their rural audiences communicated orally rather than by writing; moreover, they presented their lessons from the point of view of a fundamentally isolated society. Maury's *Elementary Geography* defined distance and direction with careful reference to familiar spots such as the rural home, church, schoolhouse, and post office. "Very often we do not need to be exact," Maury acknowledged; it was "enough to know that a place is 'very far off' or 'very near.'"[61]

Most of the examples in the spellers and the selections in the readers drew from the experience of farm life; their heroes were independent farmers, who were healthier and more patriotic than city dwellers. Cities were viewed with suspicion. Many passages emphasized the destructive atmosphere of the city, where moral constraints were looser than in rural areas or small towns. *The McGuffey Reader* told of a "decent, well-behaved" boy who moved to work in a city, soon fell into "bad company," and was doomed to a life as a drunkard. Rural texts expressed a common conception of social change and proper moral behavior. Young schoolchildren were repeatedly reminded that stability depended on strict adherence to rules. "Every thing should be put in its place," noted one text, "that you may know where each thing is."[62]

Many of the schoolbooks, especially before the 1890s, dealt gingerly with questions of social mobility and social aspirations.[63] When mentioned in textbooks, poverty was often portrayed as a virtue. One story in *The Holmes Reader* thus told of a young peddler whose parents and sister had all died prematurely because of poverty. The author did not question the justice of their fate but concluded, when the young peddler also died, that it was "much better" that he was with his family in heaven "than living here in pain and want." The readers also provided ample evidence of the consequences of excessively rapid social mobility and of movement from the countryside to the city. In the fable "Young Frog," an author described a vain frog who complained about her "dull out-of-the-way life"; she wanted to move "into company" where she could make her fortune. The frog left the security of her home and was soon devoured by a hungry duck. The story concluded with the moral that it was "a bad thing to think of ourselves more highly than we ought to think."[64]

The schoolbooks stressed what one historian has called the "secular ethic of Puritanism"—self-discipline and, above all, self-control. By the last quarter of the nineteenth century, texts included fewer direct theological references. Some 30 percent of the stories in *The McGuffey Reader*, according to one count, had religious themes in 1844; thirty-five years later, only 3 percent had a religious message. In contrast, the emphasis on secular moral behavior increased to 40 percent of the total in the 1879 edition.[65] An important assumption of the Victorian ethic was that hard work led to material success—a message that was constantly reiterated. *The Holmes Reader* included a fable about a grasshopper and an ant in which the grasshopper sang and played during the spring and summer while the ant worked hard. The moral of the story was that the hard workers of the world ultimately benefited, for those "who eat, sing, dance, in the summer, must starve in the winter." In another story in *The McGuffey Reader*, a young boy gave money to poor German immigrants, and, when his father saw him, he was rewarded for the good deed by a gift of a bundle of books. A boy in the "Fable of Insolence" received his comeuppance. One day, he abused a stranger and injured him with a brick. But the stranger turned out to be the boy's uncle, and the boy was punished by not receiving a gold watch and books which the uncle had intended to give him.[66]

Morality, the nineteenth-century schoolbooks emphasized, was self-actuating and unwritten. "We need not go to law to find out what is right," declared one writer. Upright behavior came with the strict observance of a code of morality. Breaking the rules, the texts acknowledged, was inevitable given the strength of man's baser nature, and the heroes in the readers always admitted any infractions. "Always tell when you have done anything wrong," advised one reader. "Tell the truth at all times, boldly, and all will love you for it." Obeying these constraints, the authors wrote, was important because self-control was essential for the stability of society. Even a single violation of any rule, they warned, could lead to the individual's moral degeneration. "'Only this once,'" admonished a teacher to a misbehaving pupil, "has been the first step to ruin of many who never meant to be anything but what was upright and good." Disobedience of the moral constraints of teachers and parents, the writer added, led to a "life of evil."[67]

Schoolbooks embodied the values of their environment in another important respect. They displayed the attitudes of an aggressively ethnocentric culture, which espoused the superiority of white, northern European civilization. In his *Elementary Geography*, Matthew Fontaine Maury outlined a racial hierarchy of humanity—including whites, Mongolians, Negroes, Indians, and Malays—in which whites were the master race. Indians, according to Maury, were "savages"; Arabs, "barbarous"; the Chinese, "civilized" but "heathens"; and Africans, "treacherous and savage." Whites naturally represented a higher stage of development. "People who live as we do," Maury explained to his readers, "are called *enlightened*." Another author of a geography textbook reached the same conclusion. Arnold Guyot, a Princeton professor and author of a popular text, wrote that whites were the "normal" race from which others were descended and that the extent of racial degeneration in other races depended on their proximity to the Europeans. "The degree of culture of the races," he observed, "also varies in the same order." Whites—the "central race"—were a "race of culture and progress, both now and in all ages past."[68]

Although instruction in American and Virginia history was spotty throughout the state and usually confined to graded and secondary schools, successful histories expressed this cultural orientation. For Virginians, ethnocentrism meant regional as well as racial consciousness, and schoolmen carefully chose only those histories that treated the Civil War and Reconstruction with "justice." Local school boards scrutinized texts for objectionable references to the South—particularly to slavery, the Civil War, or Reconstruction. Histories that were popular in the North, such as Joel Dorman Steele's *Brief History of the United States* (1876), were not considered acceptable because they made unfavorable references to the South. Virginia schools that included history in their curriculum probably used Mary Tucker Magill's *History of Virginia* or George F. Holmes's *School History of the United States*. Used by both blacks and whites alike, these books taught the superiority of white culture and institutions. The progress of humanity would have been impeded, read Magill's text, if America had been left to "a few savage tribes" who were "incapable" of appreciating their possessions or of improving them. "God," she wrote, "for His own purposes makes one nation superior to another, and the history of the world shows that the inferior always gives place to the superior race."[69]

Popular histories such as those by Magill and Holmes also treated other issues with proper delicacy. As Holmes wrote, his text deliberately avoided touching on the sensitive areas of slavery, the Civil War, and Reconstruction. He cited "misapprehensions or misrepresentations" of other texts whose accounts were "discolored or disguised by political, sectional, or local prejudices." Until "other years and calmer judgements" allowed a fairer assessment of the South's role in American history, he contended, his *School History* was a "serviceable" alternative. Ruffner made the same point more explicitly. No school history written by a northerner, claimed Ruffner, did justice to "the leaders, the character, the principles or the actions of the Southern people." "Would England allow France," he asked, "to write a modern History for English schools?"[70]

Rural School Pedagogy

What teachers taught as well as the texts they used varied from school to school. "Every teacher," remembered one student, "was a law unto himself" in the classroom.[71] Most teachers, of necessity, improvised. The vast majority of rural schools were held in a one-room building, with no identified age groupings. Pupils straggled in at the ages of eight, nine, or even older; in one-room schools in 1919, 60 percent of all white pupils and 78 percent of all black pupils were older than those who followed an age-graded schedule.[72]

Learning in rural schools was not a continuous process with a well-defined beginning or end. With little continuity between school sessions, recalled one southwestern Virginian, the "minds of the pupils did not hold much of the information acquired from one session to another," and each school began "at the bottom." Schools typically taught little more than basic literacy, a knowledge of arithmetic, and an elementary understanding of grammar. Adapted to these requirements, schoolbooks were designed to be self-instructional. "As matters now are," observed Ruffner, "the method of the teacher is commonly the method of the book and hence where there is a poor book there must of necessity be a poor school." Holmes informed teachers using his readers that the "varied exercises" were designed so that "even the inexperienced teacher can have little difficulty in making them available for profitable class-practice."[73]

Teaching commonly meant instruction through rote memorization and frequent use of the slate. The class "stayed with a book until we knew it from 'cover to cover,'" one former student recalled, "and the teacher decided we were ready for something else." *Holmes' First Reader* informed teachers that students learned best through "frequent and thorough review," and it recommended that new words be "pronounced plainly over and over by the pupils, singly and in concert." Spellers, grammars, and arithmetics all were designed to require constant memorization by the pupil.[74]

Numerous other observations of contemporaries stressed that the agenda of rural schooling consisted almost entirely of learning basic skills through rote memorization. Ruffner visited rural schools in one area of Virginia in the early 1870s and reported to his daughters about their apparently primitive—but typical—teaching methods. The state superintendent was shocked. Children there were required to work through a thick spelling book before actually reading the "simplest sentence"; grammar was learned through drill and memorization, "without a word of explanation." Even an advanced class in arithmetic, reported Ruffner, did not progress far beyond basic skills and "did not know what I meant when I spoke of numeration or nottation [sic]."[75] "We wrote our copies over and over; we 'ciphered' till we 'got the answer,'" recalled a former student in the Eastern Shore. The curriculum was composed of "but few subjects"—the three R's—and, if, after ample opportunity, "we could not get the answer, we were thrashed, and, after brief explanation, we tried again."[76]

Spelling was a crucial part of instruction in rural schools, both in the use of repetition and drill and as a demonstration that students were indeed learning. As Edward Eggleston reported in *The Hoosier School-Master*, spelling not only was the most apparent and practical skill that students acquired from school, it carried with it a significant mystique and prestige. Rural Hoosiers "loved spelling for its sake," and champion spellers held a special place in society.[77] The communal approval apparent in Indiana was also evident throughout rural Virginia during the nineteenth and early twentieth centuries. Learning through drill and repetition especially applied to spelling, and students and parents alike regarded it, according to one account of a white school, as "our specialty and our pride." Each class was sure to conduct a spelling session every day, and before dismissal the entire class lined up for a general "spell." The most coveted honor was to stand at the head of the class as champion speller.[78] Spelling distinguished the most literate and skillful members of each school, and areawide competitions—"spelling bees" —attracted the keen interest of the local denizens. In a society that lacked sporting events or other forms of mass entertainment, superiority in spelling signified both scholastic achievement and a sort of athletic prowess. As one Virginian boasted, he was a "champion speller" who traveled from "school house to school house to spelling bees."[79]

Such was the world that the large majority of American children and their teachers inhabited during the last third of the nineteenth century. Functioning in an environment radically different from that of towns and cities, rural schools were closely adapted to their surroundings. The local community firmly controlled their affairs, but because these communities were often poor, their schools were impoverished. Moreover, responsiveness to the community—fundamentally democratic, to be sure —did not always mean that the schools of rural America offered superior education. Indeed, because schooling was so closely adapted to the rural environment, it was nothing more than an occasional experience for teachers and pupils alike. Rural schools never played more than a part-time role, and they rarely went further than instruction in basic literacy. And although the milieu of the rural school appeared placid, content in its own inertia, and indifferent toward pervasive poverty, by 1900 it was on the eve of fundamental change.

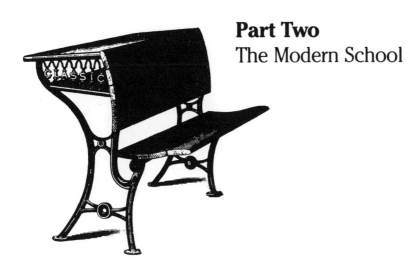

Part Two
The Modern School

Chapter Four
Sources of Change

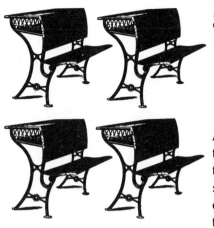

After the turn of the twentieth century, a series of related forces eventually remade the community-based
schools of rural Virginia. One obvious manifestation of change was
the heightened role of outsiders, es-
pecially the state government, in a range of decisions in which they
previously had taken little part. These changes ran against the tendencies of post-Reconstruction schools and resulted in an alteration of
power and decision making in public education. After Reconstruction,
localism was the driving force in the expansion of schools and enrollments; after 1900, dynamic expansion came from cosmopolitan centralizers, who brought innovations to schools such as modernized facilities,
diversified curricula, and new standards for teaching and learning. And
in contrast to the haphazard and spontaneous post-1870 expansion,
growth after 1900 was the direct product of a purposeful, self-conscious
attempt on the part of a group of reformers, elite in both composition
and approach, who were determined to institute a new function for
schools in rural society.

Although the need for change in country schools was unambiguously
apparent to reformers, rural Virginians were perhaps never happier with
their schools. Then and in subsequent attempts to change community
schools, they continued to regard any tampering with a combination of
indifference and suspicion. There was little evidence of popular discontent with post-Reconstruction education. Schools appeared to fulfill local expectations: they existed only if parents valued education, could
afford schools, and were willing to support them with adequate enrollments and attendance. By these measures at least, community-controlled education succeeded. The number of schools steadily increased
during the last third of the nineteenth century, as did enrollments and
attendance; an increasing level of literacy among whites and particularly

blacks suggests that rural schools served an expected, if limited, function. With no strong surge of popular resentment evident inside rural Virginia, the search for the roots of educational change must begin elsewhere.

The Urban Roots of Rural Reform

The insiders of the Virginia school system—state officials and urban educators—were prominent advocates and supporters of change. Throughout the post-Civil War decades, officials at the state superintendent's office and in the county schools were sorely aware of the impotence of state administration to affect local schools. Most of them probably became resigned to living with a system that provided few incentives for administrative zeal and energy; a significant number considered their work in schools only part-time. Still, a growing minority of state officials publicly expressed an angry discontent with the status quo in teachers' meetings, published state reports, and the professional journals, *Educational Journal of Virginia* and *Virginia School Journal*. Able to identify and to a certain extent communicate with state officials elsewhere through regional and national professional organizations, these men had little tolerance for low tax support, irregular attendance, abject school facilities, and substandard teaching—all products, they claimed, of loose school administration. Like their counterparts in the rural Middle West, dissatisfied school officials supplied both leadership and support for change.

Urban educators made up another insider group receptive to change. Unlike state officials, city schoolmen had enjoyed years of steadily increasing authority and prestige during the late nineteenth century, years that brought not only rapid growth in facilities and financial support but also witnessed the largely successful centralization of decision making and governance in the state's urban schools. Few of Virginia's major towns and cities escaped the spread of centralized, bureaucratic school organization, administration, and supervision. Well-organized school systems emerged in Richmond, Norfolk, Petersburg, Staunton, and Lynchburg, as well as in the new cities of Roanoke and Newport News. These schools produced educators who assumed the mantle of statewide leadership and who emulated national figures in city schools such as St. Louis superintendent William T. Harris and Cleveland superintendent Burke A. Hinsdale. Edwin Christian Glass, brother of Congressman and Senator Carter Glass, made Lynchburg's schools a model of educational modernization. Extending his influence through control of the statewide professional journal, the *Virginia School Journal*, he helped to establish a state-supported summer school for teachers at the University of Virginia in the early 1890s that became an arena for professionalism and reform.[1] The case of Glass was not exceptional, and much of the subsequent expertise and experience among Virginia school reformers came from urban school officials.[2]

Nonetheless, like professional state officials, city and town educators had exerted little influence statewide over public schools. For a variety of reasons, urban educators believed modernizing rural education would help extend their influence. Like most turn-of-the-century urban southerners, these men were not far removed from rural roots. Most of them were country-bred and retained a close identification with their rural roots, as well as a strong interest in rural Virginia. As early as the 1890s, some of these urban schoolmen became exposed to rural schools through attempts to introduce changes in contiguous counties. Others sought to change rural education because they realized that it was necessary for statewide centralization. Although these urban educators ultimately had an extensive influence on rural school reform, they remained isolated until they could forge a broader coalition.

Both professionals and urban educators had reached a similar conclusion by the end of the 1890s: rural schools, which educated the great bulk of Virginians, held the key to future educational development. Both professionals and urban reformers also began turning to national examples of rural school reform. Many of them favored extending city school organization to the countryside by expanding the age group in school, introducing curricular changes far beyond simple literacy and numeracy, and, above all, inaugurating fundamental changes in school administration. Yet, transplanting the urban model to a rural setting involved obvious limitations. A major challenge in city schools lay in organizing large numbers of students productively and efficiently; in rural schools, it was organizing and making efficient small numbers of dispersed students. Rural schools posed seemingly insurmountable obstacles to educational modernizers—above all, the staggering problem of geography that could be overcome only through massive state intervention and centralization.

A more satisfactory model of rural school reform, which addressed the difficulty of applying urban organization to rural schools, appeared in the report of the National Education Association's (NEA) Committee of Twelve in 1897. For reform-minded educators in Virginia, it was an appealing document. It was written by men of their ilk, primarily state officials and urban educators of the rural Middle West, such as the committee's chairman and state superintendent of Iowa, Henry Sabin. A blueprint for reform, the report of the Committee of Twelve proposed a complete transformation of the structure, pedagogy, and purposes of rural education. The committee condemned the prevalence of local autonomy and stressed the need to concentrate power in larger administrative units. It called for a significant expansion of physical facilities, consolidation of one-room schools, transportation of pupils at public expense, and the introduction of sanitary facilities in schoolhouses. And it urged the professionalization of rural teachers through stiffer examinations, expanded normal schools, and the establishment of supervisory staffs responsible to the state superintendents.[3]

The reforms outlined in the Committee of Twelve's report not only neatly matched but went far beyond urban school reform. In contrast to what reformers had diagnosed as the basic deficiency of urban education, rural schools were not alienated from their environment: rather, the report suggested, they resembled it too much and lacked the characteristics of modern urban society. Rural schools were dominated by localism, which these reformers considered a major failing. Sabin thus described the typical rural school as permeated with an "apathy, ignorance, and indifference" that hovered over the entire community like a "thick cloud." Or, as the report of the Committee of Twelve expressed it, rural schools needed the revitalizing values of "regularity, punctuality, obedience, industry, self-control."[4]

The recommendations of the Committee of Twelve fell on receptive ears among Virginia's professional educators. Following the report's publication, they began to advance a well-articulated program of school consolidation, modernization, and supervision that resembled the committee's recommendations. Influential though the support of these professionals was, it was not enough to change the school system. Indeed, they were powerless to affect rural education without broader support outside the school system.

Civic Group Activism

A crucial link between the expertise and experience of school officials and broader-based leadership and constituency became possible with the emergence of urban civic groups committed to educational change. Practicing an increasingly sophisticated brand of pressure-group politics, civic groups were a distinctly post-Civil War phenomenon. They at once provided a vehicle for mobilizing the urban middle class—a group never before involved in Virginia educational issues—and contributed a new intensity of activism and advocacy to school reform.

The emergence of civic group activists in Virginia paralleled the rise of similar metropolitan organizations elsewhere during the 1880s and 1890s. Tending to develop single-issue agendas, many of these activists focused intensely on educational reform. Urban middle-class civic groups such as the Public Education Society of New York City and the Public Education Association of Philadelphia were remarkably similar in leadership and objectives. Dominated disproportionately by business and professional classes, they believed that a participatory, haphazard system of governance accounted for the inefficiency and corruption of nineteenth-century public education. They thus proposed systematic centralization of school administration controlled by a professional, nonpartisan elite. With their leadership and political clout, the urban educational associations led the way in introducing stronger central control, eliminating partisan influence in schools, and initiating both secondary education and kindergartens.[5]

Urban civic groups resembled one another in still another respect: they were one of many expressions after the Civil War of increasing activism on the part of middle-class women. In Virginia, the Richmond Education Association (REA), a civic group that included a long list of illustrious citizens, was dominated and run by women and eventually became an important element of the reform coalition. The women who founded and then ran the REA—Landonia R. Dashiell, Lila Meade Valentine, and Mary Cooke Branch Munford—had first become active in Richmond's public life when they organized a woman's club in the early 1890s. Like their counterparts around the country, these Virginia women aggressively asserted a new definition of the proper feminine public role, but they remained within the accepted sphere for Victorian married women by choosing the feminized church, home, and, above all, school. These were "earnest, devout women," as a Richmond newspaper observed, who felt that there was "something in life for women to do beyond the home circle and the social circle."[6]

Mary Cooke Branch Munford and Lila Meade Valentine were typical REA reformers. Both blended traditional gender roles and social reform feminism. Both were born to prominent Richmond families in 1865, and

Lila Meade Valentine
(courtesy of the Virginia Historical Society)

Mary Cooke Branch Munford
(courtesy of the William Byrd Press, Inc.)

their adolescence and early adulthood were similar to those of many women social reformers of their generation. Like other activist women of the late nineteenth century, Valentine and Munford experienced emotional crises that arose from conflicts between their traditional roles as women and their desire to lead, direct, and refashion society. After marriage to Benjamin B. Valentine in 1886, Lila faced an emotional crisis two years later with the birth of a stillborn child. She underwent a protracted convalescence and experienced general depression, indigestion, and migraine headaches, from which she emerged only after a trip to Europe in 1892 and, a year later, a commitment to social activism.

Munford, who experienced an emotional crisis of a different sort, joined Valentine in spearheading feminine activism.[7] After suffering a nervous collapse prompted by her family's refusal to allow her to attend college, in 1893 she married Beverley Bland Munford, a lawyer of distinguished stock who had served as a Democratic member of the state legislature. A year later, Munford helped to organize the Richmond Woman's Club, and, although it began as an organization of upper-crust congeniality, its members were soon involved in citywide reform.

In ways that appeared to reinforce Victorian gender roles, both Valentine and Munford probed, tested, and even challenged their position as southern women in a male-dominated society. The move from home to school was a "short and natural one," wrote Munford. Urban women should feminize the school into "an efficient partner of the home" and thus develop a "broader life and more purposeful citizenship" among southern children. Although Valentine and Munford agreed that a group "organized and promoted almost entirely by women" could properly lead and direct school reform, they diverged—as did most REA women —on the limits of activism. Valentine later became Virginia's most important advocate of equal suffrage; Munford's activism, in contrast, was confined to educational and civic reform. Yet, like many other women across the South at the turn of the century, Valentine and Munford could agree on an activism that concentrated on increasing women's role in public life through educational reform. And like other upper-class urban women in the South, their first taste of school reform was a mixture of respect for the traditional with an assault on the role of women in southern society.[8]

Munford, Valentine, and three other woman's club members founded the Richmond Education Association in 1900 as an organization of mothers of schoolchildren who met once a week, without any specific agenda for change. Within two years, under the leadership of Valentine and Munford, the REA had inaugurated a strategy for changing Richmond schools. In 1902, the REA formed a Publicity and Press Committee to focus the attention of the Richmond dailies on educational issues. Soon the REA, functioning as an active interest group, was applying effective pressure through the press, public meetings, and the political process. Within a decade, its intense pressure on the city council and school board yielded results in the introduction of vocational training, the inauguration of a city kindergarten, and the construction of the new, central John Marshall High School.

While it was enjoying significant success in Richmond, the civic group began to turn its attention to assembling a statewide reform coalition.[9] Superficially, the Richmond women had little to offer the cause of school reform. Their experience with city schools was only recent; they knew next to nothing about schools in hinterland towns and cities, let alone about rural schools. Yet in retrospect it seems unlikely that school reform would have been effective without the participation of the REA women, for they brought political savvy, organizational ability, and activist zeal to educational reform.

The Intersectionalists

Like civic group activists, Virginia intersectionalists were another group of outsiders who were attracted to the cause of reform. Although many of them possessed long experience in southern schools, they regarded educational reform as only a means toward a more pressing end: remaking southern society. Acutely aware of the failure of Reconstruction to alter the regressive inertia of southern folkways, they believed that schools could help reintegrate the South into the nation. Virginia intersectionalists thus energetically promoted contacts among reformers in the region and, more important, among interested northerners. And they sought to fulfill these objectives by fostering native white southern leadership working in active cooperation with northern financial power and organizational skill.

Northern and southern intersectionalists were a product of an impressive network that came into existence during the late nineteenth century. Following the establishment of southern public schools in the early 1870s, northern missionary educators largely withdrew from elementary education but broadened their participation in black secondary and higher education.[10] Former northern abolitionists retained a strong commitment to the advancement of black education through organizations such as the Slater Fund, which encouraged the extension of elementary and secondary schools for blacks, and the American Missionary Association, which promoted and financed higher education for freedmen.[11] Many other northerners had strong links to the South through philanthropic organizations such as the Peabody Education Fund, which became a major private sponsor of southern educational expansion after Reconstruction.[12]

Philanthropy in the post-Reconstruction South bred an entire generation of leaders—some northern, others southern—with an informed perception of the realities of southern education. The veterans of the lean decades of the 1880s and 1890s had developed a deliberate and cautious style. An unwritten rule, a consequence of Reconstruction, was that northerners—particularly philanthropists—did not involve themselves directly in southern affairs. Instead, they often worked through ambassadors, intersectionalists able to bridge the gap between regions through a common interest in education. Barnas Sears, the first general agent of the Peabody Fund (and earlier the successor to Horace Mann as secretary of the Massachusetts Board of Education), acted as liaison between the philanthropists and southern educators. Amory Dwight Mayo, another northerner, became absorbed in the improvement of southern education during the 1870s while he was a Unitarian minister in Cincinnati. By 1885, he was devoting full time to the study and reform of southern schools—his "ministry of Education in the South"—and was bringing his message back north to educators and philanthropists.[13]

Although these intersectionalists took a regional approach, within several decades they had established bases in Virginia. One such stronghold was established by a son of missionaries to Hawaii, Samuel Chapman Armstrong, who founded Hampton Institute in 1868 after several years' experience in educating freedmen in southeastern Virginia. Within a decade, Armstrong was attracting a steady stream of funds from northern benefactors and making Hampton not only a model of industrial education but also a center for contacts between white southerners and sympathetic northerners. Among its generous northern benefactors was Robert Curtis Ogden, a partner of John B. Wanamaker in the department store business in New York City and an evangelical Presbyterian. Upon Armstrong's death in 1891, his successor at Hampton, New Yorker Hollis Burke Frissell, continued to cultivate white southerners and wealthy northerners.[14]

Most intersectionalists were native southerners, actively supported by

Robert Curtis Ogden
(courtesy of the Southern Historical Collection)

northerners. Jabez Lamar Monroe Curry, who succeeded Sears as general agent of the Peabody Fund, became a sort of educational elder statesman during the 1880s and 1890s, when he established extensive contacts among southern educators by regularly touring the South, encouraging the establishment of urban secondary schools, sponsoring local teacher training, and lobbying for increased state educational appropriations. Although he reported regularly to his northern superiors, as a former Confederate general and Alabama cotton planter, Curry was able to portray the cause of schools in unthreatening tones that soothed and reassured white southerners.[15]

Curry also served as mentor of a younger generation of southern leaders and intersectional ambassadors born during the Civil War era who reached maturity after Reconstruction. These younger southern intersectionalists had a variety of backgrounds. North Carolinian Walter Hines Page became an expatriate southern journalist, publisher, and publicist who won over and then maintained a formidable array of friends and supporters. Another Tar Heel, Edwin Anderson Alderman, served as a normal school educator and then, successively, as president of the University of North Carolina, Tulane University, and the University of Virginia. A close friend and contemporary of Page and Alderman, Charles Duncan McIver, helped to found the first state normal school in North Carolina, and, as its president, acted as consummate intersectionalist and southern educational statesman.[16] Among other prominent intersectionalists by the late 1890s were Virginians Charles William Dabney and Samuel Chiles Mitchell, both university presidents, and the influential Episcopalian minister and social reformer Edgar Gardner Murphy.

Unlike either reform-minded school officials or civic group activists, these intersectionalists emphasized the total, systemic change of Virginia's rural way of life. In contrast to social reformers elsewhere in early twentieth-century America, they identified underdevelopment, rather than excessive industrialization, as a fundamental cause of their region's social problems. The rural South was an "isolated, individual, conservative" society that held itself "proudly aloof from the ferments of modern society," wrote Alderman. Underdevelopment, according to Page, imprisoned the South in the most backward social structure and economy in the English-speaking world. Its inhabitants permanently retained "the qualities of the frontier civilization long after the frontier has receded and been forgotten."[17]

Intersectionalists saw national reintegration and sectional reconciliation—to nationalize the rural South "in politics and liberalize it in

Charles William Dabney
(courtesy of the Southern Historical Collection)

Walter Hines Page
(from Charles William Dabney, Universal Education in the South *[Chapel Hill: University of North Carolina Press, 1936], 2:35)*

Edwin Anderson Alderman
(courtesy of the University of Virginia Library)

thought," according to Mitchell—as crucial to future development.[18] Nationalization would come only when southerners discarded traditionalism, individualism, and, above all, localism. It would come when the region adopted entirely new values and attitudes toward its past and its future and wholeheartedly adopted a program of industrialization, urban development, and commercial-scientific agriculture. Yet the intersectionalists were also realists, and they believed that only long-term changes in the social and political institutions of southern society could overcome the instinctive conservatism of the rural South.

Intersectionalists were realists in another sense: they understood that any North-South alliance would have to overcome the nagging problem of the southern caste system. But although nationalization depended on an acceptable compromise on the "Negro question," the burden of compromising lay with northerners, who by the 1890s were making it clear that they would ignore white supremacy in the interests of regional progress and sectional reintegration.[19] Indeed, intersectionalists, northern and southern, greeted disfranchisement and legally enforced segregation as forward steps and lent influential support to both. Frissell endorsed disfranchisement as "a thing to altogether be desired," and Murphy held that the restriction of the electorate would end political violence and corruption and do justice to blacks "educationally and industrially." Many of these reformers soon regarded disfranchisement as distasteful, but some, such as Alderman, found it—despite its "ragged edges and incidental injustices"—a "wise and philosophical" reform.[20]

Although comprehending the gravity of racial problems, Virginia intersectionalists believed that the key to regional uplift lay with the white South. Much of Virginia was only "semi-civilized," wrote an intersectionalist, and "human life, whether white or black[,] is held cheap." Another Virginia intersectionalist was more explicit. Most rural whites, he wrote, were "poor and ignorant," had little conception of the need for progress, and were at a "stupid stand-still"; worse still, they were "satisfied with their stand." Ignorant whites were a dangerous element in southern society, for they obstructed the development of a "wholesome life" like a "stagnant and saltless sea." They were a "dead weight," a "menace" to their society.[21]

Intersectionalists concluded that systemic change depended on institutional change, which in turn depended on transforming public education. As Page wrote in *The Rebuilding of Old Commonwealths* (1902), energizing the rural South required the "training of the untrained masses" to "release" them for "usefulness" in a democratic society. Such training and the subsequent "building of a new social order" could come only after educational reform with far-reaching and long-lasting effects. It would place schoolteachers "on the level of constructive statesmen," making them "servants of democracy in a sense that no other public servants now are."[22]

A Reform Program

By the turn of the twentieth century, educational professionals, civic groups, and intersectionalists, all for different reasons, had converged on the issue of schools. In the 1890s, each offered distinctly different approaches and outlooks and envisioned a different outcome for school reform. The professionals were concerned almost exclusively with modernizing the administrative structure and beginning qualitative improvements; civic group activists and intersectionalists were less concerned about schools than about their impact on outside society. Yet once the reform coalition began to come together, these differences were muted. The coalition's strengths were the expertise and experience of the professionals, the organizational skill and activism of the civic groups, and the prestige and national and regional influence of the intersectionalists.

All were also in general agreement on the deficiencies of rural schools and the changes that would properly remedy them. They agreed that country schools posed the most serious obstacle to reform; changes in state administration were impossible without fundamental changes in country schools. Yet these schools also offered considerable opportunities for reformers, for changing them would mean not only the final triumph of the professionals but might also provide, as one southern educator phrased it, a "convenient point of contact for all constructive social forces." Or, as a Virginia reformer wrote, progressive rural schools would serve as a "headquarters" and "co-ordinating agency" of diverse types of social reforms.[23]

This vision of progressive rural schools leading regional uplift and development contrasted with a starker reality. Reformers believed that the institutional deficiencies of schools—especially undereducation and impoverished public support—were but prominent expressions of a larger southern malaise and the endemic social problems that accompanied poverty and underdevelopment. Reformers painted a dark but well-documented picture. Their investigations, surveys, and reports, which have survived as indispensable sources on southern rural education,

constituted a full-fledged attempt to examine the role of school in society, using social-scientific methods. Studying the rural schools revealed an array of social problems—poverty, underdevelopment, and
malnutrition—which public education did little to change and appeared
to abet.[24]

Yet because school reformers were imbued with a cultural imperiousness common to their era, they examined rural society exclusively on
their own, highly subjective terms. The result was a mixture of rich description and distorted analysis, an obsession with detailed description
combined with conclusions shaped by their own experience. Through a
perspective that was both highly empirical and highly subjective, reformers agreed that the main problem of rural education was its close symbiosis with rural society. In particular, schools and the society that shaped
them were unable to transcend the powerful force of localism. Few reformers would deny the tight cohesion between school and community,
wedded by a decentralized, participatory, and highly responsive system.
Yet such cohesion brought fortified resistance to change in the schools
and modernization of society. As one reformer claimed, localism, by
encouraging parochialism and discouraging a holistic, cosmopolitan
approach to life, threw up formidable barriers to change.[25] As serious
for reformers were the extended consequences of localism. Nepotism
and the participatory nature of school governance were also perceived
as obstacles to reform, as was a curriculum that did not attempt to teach
much more than the three R's. Perhaps most disturbing was the impermanence of rural education, both in the high rate of transience among
teachers and in irregular attendance among pupils.[26]

Reforming rural schools thus hinged on limiting, and ultimately ending, the influence of localism over education and society. Instead of
buttressing traditionalism and rural conservatism, schools should be future-oriented. The school of the modern rural South, wrote an agent of
Rockefeller philanthropy, Frederick T. Gates, should be a "microcosm of
the life of the whole community." Clearly distinguishing between present
status and future needs of the rural community, Gates maintained that
modern country schools should not reflect their environment but represent "a picture in little of the community as it is to be."[27] Inside the
schoolroom, lessons would go well beyond simple literacy and numeracy. Students in the reformed rural school would be taught a code of
responsible citizenship, political conduct, and productive participation
in a commercial market economy. Projecting themselves outward into
the community, modern schools would serve as a "nucleating center for

social progress."[28] Reformers expected that modern schools could occupy a commanding position only by extending their functions to a variety of specific activities. By offering vocational agricultural education
and adult education, wrote Dabney, schools could enlarge their usefulness in the rural economy and bring the "life and work of the people"
into the schools.[29]

Modernized rural schools would perform these functions with deliberately ostentatious visibility. They would become the physical and geographical center of the rural community and, unlike makeshift and transient nineteenth-century schools, would permanently project the power
of the state and symbolize a modernized society. Reformers believed
that school boards should hold clear legal title to buildings and facilities and that the nebulous distinction between private and public power
so common in the late nineteenth century be sharpened. They even insisted that schools follow a standardized architectural design. They
should be large enough to include a commodious assembly hall for
students and their parents. Most important, the rural school should
serve as an example of permanence and attractiveness.[30] "Its trees," said
one educator, "should be the handsomest, its trailing vines the most
tasteful, its shrubs the most thrifty and its flowers the most beautiful."[31]

A Cooperative Democracy and the Public School

It was obvious to most reformers that their vision of a future modernized
public education tensely coexisted with the inescapable reality of the
power of localism in school and society. Democracy and decentralized
education brought high enrollments and popular participation, but to
reformers they also brought undereducation and a host of social problems. These problems and the whole scheme of transforming the role of
school in society thus required broad changes elevating public institutions above individual license and extending community restraints over
the power of localities. Rural Virginia and the rural South, they believed,
could enter the world of cosmopolitan development only if community
power and unrestrained democracy were limited in areas as various as
race relations, governance, and economic organization. For reformers,
cooperation became an organizing concept for change.

It was urgent that rural Virginians move forward out of a world of
inertia, poverty, and parochialism and into an environment of energy,
growth, and cosmopolitanism. "No civilization can grow great in pov-

erty," declared Alderman, "any more than a man can grow and work when he is hungry." The South was on probation as a "member of the modern world"; its greatest need was to develop a "higher" form of social organization. Alderman explicitly rejected the individualism of the nineteenth-century South. Development came not through "personal courage or raw individualism," he wrote, but through organized interaction, a "public spirit," and "civic unity." Other southern cultural leaders who thought similarly pointed to the examples of European nations that had successfully transformed themselves from agrarian to urban economies. As a Virginia school official said, Holland and Germany had undergone these changes through national will and self-discipline; the key in each case had been organization, direction, and a "spirit of progress and social service."[32]

These changes, in turn, depended upon altering long-held concepts of the function of politics and the role of community institutions in a rural society. Again and again, school reformers saw the need for basic political changes to pave the way for a cooperative and regulatory, as opposed to a participatory and distributive, system of politics and policy making. Yet the logic of this analysis led them to a contradictory conclusion: extending a cooperative democracy could be possible only by limiting popular control over public schools. Cooperation, Mitchell told the Southern Sociological Congress in 1913, was a concept that went beyond mere democratic politics. Standing for "something infinitely larger and more complex" than universal suffrage and political representation, a cooperative democracy embraced "all the basal interests of man in community life, whether economic or educational."[33]

Like social and political reformers elsewhere in early twentieth-century America, school reformers agreed that basic changes in both politics and policy making were a prerequisite. From a variety of quarters during the turn of the century, national opinion makers blamed mass democratic politics and localistic governance for the failures of the nineteenth-century polity. Many of these same opinion makers advocated adjusting the political system to make it responsive to new economic realities. Democracy, as Alderman wrote, no longer meant the "interpretations of constitutions"; it required an understanding of "the very nature of the social order." Southerners and all Americans now faced an important and new "question in human liberty": how to keep the "priceless glory of individual excellence" and, at the same time, to control the "great cooperative forces which the plans of this giant age demand."[34]

Most reformers came to conclude that the Jacksonian political structure had outlived its usefulness. A large majority remained ill educated, poor, and uncivilized; participatory democracy in a modern society fostered political chaos and social disintegration. The voice of the majority, declared Dabney, was not "always the voice of God." Frequently popular democracy was neither wise nor safe, for "passion and prejudice" often broke "their fetters and the Demos work[ed] great destruction."[35] Reformers advocated instead a new system of politics and policy making better adapted to twentieth-century social and economic realities. They believed that the flow of power—bottom to top in the nineteenth century—should now run top to bottom. Such a cooperative democracy necessitated the end of decentralized decision making and a new role for expertise and interest groups. But it also necessitated a fundamental reorientation of the definition of citizenship. Whereas in the mid-nineteenth century republican citizenship represented a cluster of passive, even negative, political values protecting individuals from concentrations of power, in a cooperative democracy it required training provided through governmental intervention. And responsible citizenship was especially crucial to southern development. Modern southerners needed an independence and autonomy that were impossible when they were provincial, poor, and ignorant. Once southerners were freed from this condition of dependence, wrote a Virginia educator, they would be able to see "those larger and deeper social things that mean life, and hope, and joy." No persons, if "in a state of bare existence, or economically dependent," could comprehend a larger vision of society necessary in the modern world.[36]

By the first decade of the twentieth century, therefore, reformers were frankly acknowledging that this social transformation would not come democratically. Rather, such changes would come from above—from the South's natural, enlightened leaders, who would reshape the region's society and polity along cooperative lines and usher in a new, harmonious modern era. Such was the vision of Edgar Gardner Murphy, who foresaw a progressive leadership, acting as regional peacemakers to reform the economic system and reconstitute "a new sense of nationality." With such leaders at the helm, he envisioned the end of "class suspicions" and "race antipathies." Public education was a key ingredient of progressive governmental intervention and social policy. As Page put it, the reformation of public education was the "central secret of human progress" because it extended training and direction without coercion. "Since civilization began," wrote Page, "religions and statecraft, priests and conquerors, cliques and classes, sects and sections" have vied for the "leadership of man." Early twentieth-century reformers differed only in results; they held "the master trick against them all." With the public school, reformers could direct without coercion, could fashion a cooperative citizenry in a democracy. And, Page added, "when we win, man leads himself."[37]

The new progressive school would "inculcate the sense of duty to society" and hence dissipate the threat from "mob minorities."[38] Its enlightened product—the progressive citizen—would begin to transcend localism, indifference, and perhaps even class and racial differences. As a new center of the community, the reformed rural school, wrote a school official, brought together disparate and isolated groups of children and citizens. In this way, it would also break down parochialism, socialize isolated rural southerners, and take rural children and their parents out of their "small and narrow environments."[39] By enriching the community with the "ideas, influences and conveniences of urban life," declared Mitchell, the modern rural school relieved the countryside of "loneliness, stagnation and inefficiency."[40] Above all, the school would transform a turbulent society with a precarious future. It would train leaders for the future—men and women, according to one reformer in Virginia, "shot through with social insight, social sympathy, and social efficiency."[41] But progressive rural schools would do more than educate an elite; they would prepare the masses for participation in a cooperative democracy by inculcating in each citizen a sense of responsibility and civic training. As one reformer put it, it was far better to spend money "making cultured citizens than in maintaining great prisons and armies of policemen."[42]

The Emerging Polity

The timing of school reform—and in particular its translation into policy—depended upon important changes in politics to end the long-standing hostility of Virginia's leadership to public schools and open the way for greater state involvement in local affairs. V. O. Key in 1949 wrote that twentieth-century Virginia was a fascinating subject for students of history and politics because it was a "political museum piece." More than any other state in the Union, the commonwealth was firmly under the thumb of an oligarchy. This small but well-organized coterie of politicians restricted the suffrage, dominated the electoral process, and ran state government by means of a "tightly articulated hierarchy of power."[43] Originating some sixty years before Key's description, the Virginia machine played a pivotal role in school reform in at least two respects. First, the political rulers of early twentieth-century Virginia, although firmly in control, softened their impact by expanding public services in various limited areas, including public schools, and long-standing opposition was replaced by a limited degree of toleration. Second, reformers benefited not only from the new attitudes of policy makers but also from monumentally important changes in the political system itself. By ending partisan politics and diminishing the impact of popular participation upon policy making, the new closed system of politics maximized the power of pressure groups like school reformers and minimized the ability of potential opponents to coalesce.[44]

Throughout the post-Reconstruction era, Virginia public schools functioned in a precariously hostile political climate. The ruling Democrats gave public education only qualified approval, and the system verged on extinction during the 1870s; for the rest of the century, schools were tolerated without substantial political approval, and, with the emergence of a tightly structured Democratic organization in the mid-1880s composed of men such as John S. Barbour, Thomas Staples Martin, James Hay, and Harry D. Flood, they faced a bleak future.

By the first decade of the twentieth century, the organization's agenda included support of public education. Political realities dictated this transition. Leaders of the Democratic party, which since Andrew Jackson opposed any form of governmental interference in local affairs, faced a challenge from within their own party that forced them to recast their position. In 1899, insurgent Democrats such as Andrew Jackson Montague, J. Hoge Tyler, and William A. Jones attacked the organization and its allies by calling for a system of nomination by primaries, restriction of the suffrage, and modernization of public services in roads, public health, and schools. Their challenge culminated in the election of Montague as governor in 1901 and the constitutional convention of 1901–2. The new constitution ensured a closed form of governance by limiting political participation through a poll tax and complicated voter-registration requirements. It also provided for the modernization of the school system through the expansion of the powers of the State Board of Education and the establishment of legal compulsory education.[45]

On the surface, it appeared that the convention represented a significant victory for insurgents. Actually, both for the short and long term, the new constitution helped to initiate a closed political universe well suited to the needs of the Martin organization. Martinites realized that the best response to the insurgent challenge was to support limited political reform and to co-opt the reform program through superior organization and leadership. Not only did Martinites endorse political reform, they also learned to exploit the issue with remarkable speed and agility. Reform, they found, consolidated their hold on state government: suffrage restriction legitimated and widened their de facto political control; expanding governmental services widened their popular base. Martinites acted for the most part out of a need to maintain power—certainly, more than out of a strong interest in reform—and they were determined that they, rather than the insurgents, receive due credit as reformers and that they tighten their grasp over the twentieth-century polity through reform.[46]

By 1905, when Martin defeated Montague in the state's first senatorial primary, the former railroad lawyer openly supported railroad regulation, educational expansion, and better roads. In the senatorial primary campaign of May 1905, Martin described rural education as of "vast importance"; several days later, he endorsed a longer school term. Not only did the machine politician support public schooling; in a thinly veiled reference to the political impotence of Montague and his supporters, he also promised results. As he explained to an audience in Lynchburg, despite the promises of insurgents, the roads were "just as full of holes and the school terms are just as short as before." Hot air, he remarked, would not "aid in bettering the conditions much."[47]

Contemporaries and recent historians have remembered Montague as Virginia's "education governor" and Martin and his allies as the public schools' leading opponents. But it was Montague's successor, Claude Augustus Swanson, who successfully sponsored the most important reform legislation. Swanson was typical of the new organization politician. Born in 1862, he had become an effective campaigner and organizer as a Southside congressman and had struck an alliance with Martin before the end of the century. Although losing to Montague in the gubernatorial election of 1901, Swanson won resoundingly against another opponent four years later and immediately acted on his mandate by pushing a state highway commission act through the legislature.[48] A strong proponent of the expansion of governmental health, highway, and educational services, Swanson enlarged the power of the State Board of Health, expanded the Department of Public Instruction, and instituted a stream-lined system of revenue appropriation. The greatest beneficiaries of the Swanson administration were the public schools. The Southside politician was the most vigorous of a new generation of machine leaders who combined oligarchical rule with the modernization of governance. A former schoolteacher—he recalled as governor how he was "scorched by the summer suns and shivered by the winter winds"—Swanson was also genuinely concerned about the improvement of public education.[49]

As J. Morgan Kousser has shown, the transformation of the southern political universe was a pivotal development, making possible a system of government dramatically less responsive to popular participation and pressure and paving the way for legally enforced racial segregation.[50] For educational reformers, especially, disfranchisement and the restriction of southern democratic politics were of utmost significance. From their perspective, these changes offered potential for the building of a forward-looking, cooperative society, energized and modernized; in southern schools, from another perspective, they meant the further restriction of local control and democratic governance. But effecting educational change needed more than the limited enthusiasm of the new political rulers of the twentieth-century South. It required the coalescence of a reform leadership, able and willing to reach an accommodation with the new system and to adapt it to their advantage. It required enough popular support to advocate and then guide change on the local level. Not the least important, it required the permanent alteration of the educational polity.

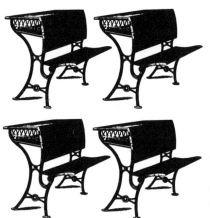

Chapter Five
From Evangelical Reform to Bureaucratic Management

In spite of their aggressive rhetoric and confident optimism, school reformers confronted a sobering social and political reality. Late nineteenth-century rural Virginians had successfully resisted attempts by the Reconstruction generation of reformers to impose an educational polity; even in 1900, a pervasive hostility remained toward increasing state control at the expense of local autonomy. Whether reformers could effect real change or whether their vision would remain an empty pipe dream depended on the inauguration of centralized, coercive school governance. Without this crucial change, it made little difference what other policy changes reformers advocated; what really mattered was their ability to articulate and command the entire system, from top to bottom.

The realities confronting reformers were sobering enough, but surely even more frustrating was a pervasive but corrosive indifference. School modernizers needed "all the help we can get," as a Virginia reformer observed; the most serious problem confronting them was "an inertia well nigh irresistible."[1] For reformers, inertia meant inaction, perhaps even resistance to innovation; to rural Virginians, it meant equilibrium and stability. That this system worked and satisfied a large portion of rural Virginians probably accounts for the absence of any mass uprising from below. It also accounts for the coalescence, despite grass-roots appeals, of an elite group of intersectionalists, public school educators, and civic groups after 1905. What, then, were the sources of change? In the face of a system that worked, the strength of localism, and at least mass indifference, how could reformers effect wholesale changes in rural education? Equally important, why did reformers eventually turn to bureaucratic management to guide new forms of rural school education?

98

A central paradox of rural school reform is that change became possible because of the innate conservatism of rural Virginia society. Reformers possessed obvious advantages. They were endowed with superior powers of wealth, organization, and articulation, whereas their potential opponents in the countryside were comparatively poor, disorganized, and inarticulate. And when reformers eventually united around a program of change, rural Virginians remained divided and isolated from the outside world and each other. Rural Virginians considered schools a community issue of no concern to outsiders, even fellow rural Virginians; to them, rural schooling was not a system which included anything beyond their own neighborhoods, and they harbored deep suspicions of other localities. In the heartland of community-controlled education, moreover, progressive school reform probably meant improvement and modernization, sometimes at the expense of local autonomy, but usually with substantial benefits. Reformers thus campaigned against localism by taking advantage of it—by dividing before conquering, reforming within the post-Reconstruction system.

But by itself, the inability of rural Virginians to unite against change only partly explains this crucial shift in the bases of power. Outside of the South, in spite of similar isolation and localism, opponents of reform were sufficiently united during the first half of the twentieth century to stall modernization and prevent the complete triumph of reform. Reformers in Virginia and the South, in contrast, possessed a crucial advantage in a closed political system and a one-party state. Educational progress as southern reformers defined it meant an end to participatory democracy and the traditions of absolute local power, and the restriction of nineteenth-century democratic politics and governance worked to their advantage.

Making these objectives effective required another significant transfiguration—this one concerning school reform itself. In 1905, a school reform coalition formed with prominent support and leadership from school professionals, civic groups, and the intersectionalists. Organizing around the guiding leadership of intersectionalists in the Southern Education Board (SEB), this coalition searched for ways to extend its influence over educational policy. Needing wider support than these three elite groups could provide, the fledgling reform group emulated the most familiar model of popular organizing, the evangelical revival.

Early Virginia school reform, like most nineteenth-century social movements, accepted several key assumptions. Evangelicals and those who adopted their methods believed in reform through social conversion, which they thought possible through staged manipulation—effective use of grass-roots, popular meetings, control over the media, and mobilization of other means of mass persuasion. But evangelical-style reformers were also political realists who adeptly functioned in interest-group, give-and-take politics. By the 1890s, indeed, many of the interest groups emerging with evangelical roots were beginning to express this political realism by rejecting partisanship, by viewing their interests as above those of political parties.

The central component of the evangelical world view, the conversion experience, deeply shaped the approach of early school reformers. The centrality of conversion determined evangelical reformers' view of society, change, and the motives of individual behavior. Because reform as applied to society was simply personal salvation writ large, a host of further assumptions followed. Social change came suddenly and convulsively; it might even be part of a larger perfected human society. As they applied this evangelical-style crusade to public education, reformers focused directly on individuals and the conversion of public opinion.

Although their early successes confirmed the utility of an evangelical crusade, Virginia school reformers discovered that systemic change required much more than altering popular attitudes. If reforming public education in Virginia reduced to reforming rural schools, reforming rural schools reduced to overcoming isolation, bad communication, and population dispersion. Inevitably, centralizing control over a decentralized system meant establishing permanent, continuous agencies that first effected and then controlled change. Another implication of this path from evangelical crusade to bureaucratic management was the example it set for social and political relationships in the rural South. In both implementation and practice, reform set a new pattern for civic-minded leadership and for harmonious intersectional relationships. "It's not so much education," a northern visitor to Virginia declared, "as the struggle for education that educates."[2]

Origins of the Southern Education Campaign

A crusade emerged in Virginia between 1902 and 1905 that brought together a reform coalition known collectively as the southern education campaign. It practiced the style and reflected many of the organizational characteristics of progressive reform movements elsewhere. It relied heavily on exposure by reforming journalists and political progressives. It was dominated by upper-income groups, and power and decision making flowed from the top down. Most important, southern educational campaigners, lacking a clear idea of how to implement change, relied on a familiar nineteenth-century organizational model, the Protestant revival.

Emerging from strongly evangelical roots, the crusade—and the reform coalition that it embodied—was the handiwork of the intersectionalists, whose main instrument became the Conference for Education in the South and then the Southern Education Board. The conference was originally the idea of a small group of largely unnoticed southerners, who convened its first meeting in June 1898 in the mountain resort of Capon Springs, West Virginia. The Capon Springs conferees held an innocuous meeting. Attendance was small and deliberately restricted, but an agenda of Christian education, black schooling, and mountain white education placed it squarely in the mainstream of post-Reconstruction missionary education.

The meeting ended with a resolution expressing a "deep and abiding interest" in the advancement of "moral and religious education" in the South "along Christian lines," and it warmly welcomed the continuing presence of northern "friends" who saw "promise for unity and harmony of our common country" through education. Yet the conference went beyond the familiar goals of missionary education to turn its attention to larger, regional problems. In a significant resolution, the missionary educators endorsed a program that ignored further support for denominational and private education and proposed renewed attention to public schools through the expansion of the school term, creation of tougher standards for teachers, and expansion of the curriculum beyond literacy.[3] Subsequent conferences went even further. By consensus, the following year's meeting dropped its religious affiliation and ended any identification with denominational or missionary education. More important, beginning in 1899, the conference clearly began to come under the domination of intersectionalists, especially the department store magnate Robert Curtis Ogden.[4]

Serving his apprenticeship in southern education as president of the board of trustees of Hampton Institute, Ogden was the movement's leader and a consummate intersectional mediator. With Armstrong and then Frissell, he had made Hampton, according to Charles Duncan McIver, an "inexhaustible mine" of philanthropic funds and a center for the training of a future generation of southern educational leaders.[5]

Convinced of the benefits of industrial capitalism, Ogden was also the quintessential northern philanthropist. But his main contribution to the conference was his considerable organizational ability. An "accomplished organizer of social functions," as one intimate described him, he led an annual railroad car excursion to the conferences, which he hired at his own expense and used to foster intersectional contact among the "best men" of both regions.[6]

To these northern guests and their southern allies, Ogden pressed a program of sectional reintegration through public education on the conference. He not only regularly transported northerners to the conferences but also insisted that their southern hosts provide them with "some particular part" in the proceedings of the meetings.[7] He was equally determined to avoid what he saw as the tragic estrangement and bitter division during Reconstruction of northern and southern whites of similar class and political outlook. Building intersectional trust and cooperation, Ogden and other intersectionalists believed, depended on a crucial concession: recognizing southern sensibilities about outside interference in the region's internal affairs. Indeed, not only intersectionalists but most educators were convinced that any attempt to change the school system without substantial and visible southern participation would surely collapse. As United States Commissioner of Education William T. Harris warned, northern attempts to dominate school reform would provoke suspicion and "furnish . . . poisoned arrow heads" for opponents of the movement, who could attack it "as fathered in Northern hatred and prosecuted by Northern investigators."[8] Such opinions were not unique to northerners. The crusade's fate, agreed a Virginian, hinged on the involvement of "men who are known to us, our feelings, our customs, our needs." "We are willing, desirous and even anxious to receive aid from the North," wrote another southerner, but only if it came with the understanding that the South would not "modify the form of education we deem necessary for any one."[9]

Northerners thus eagerly made concessions to placate southern opinion. Avoiding direct interference, they remained behind the scenes, working, as Walter Hines Page put it, with "reverend enthusiasm" to establish a "celestial machinery" operated by southerners. Ogden, although clearly the movement's dominating presence until his death in 1913, carefully delegated power, insisting that the details of the campaign remain in local hands. "My relation to the entire movement," as he once described it, was "to inspire if possible," but to be guided "in all practical matters" by the judgment of southerners more familiar with local situations.[10]

Abandoning a long-standing commitment to black education, Ogden and the northerners tolerated and even approved of southern white racial attitudes. It was a choice made carefully and consciously after persuasive arguments from southern intersectionalists. Thus when J.L.M. Curry told the conference's meeting of 1900 that a greater need existed for white schools—even at the expense of black education—because whites had "directive control" over southern affairs, he provided a formal statement of the intersectionalists' intentions. Ogden and other northerners—the only ones present who needed convincing—now concurred that southern progress depended on the end of racial antagonism on white terms, and with northern support, the meeting passed a resolution describing white education as the region's "pressing and imperative need."[11]

A major consequence of the intersectionalists' focus on white schools was, as Louis R. Harlan has shown, that disparities in the Jim Crow system of public education grew even larger during the first quarter of the twentieth century. The conference's decision reflected a national, fin de siècle tendency to accept southern mores on race. It also reflected a political realism on the part of the northerners, who exchanged acquiescence in segregation and educational inequality for an alliance with native southern white leaders. One southern educator believed the intersectionalists had no other choice. Any North-South alliance had first to overcome southern fears about northern interference; as a token of renewed trust, northerners needed to abide by "an intelligent Southern view of races."[12]

If reformers held any doubts on this subject, experience soon dispelled them. Dabney, accused in Tennessee in 1901 of sanctioning social equality through education for blacks, faced widespread popular outrage. His experience was not exceptional. Edgar Gardner Murphy's suggestion in Montgomery, Alabama, that the improvement of white public education was actually in the interest of blacks provoked a similar controversy. The lesson to these men and their allies was clear: avoid overt associations between the southern education campaign and the cause of black education.[13]

The intersectionalists' compromise with Jim Crow meant that the annual meetings of the conference and the subsequent meetings of the Southern Education Board were strictly segregated. The whites-only character of the movement went further than the segregation of these meetings, as white members carefully avoided any interracial contacts that implied social equality. When Page dined with Booker T. Washington, he was intensely criticized by fellow southerner Edgar Gardner Murphy, who thought it "unwise" to dine with blacks "publicly."[14] Contacts between reformers and blacks were either surreptitious or, more commonly, were made through intermediaries such as Frissell. Yet even Frissell was careful to urge the exclusion of black education from the southern reform agenda. "Intelligent and educated white men" understood the problem of black education and could improve it, he told a group of Virginia whites; white reformers were best advised to avoid connecting their crusade "too closely" with "the negro side."[15]

By 1901, well before the intersectionalist-dominated Conference for Education in the South had expanded beyond the cloistered atmosphere of Capon Springs, its character and that of the reform coalition it would orchestrate was coming into focus. It differed from anything yet seen in the South, a region not known for its social movements. It contrasted diametrically with the major popular uprisings of the post-Civil War period—the Ku Klux Klan, the Farmers' Alliance, and Populism—for, unlike any of them, its motive force was not dissatisfaction with change but an eager desire to turn away from the past and embark the South on an all-out program of modernization. There was little that was democratic about the Capon Springs meetings or later school reform; for reformers, nineteenth-century-style democracy meant social and political chaos, the triumph of localism, and the end of any possibility of progress. Reformers, seeking the participation of an intersectional elite and embracing industrialism and its values, prepared to transform a rural system of schooling.

The Southern Education Board

The same internal dynamics that transformed the Conference for Education in the South from a sleepy meeting of Christian educators into a growing force for change also pushed it into regional prominence. Perhaps most significant was the decision in 1901 to move the site of the meeting from Capon Springs, a change that marked the beginning of an attempt to reach out and build a wider coalition. As Dabney later wrote, the conference had "now broadened out" to include "the interests of the whole South." Because the best way to attract wider participation in the

Hollis Burke Frissell
(from Charles William Dabney, Universal Education in the South *[Chapel Hill: University of North Carolina Press, 1936], 1:122)*

meetings was to increase their accessibility, the leaders of the conference determined that in the future they should convene "in more central places," each year in a different location. Accordingly, the fourth Conference for Education in the South met in April 1901 in the chapel of Salem College in the bustling city of Winston-Salem, North Carolina.[16]

The Winston-Salem meeting was of pivotal significance for southern educational reform. The city represented the best of the dynamic New South; it would serve as a showcase of the region. Northerners transported in high style aboard Ogden's special train wasted little time becoming acquainted with their exotic surroundings. After its departure from New York, the train proceeded at a leisurely pace, stopping at Hampton, where the guests were elaborately entertained. Most of the northerners were favorably impressed. One guest, John D. Rockefeller, Jr., was so deeply moved by the experience that he became firmly committed to the cause of southern education; another notable, the New York City moral reformer and Ogden's spiritual adviser, the Reverend Dr. Charles H. Parkhurst, reacted similarly. In Winston-Salem, Parkhurst visited blacks in their homes, schools, and the city's tobacco factories, where firsthand exposure to the race problem moved him to tears. His main conclusion, however, was that the resolution of race problems lay properly in the hands of southern whites. He had never before understood the problem of race; now, he claimed, it seemed clear that southern whites were "doing wonderfully" with blacks. Never again, he promised, would he criticize the South.[17]

Along with intersectional bliss, the conference at Winston-Salem brought further results. Outlining the deficiencies of southern public schools, Dabney proposed the establishment of a "central propaganda agency" to convert the white South. The Conference for Education in the South had succeeded in dramatizing the need for change, but the time had now come for more ambitious measures. The broadening process— symbolized by the move from Capon Springs—required extending the narrow reach of the conference and building a coalition through the active evangelization of the public. Dabney here introduced another novel but immediately captivating idea: a central board, responsible to the conference, that would lead a regional school reform campaign. The Winston-Salem meeting responded by overwhelmingly endorsing Dabney's school reform program and specifically supporting the creation of two new agencies—a propaganda bureau to be led by Dabney and an executive arm of the conference, the Southern Education Board.[18]

Feverish efforts on the part of the conference's leaders to define the

Southern Education Board, 1901
(from Charles William Dabney, Universal Education in the South [Chapel Hill: University of North Carolina Press, 1936], 2:69)

apparatus of reform followed. Ogden, whom the conferees designated as the president of the new board, met throughout the summer and early fall of 1901 with Dabney, Curry, Alderman, Frissell, and McIver.[19] The dispositions of the SEB were, clearly, those of the conference, and its early organization reflected both intersectionalism and an emphasis on white education. The board divided itself into two wings, northern and southern. In the South, it vested authority in Curry as the "general southern agent" and McIver and Frissell as "field agents" to preach the cause of public education. The central propaganda agency was located in Knoxville and served as the investigative and public relations arm of the board. Edgar Gardner Murphy, who became executive secretary, opened an office in Washington, midway between the board's northern and southern wings. He exerted general supervision over the campaign, but his special duties were as aide-de-camp to Ogden and as a promoter of "interest in Southern education" in the North.[20]

As Ogden often stressed, the SEB's main purpose was to publicize and inform—"to reach the public mind, quicken the public conscience, and stimulate [the public] to self-activity."[21] During its fourteen-year history, the board ran on a shoestring, and, unlike the subsequent Rockefeller-financed General Education Board, the SEB, with no regular source of income, depended on the generosity of Ogden and the board's treasurer, George Foster Peabody. The SEB rarely gave direct grants, so its main expenditures were the salaries of the field agents and the costs of publicity.[22]

With the formation of the SEB, attention shifted away from the meetings of the Conference for Education in the South to the board's aggressive evangelization campaign. Evangelization, in this context, had two meanings. It meant employing evangelical methods in the organization of the SEB, the approach of its agents, and its use of funds. As its main objective, early school reform also borrowed from the revival the concept of conversion—that changed public attitudes toward schools would remake the character of education. Such was the approach of the SEB when it began to organize early in 1902 in four states—Louisiana, North Carolina, Virginia, and Mississippi—and when, within two years, it had expanded its net over all the former Confederate states.

The Crusade Begins in Virginia

An important quality of nineteenth-century revivals was their orientation toward the short term. Only if they brought quick and recognizable results were they considered successful; conversion and the spread of evangelicalism were steps toward a future Golden Age. Although evangelists were skilled mass organizers, they believed that such innovations were only temporary instruments to further the coming millennium. The early years of the southern educational crusade appeared to confirm these assumptions. "This southern country," one intersectionalist wrote about Virginia in 1903, "is alive with educational energy." Agreeing with this assessment, the SEB's field agent in Virginia described the enthusiasm for public schools which he elicited from one Southside Virginia "thrifty farmer," who declared that the world was "turned upside down about the schools."[23]

The early results of the SEB's campaign in Virginia seemed to support this optimism. In 1901, the board appointed two field agents, Robert Frazer and Henry St. George Tucker, both of whom were responsible to the state agent, Frissell, and to McIver, the chairman of the SEB's regional campaign committee.[24] Frazer, then sixty-four years old, had had a long career in education. After the Civil War, he served as a county superintendent in Virginia and then became president of normal schools

Charles Duncan McIver
(from Charles William Dabney, Universal Education in the South *[Chapel Hill: University of North Carolina Press, 1936], 1:188)*

in Alabama, Mississippi, and then Virginia. Tucker, a former congressman from a family of distinguished lawyers, brought a reputation for tact and wide political influence. He was also a renowned orator able, according to one contemporary, to "wrap a country audience around his finger."[25]

Frazer and Tucker were instructed to campaign using these very different skills. Frazer was to investigate the conditions of rural schools, to compile the results in the form of a survey, and to publicize their inadequacies and insufficiencies. Exposing the unpleasant realities of Virginia rural schools would mobilize state officials and teachers and also "rouse the people up to do their duty toward the children."[26] Concurrently, using his contacts and rhetorical skills, Tucker was to establish friendly relations with the governor and other political leaders and lobby for educational legislation.[27]

Within several years, Frazer and Tucker were reporting significant progress, especially in converting local elites and state leaders. As McIver wrote, both had created a "better educational spirit on the part of [the state's] cultured people and a broader sympathy with the public school system."[28] Particularly noticeable was the effect of the campaign on newspapers and churches, influential people in several communities, and the state's institutions of higher education.[29] By the end of 1903, Frazer had visited sixty of the state's one hundred counties and six of eighteen cities.[30] Tucker claimed similar success in addresses to religious and educational meetings, as well as gatherings at local courthouses, and he reached between twenty-five and thirty thousand people during 1903 alone.[31]

Nonetheless, the leaders of the educational crusade were soon reaching the limits of evangelical methods.[32] Tucker's main interest remained politics and his commitment to school reform was only halfhearted, and Frazer's enthusiasm was provoking opposition among potential allies—State Superintendent Joseph W. Southall and his secretary, Frank P. Brent. When, in an article that appeared in the *Richmond Times* in the spring of 1902, Frazer charged that the state's rural schools were in a "contemptible" condition, Southall complained that he was "surprised" at the charge and that he had been excluded from the organization of the SEB's campaign in Virginia. Brent repeated these countercharges, adding that Virginia's schools were among the best in the South.[33]

The conflict between school officials and educational crusaders posed a major obstacle to coalition building. The defensive reaction of Southall and others, despite the general receptiveness of state school officials to the SEB program, suggested not just indifference but the possibility of outright opposition. SEB operatives unanimously condemned Southall's response. About a week after the incident, Joseph D. Eggleston, formerly a protégé of Dabney and later elected state superintendent of education, wrote that Southall was a "mere figurehead, put into office because he had pull and because he was growing old." With similar flourish, Eggleston dismissed Brent as a "secret enemy," who had assumed the "role of a priest" and absolved "every evil in the school system from the moment the matter is brought to his attention." Both officials, Eggleston charged, regarded any criticism of the school system as a "personal affront."[34]

Other SEB agents, though agreeing with Eggleston, muted their criticisms. McIver described the situation in Virginia as "bright in every way." The progress of civilization usually encountered the opposition of the "local patriot," who pandered to ignorance and was threatened by "any one who wishes to make a change."[35] Yet McIver's optimism masked a reality about the reaction of Virginians toward the SEB campaign: defensiveness toward outsiders, deeply rooted resistance to change, and indifference toward the question of educational reform. Worst of all, even the optimists would concede that these characteristics permeated the school system. Expressing a realization about the enormity of these problems, Frazer described inefficiency among local school officials as an impediment to "real progress." Later, making the same complaint, he reported the general indifference of county superintendents to aiding educational reform.[36]

An equally serious problem was that the SEB campaign was generating public hostility. In the spring of 1904, newspapers across the South participated in a well-orchestrated attack on the SEB, which was promoted by the New South ideologue and publisher of the influential Baltimore *Manufacturer's Record*, Richard Hathaway Edmonds. Along with his associate, Edward Ingle, Edmonds charged that the SEB masked a movement determined to impose child labor restrictions on the region. More seriously, Edmonds and Ingle raised the specter of northern interference in southern "internal"—that is, racial—affairs.[37] By relating educational reform to the bugaboo of northern interference in race relations, Edmonds's attack seemed to bear out the fears of southern reformers. Equally serious was the appeal to the southern agrarian tradition against monopoly, a theme that carried substantial popular support and could serve as a rallying point against reform.

The Edmonds attack had considerable impact in Virginia, where the charges were "industriously circulated" to every state legislator. The anti-SEB campaign also affected the state's leading newspapers, previously supporters of reform, which now, "through appeals to prejudice and otherwise," maintained a cautious distance. The attitude of local school officials, previously lukewarm, was "visibly affected," the support of state officials, "if given at all," lacked "earnestness and cordiality."[38]

The combination of limited results and Edmonds's attack forced the SEB's hand. Whether its claim that the early campaign was only an experiment or whether the board accepted the need for a fresh approach,[39] the intersectionalists were looking for alternatives. One change was the decentralization of the board's operations. After 1903, the propaganda bureau headed by Dabney in Knoxville played a less significant role, and, within a year, the SEB unveiled a new mode of operation which involved a "general enlargement" and more attention to local public relations.[40]

In spite of these changes, direct intervention by the SEB increasingly encountered major obstacles. Even an eternal optimist like Ogden, though confident about the ultimate triumph of reform along "the teachings of the New Testament," confessed "very serious anxiety" about the long-term prospects for educational change. Indeed, the path to the "Golden Age" appeared "long," the steps "painful and slow." The impact of popular indifference and resistance to the top-heavy SEB campaign drove home several points. First, based on their experience with the SEB, intersectionalists began to comprehend the enormity of rural school reform. That there would be no quick and easy solution to the problems of country schools, no sudden reform, had become clear to the SEB agents exposed to the conditions of rural Virginia. Second, the potential strength of opposition and the indifference of Virginians toward reform convinced the intersectionalists of the need to cultivate the support of potential allies. The SEB, a regional organization, needed a state-level coalition led and supported, as one Virginian put it, by men of "tried ability & demonstrated power."[41]

The Co-Operative Education Association of Virginia

The new approach ultimately endorsed by Ogden and others was less a crusade to uplift public opinion than an effort to transform the system itself by working through alliances with local civic groups, political leaders, and school officials. In Virginia, the mechanism of this new approach soon became the Co-Operative Education Association (CEA), an organization founded in the spring of 1904, which sealed this tripartite alliance. Contacts between the SEB and the Richmond Education Association began as early as the winter of 1902, when Tucker met with the Richmond women and encouraged them to expand their activities outside the confines of Richmond. He suggested that the REA amend its constitution so as to sponsor a central organization with affiliates across the state whose purpose would be to press for rural school improvement. A month later, addressing the REA, McIver made the same point. Urging the Richmond women to unite with "our forces," he proposed the creation of associated local organizations, modeled on the REA, to improve conditions and to increase attendance. The "most wholesome kind" of compulsory attendance, he declared, could result from these "associations of women." Throughout 1902 and early 1903, pressure to create a statewide organization came from like-minded urban women and their educator allies.[42]

Nonetheless, it remained clear that, as far as the male leaders of the SEB were concerned, the female-dominated REA would be unable to provide broadly based leadership for the educational campaign. As Frazer wrote, the "educational forces" in Virginia needed the "counsel & the cooperation of our wisest & most patriotic citizens—especially of men." Early in 1904, therefore, a group of reformers met and decided to form an expanded organization modeled on, but not officially connected with, the REA. In March, Ogden gave official sanction to the new organization as an "auxiliary" to the SEB's campaign in Virginia. Throughout that month, the organizers met and made plans for the new group, and by the end of April, a conference among SEB reformers, members of the REA, and the governor was held at the capitol. The group announced an ambitious program: extension of the school term, creation of high schools, expansion of facilities for teacher education, and introduction of "expert" supervision into schools. During the rest of that year, the new group, now known as the Co-Operative Education Association of Virginia, laid careful plans for an educational campaign, and at a well-publicized conference at Norfolk in early December 1904, the group agreed to inaugurate the "May Campaign" during the following spring.[43]

The organizers of the campaign—later described as a "combination of crusade and a glorified picnic"—succeeded in several important respects. They attracted the attention of the press to educational problems, both in Richmond and in the provincial towns of the state. Perhaps most important, the May Campaign galvanized a new reform coalition composed of the SEB, civic groups, political reformers such as Montague, and machine politicians such as Martin and Swanson. The campaign also provided a way to include school officials and urban educators in school reform and to end the domination by outsiders. Indeed, by the end of the campaign, local reformers, technically independent of the SEB but deriving support and leadership from it, were exerting considerable influence over the state educational bureaucracy. Local organizations, some three hundred of which were created during the campaign, now began to apply pressure on county superintendents to modernize and upgrade facilities.[44]

Whatever the immediate results of the May Campaign, the alliance for educational reform gained permanent form in the CEA. The CEA expanded the movement to the grass roots by creating local "school improvement" organizations to supervise school officials and to put pressure on them to improve conditions and modernize facilities. Often the leagues worked with reform-minded teachers, and, in general, women dominated the local organizations. According to Mary Munford, women involved in the school leagues were like fans at a baseball game; they organized the crowds, cheered the speakers, and served as the backbone of the leagues. Most of the league presidents were women. As the CEA coordinator of the leagues, Landonia R. Dashiell, wrote in 1906, no community was without "one influential, intrepid woman" who served as league president. Under such leadership, "ten more" women became interested, and female enthusiasm grew "in ever widening circles." Men, added Dashiell, usually took part because "no work will prevail without their countenance and support." Until "some unwary man" became involved, there was little hope of progress. Yet the group was clearly female-run, and men usually held only nominal positions of vice-president and treasurer. Dashiell further concluded that the dominance of women brought another, unanticipated result: although Virginia men participated, women received "all the credit."[45]

Rural school improvement leagues closely followed the REA's model of organization, leadership, and interest-group politics. The leagues drew support and leadership from woman's clubs where they existed, and, with the backing of Richmond reformers and state school officials, they launched local-initiative campaigns to press for modernization of school facilities and curricula. When they lacked the active cooperation of school boards, they frequently improved facilities on their own. By 1910, local leagues had become key factors in the transformation of a top-heavy, state-level crusade into a locally based, grass-roots reform movement, with supporters in rural counties and provincial towns, all under the direction of CEA leaders and SEB agents.[46]

The organization of the CEA also gave a structure to the alliance between the SEB, indigenous civic groups, and politicians. In 1905, the simultaneous election of Eggleston to the state superintendency and of Swanson to the governorship led to a close working relationship between the two men and to an unprecedented spate of educational reform. In 1906, the legislature enacted a high school bill written by school reformers; legislation passed during the 1908 session provided impetus for the improvement and expansion of school facilities. The CEA also worked closely with school officials—county superintendents and especially the growing number of state supervisors attached to the state department of education—and helped them supervise and even raise funds for rural school modernization.[47]

The CEA's success taught Ogden and the SEB a valuable lesson: decentralization of the crusade was both appropriate and advantageous. Because the CEA was a state organization under native white control, the campaign could be impervious to charges of northern domination or of posing a threat of an educational monopoly or a challenge to white supremacy. It also overcame the entrenched conservatism of state officials and the Democratic organization by expanding, rather than reducing, their control; at the same time, it adapted itself to rural localities by soliciting their participation. As early as March 1904, Ogden had concluded that for all of these reasons the CEA-style approach offered the best future for reform.[48]

The formation and early successes of the CEA and the reform alliance it represented marked a significant transition in the nature and direction of the educational crusade in Virginia. In the CEA, reformers discovered that the transformation of public education required more than a brief popular campaign. Ironically, the success of the May Campaign brought a shift in focus. Reformers realized that future revivals were unnecessary; the May Campaign had exhausted this possibility. Instead, reform would come over the long term through the active yet continuous guidance of governmental agencies. With the successes of the CEA, the new reform coalition turned increasingly to the use of permanent governmental institutions—bureaucracies, as they have come to be called—for the uplift of the public schools.

The General Education Board and the Evolution of School Reform

This new, bureaucratic approach in part reflected the growing influence of the philanthropic intervention of John D. Rockefeller and his progeny in the early twentieth-century South. At first glance, the differences between the General Education Board (GEB) and the SEB seem trivial. Both were outgrowths of the Winston-Salem meeting of 1901. Traveling as a guest on Ogden's special train, John D. Rockefeller, Jr., returned North determined to finance a wholesale effort to further education in underdeveloped regions of the country.[49] Intimately associated from the outset, the two organizations included some eleven common members—a "community of interest," as Ogden put it, directing school reform. The Wall Street capitalist and philanthropist George Foster Peabody served as treasurer for both organizations,[50] and the GEB and SEB shared similar attitudes and assumptions. Rockefeller philanthropists, along with SEB leaders, believed that southern whites controlled the destiny of black education, and rightfully so. The role of philanthropy was to help "intelligently and sympathetically" by cultivating alliances with native white leaders, southerners "strongest in wealth, intelligence, and power."[51]

Although the boards shared leadership and attitude, their approach to school reform differed fundamentally. Where SEB agents experimented and improvised, GEB agents entered the field with clearly articulated prescriptions for rural education. Where the SEB drew from an evangelical model of popular mobilization and reform, GEB leaders consciously looked to the standards of the modern corporation. Like combinations in industry, the GEB operated as philanthropy's "benevolent trust." Because its guiding organizational principles were corporate rather than evangelical, the GEB managed the cause of educational reform through the introduction of economies of scale and the application of the objective of efficiency.[52] The GEB functioned in efficient and streamlined fashion in part because there was no doubt about who dominated the board, for the only northern capitalist involved was Rockefeller himself. Nor was there, given the almost limitless resources of the Rockefellers, ever much question about money.[53]

GEB agents used these resources according to the principles of scientific philanthropy as established by Rockefeller lieutenants and Baptist ministers, Wallace Buttrick and Frederick T. Gates. The experience of these men, along with Rockefeller himself, in the founding of the University of Chicago in 1893 and in the establishment of the Rockefeller Institute for Medical Research in 1901, led them to follow explicit criteria. Viewing "scientific giving" and philanthropy as only temporary, Buttrick and Gates insisted on the long-term, bureaucratic management of social problems. Rockefeller philanthropy thus usually went to institutions rather than individuals, especially institutions that demonstrated their efficiency and usually, though not invariably, operated in tandem with governmental agencies. Along with other Rockefeller philanthropies, the GEB donated conditionally and thereby promoted giving by others. A final assumption behind scientific giving was that the recipient of the gift would eventually be weaned from dependence.[54]

The GEB's distinctive characteristics were clear from the outset. In the spring of 1905, three years after its founding, the board began to finance agents to promote and guide the development of southern high schools. In contrast to the early SEB agents, these educators were insiders. Not only were they natives of the states in which they operated, they also held official positions as professors of secondary education at state universities. In reality, these men did little teaching, and their primary responsibilities were to represent the GEB and to agitate for new high schools. They served two additional functions: as "critical students" of educational conditions who reported to the board and to the state departments of education, and as "high school evangelists" who prompted, cajoled, and encouraged the spread of high school education.[55]

Bruce Ryburn Payne, appointed as professor of secondary education at the University of Virginia, brought ample educational experience to this position. Earlier he had served on the faculty of the College of William and Mary and as chairman of the May Campaign's publicity committee and in the latter capacity had developed strong rapport with the new reform coalition. Soon after his appointment, Payne launched a two-pronged attack. During the spring of 1906, he lobbied strenuously for expanded and state-funded high school facilities and wrote the state's first high school act in March. At the same time, Payne worked closely with the state superintendent, state inspectors, and teachers and county superintendents in inaugurating the new high schools.[56]

Payne used the resources of the University of Virginia as a base of his own operations and as a permanent institution committed to the expansion of the entire school system. Beginning in 1908, he initiated a series of rural life conferences at the university which attracted educators and other reformers from across the country.[57] Payne also linked the university with the state high schools by insisting that it accredit secondary schools and by creating a scholarship fund for "efficient" high schools.[58] In all of these efforts to link a long-isolated university with the public schools, Payne and the GEB enjoyed strong support from the university's president, Edwin A. Alderman. The North Carolinian reaped huge benefits from his association with Rockefeller philanthropy; because of his connection with Buttrick, Alderman won a large donation to the university's endowment from the GEB. But Alderman had another motive: he was determined to establish the University of Virginia as the locus of educational expansion, and the professorship of secondary education provided him with a power base and a large stake in secondary school expansion.[59]

Events, however, did not work out either to Payne's or to Alderman's liking. Instead, by World War I the transformation of Virginia rural schools had begun to slip from the grasp of Alderman and other like-minded early school reformers. In part because of the influence of the GEB, in part because of the acknowledged need for a regular, systematic approach to school administration, and in part because other modernizing school systems had adopted centralized units of control and inspection, bureaucracy was replacing evangelical fervor as the motive force in educational expansion.

By the time Payne left in 1911 to become president of the George Peabody College for Teachers in Nashville, the position of the professor of secondary education illustrated this larger transformation. As early as the summer of 1907, Payne had begun to discover that his role was more bureaucratic than evangelical. "I do not believe that I should give my life over to the task of acrrediting [*sic*] and inspecting high schools for the University of Virginia," he complained. Yet that was what his work had rapidly become.[60] These trends were not reversed during the tenure of his successor, Charles G. Maphis, and, over time, the position came more under the control of—indeed, became a part of—the state educational bureaucracy, as Maphis spent less time in the field and more time accrediting and standardizing secondary schools.[61]

Indeed, by 1919, bureaucratic control of high school inspection had become, to Alderman at least, a lamentable development. Because of growing state control in public education and health reform, he complained, southern universities were now in "a difficult and dangerous situation." Bureaucratic agencies, tending to "devitalize the state universities," deprived them of "power and [the] opportunity to direct and

Wallace Buttrick
(from Charles William Dabney, Universal Education in the South *[Chapel Hill: University of North Carolina Press, 1936], 2:35)*

guide in technical ways the industrial, economic and educational life of the States." What all of this meant was not only greater bureaucratization, but that universities would also become "Olympic sorts of places," which existed outside of the "advancing life" of the "turbulent democracy." Alderman's protestation went unnoticed, however, and in 1919 the state department of education acquired complete control over accreditation. It promptly changed the name of the position to "state high school inspector."[62]

The GEB and Rural Elementary Schools

The GEB eventually involved itself in almost every area of southern education, including that of black and white elementary school students. After initial success in high school expansion, the board in 1910 began an active intervention in rural white education. This involvement, closely paralleling its role in the expansion of white high schools, stressed greater bureaucratic and eventually greater governmental control.

As was also the case with secondary education, the GEB worked with local reform groups, the most important of which in Virginia was the CEA. Since its founding, the CEA had organized local school improvement leagues—including patron-run "citizen leagues" and student-run "junior leagues"—in about five hundred "strategic centers."[63] Dominated by rural women, the leagues became instrumental parts of the reform apparatus. Leading fund-raising drives and seeking to elevate local expectations and standards, they also served as vehicles for activism by women. As CEA leader Landonia Dashiell expressed it, the leagues' function was to "bring the home and school nearer to each other" by enlarging the significance of the common school "in the minds of the people" and by transforming the "bare, unbeautiful places of drudgery into more pleasing and homelike conditions."[64]

The CEA leagues also propagandized the reform cause on the local level. From Richmond, the CEA sent out lecturers equipped with advanced methods of communication, including lantern slide and stereopticon presentations, to towns and villages. At the same time, the CEA provided copy and photographs for the state's newspapers detailing abject conditions in rural schools and also regularly informed them about the successes of reform.[65] Throughout, according to one CEA official, the objective was to mold "sentiment for improving school conditions."[66]

About five years after its founding, the CEA began an important shift in emphasis that reflected a larger transformation from evangelical reform to bureaucratic management. The organization's original objectives directly emanated from the SEB and the fervor of the early school reformers. Its essential purpose was inspirational—to reach the community and to enlist its "constructive interest," as one reformer declared. Early CEA leagues sought to expose, awaken, and convert; the objective of reformers was to "stir the interest of the citizens," enlist "their resources," and vitalize every neighborhood. As another reformer wrote, the CEA was a "popular, unofficial" organization; he believed that it should not become "officialized" or abandon its "popular and spontaneous spirit."[67]

Although founded by evangelical school reformers, the CEA became increasingly committed to bureaucratic means and methods. This transition coincided with the rising importance of two groups in the organization—professionalizing state officials and the GEB. For different reasons, both saw reforming rural schools as the product of organizational and institutional change rather than of publicity campaigns or the conversion of public opinion.

The changed nature of the CEA and its shift away from evangelical school reform acquired greater focus in 1909, when the newspaper magnate and civic leader John Stewart Bryan was elected president. According to a contemporary, Bryan's election not only signified that men now possessed a larger share in the operation of the CEA, but also a shift in the organization's approach to reform.[68] Attempting to instill professionalism in the organization, Bryan appointed a permanent executive secretary, Jesse H. Binford, who was paid an annual salary, had impressive qualifications, and was given considerable power in running the organization. Bryan and Binford then linked the CEA and the leagues more closely with state officials by sponsoring the creation of the office of rural school supervisor of white schools, a position financed by the GEB and the Peabody Fund but responsible directly to the state superintendent.[69]

These organizational changes reflected a blossoming alliance between the CEA, Rockefeller philanthropy, and the state department of education. Through the rural school supervisors, relations between the CEA and the GEB, on the one hand, and public school officials, on the other, grew intimate. The supervisors consulted with county superintendents frequently and often gave advice about school construction and consolidation. They also worked closely with the school leagues by co-sponsoring various activity days, such as Patrons' Day, Good Roads' Day, Better Health Day, and Better Farming Day. Supervisors provided a regular form of inspection, but even more important, they aroused local interest and attempted to involve the community through the school improvement leagues.[70]

The rapprochement between the CEA and the state educational bureaucracy expanded as the influence of the GEB grew.[71] After the SEB disbanded in 1914, the GEB financed the CEA and the state rural school supervisor. The board soon moved to strengthen state influence and control in the CEA by financing it through the state department of education, rather than directly as had been the case under the SEB. Increasingly, the activities of the leagues and of the supervisor, as with the professor of secondary education, came under the direction of Richmond state officials.

An almost inevitable consequence of the CEA's new, semiofficial character was the displacement of early educational reformers, especially women activists. Although bureaucratic dominance expanded job opportunities for women as teachers, it also caused a steady decline in the influence of elite women. It was a subtle shift that did not escape the notice of pioneer reform women. Just as Alderman decried the declining role of universities, so too did Mary Munford grasp the new realities of educational change. The CEA was becoming less a citizens' organization, she complained to GEB officials in 1914, and more an arm of the state department of education. Much of its strength derived from its nonpartisan, unofficial appeal. Just how far this would be possible under bureaucratic dominance would be problematical.[72] In spite of Munford's protest, the GEB shifted control of the office of rural school supervisor to the state educational bureaucracy in 1914. Indeed, as the Rockefeller official Abraham Flexner put it in 1914, such a shift from the private to the public sector was natural and inevitable. "Every [state] superintendent is to be the judge as to what is wise and feasible to attempt in his own state," he wrote, but whatever the case, the rural school supervisor would be an agent of the state.[73]

The increasing role of the GEB in Virginia rural schools dramatized an important but paradoxical process of change. Because its success made reformers unnecessary, it tended to accentuate a shift in leadership and control over rural school modernization out of the hands of the pioneer generation. Emphasizing expertise and systematic organizational changes, the GEB accelerated the redundancy of the original reformers. By the 1920s, those portions of the reform coalition that had exercised the greatest influence—intersectionalists and civic group activists—had little influence over decision making. Steadily more influential in directing the path of educational change were professionalizing school officials. Relying on changes in school governance made possible by the reform coalition, school officials began a wholesale effort to modernize the structure and experience of rural education.

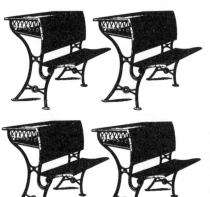

Chapter Six
Modernizing the Rural School

Important changes in rural education were evident by the eve of World War I. In the space of a decade, reformers had mobilized a revival-style campaign and in its wake created permanent reform agencies. They had converted state politicians, struck an alliance with the one-party state, and laid the basis for a coalition that attracted support at state and local levels. But reformers eventually discovered that effecting change required more than enthusiasm. Ending the traditional physical isolation and improving the appearance of rural schools, establishing statewide standards for teachers, and projecting state power over the upbringing of rural children through school consolidation were all long-standing objectives of rural reformers, but they were possible only through a wholesale modernization of the structure and experience of education.

Bureaucracy and the Rural School

Explaining the evolution of rural schools in the twentieth century as a process of modernization implies that it was both inevitable and completely beneficial. It was neither. By 1920, rural schools had undergone only a hesitant transformation; far from being fully modernized, they still operated under the constraints of the nineteenth-century system. Such modernization as had occurred affected teachers, parents, children, and school officials in distinctly different and often uneven ways—in increasing central power at the expense of localities, in encouraging rather than eliminating traditional disparities between have and have-not schools, and in fostering the persistence of transiency as a main characteristic of rural teachers.

124

What gave rural school modernization its distinctive influence was the central role played by bureaucratization, a term enveloped in conceptual vagueness and pregnant with meaning for our own time. Recent historians of public education, employing local studies of urban school systems, have concluded that the augmentation and centralization of school administration and the creation of impersonal agencies to direct it were avoidable, short-term phenomena consciously initiated by reformers. To these historians, the coming of bureaucracy meant the loss of local power and parental participation, the creation of a pedagogical hierarchy, and the institution of a new agenda of education designed to maintain dominant class relationships.

The same case has been made about rural school reform.[1] Reformers considered centralizing administration and establishing permanent agencies of state power instrumental preconditions of change, and, as much as urban reformers, they sought to replace community education with impersonal bureaucracy. Not unlike city school officials, rural modernizers did not conceive of public education as a vehicle for ending social, racial, and gender inequality.

But such a view of bureaucratization and modernization explains only one dimension of twentieth-century educational change. It assumes that the transition from an ideology of reform to the implementation of that policy was smooth and logical and that the result—bureaucratic governance—constitutes evidence of self-conscious intent and clear responsibility. In rural Virginia, the transition from evangelical reform to bureaucratic policy, which was more abrupt than smooth, displaced the original cast of reformers and brought to prominence modernizing state officials. In short, a wide gap existed between the emergence of school reform and the actual transformation of public education.

Beyond the issue of responsibility for bureaucratization lies another question: what alternative models of school organization did modernizers possess? A leading critic of twentieth-century school bureaucracy, Michael Katz, has suggested three alternative models of school organization: bureaucracy, paternalistic voluntarism, and democratic localism. Paternalistic voluntarism, involving private control of education, abjured publicly supported education in favor of free schooling only for the very poor. Democratic localism, in contrast, was a model that expressed absolute community control of education and was diametrically opposed to central state control.[2]

The reality was that Virginia school officials had no alternative but to

A modern rural school, Frederick County, Virginia, 1912
(courtesy of the Virginia Department of Education)

embrace bureaucracy, a model of educational adminstration that had already been successfully practiced in every modernizing school system in the world. By the early twentieth century, Virginia had exhausted the last two models of schooling. Paternalistic voluntarism aptly character- izes the elitist antebellum system; democratic localism describes Vir- ginia schools after Reconstruction. Confronting a sprawling system of rural education, Virginia school officials, empowered with a mandate for change, saw centralized administration and the use of supervisory per- sonnel as ways to end decisively what they considered to be the blight of localism in education. These modernizers did not invent bureaucracy. Nor did they use it exclusively to impose their class and racial atti- tudes; rather, their main concern was eradicating localism from public education.

This brings us to another fundamental question: what explains the motives of school reformers? In recent studies of urban schools, histori- ans have emphasized the power of class, economic status, and ethno- cultural values in school modernization. Modern schools were to serve as filters for the imposition of Protestant and middle-class values on recent immigrants and the working class. Historians of the South have reached similar conclusions about southern social and educational re- formers. In a recent study of child labor reform in South Carolina, David

L. Carlton has forcefully argued that reformers were guided more by class than by humanitarian motives. Child labor restriction reflected an attempt to extend middle-class, town values upon working-class children by separating them—against their parents' will—from home and work and substituting the socialization of public education. By detaching childhood from devitalizing parental control, they intended to remake folk culture and popular attitudes toward work and life.[3]

A major difficulty in all of these analyses is that they assume a degree of exclusivity. If these interpretations are correct and reform and modernization were imposed for economic, class, and ethnocultural reasons, then the use of schools as a tool of social control to shape future behavior should appear only in urban-industrial settings. Yet in reality the objectives of rural modernizers closely resembled those of urban modernizers. Bureaucracy and modernization were not imposed exclusively on non-Protestant immigrants and workers; they were also imposed on Protestant rural white southerners. Virginia school officials were as concerned about the southern countryside as northern city officials were about immigrants, and they were equally willing to judge both "backward" and "unprogressive."

The Rise of Bureaucratic Governance

Modernizing rural education required a transition from localistic to bureaucratic governance. With open support from a broad-based reform coalition, a new generation of officials dominated school administration during the early decades of the twentieth century and supervised the beginning of fundamental changes in school governance. Yet the success of these modernizers depended on other changes that began to affect school administration. Under powers granted in the new constitution of 1902, the State Board of Education expanded its membership from three—the governor, attorney general, and state superintendent—to eight, including one city superintendent, one county superintendent, and three "experienced" educators who represented the state's higher educational system. The reinvigorated board made the office of its chief executive officer—the state superintendent—more important and virtually decreed the appointment of a professional administrator.

The office of county superintendent also underwent change. The constitution of 1902 renamed the position "division" superintendent and provided for the amalgamation of small counties into larger units of school administration. In 1908, the legislature further allowed counties to supplement the salaries of division superintendents, and their pay nearly doubled during the first decade of the twentieth century. These structural changes reflected a wholesale transformation of the office. Whereas nineteenth-century superintendents tended to be part-time and unprofessionalized, those of the early twentieth century were better qualified. By World War I, clear generational differences among superintendents were evident. Younger superintendents usually possessed stronger professional qualifications and considerably more educational expertise than their predecessors. About half of the superintendents appointed in 1909 considered the office their only vocation and had no other occupation, and three-fourths viewed education as their primary occupation. Forty-two were under forty years old, and, of these, all but four had attended college. In contrast, nineteen of the forty-two above fifty years of age had never attended college.[4]

Centralized administration began to place additional demands on the county superintendents. In 1910, rural superintendents spent, on the average, about a third longer on the job than they had twenty years earlier. Fortified by a stronger state department of education, with more effective powers of enforcement and a willingness to intervene in local affairs, superintendents now had larger clerical staffs and a greater opportunity to supervise the schools. In the thirty years between 1890 and 1920, rural superintendents spent substantially more time visiting, supervising, and inspecting rural schools. The number of schools never visited in 1920 shrank to more than half that of 1890. Moreover, increased activity on the part of rural superintendents were qualitative as well as quantitative; not only did they visit more schools, they visited them more frequently. The proportion of schools visited more than once was close to three times greater in 1920 than thirty years before.[5]

Expanding state supervision also depended on the creation of a strong force of school inspectors loyal to Richmond. By 1920, a diverse number of state rural school supervisors and other bureaucrats inspected schools to ensure compliance with state regulations in areas such as sanitation, teacher training, and school construction standards. In that year, most of the schools of rural Virginia had had contact with a visiting official; about two-thirds of them were regularly inspected by state supervisors.[6] The presence of supervising personnel decisively affected school governance. Lines of authority became less ambiguous, more formal, and increasingly standardized, and the locus of power and decision making shifted to the central state government, which worked through superintendents and supervisors to assume responsibilities previously shared by district boards and patrons.

Modernizing school governance was partly connected with the rapid expansion of public school facilities and tax support. Twentieth-century growth, following nineteenth-century patterns, brought steady increases in the numbers of schools, teachers, and enrolled and attending pupils. Between 1900 and 1920, the number of teachers thus grew from 8,954 to 14,904; schoolrooms from 8,922 to 14,476; and attending students from 216,464 to 286,111. In more important respects, however, growth after 1900 brought significant changes to schools. Lacking large public outlays and relying on nontax community support, post-Reconstruction schools expanded in the areas of enrollment, attendance, and number of schools. Post-1900 expansion, in contrast, occasioned explosive increases of 900 percent in school revenues and of 33 percent in the length of school terms.[7]

The increased school term and growth in public financing were accompanied by increased interregional standardization. Educational disparities did not end after 1900, but statewide conditions were such that wealth and population density tended to have similar effects. Two different measures—average length of school term and district funding in 1920—illustrate this tendency. Outside of the urbanized counties, the differential among regions in both categories significantly contracted. In part, the leveling of interregional differences resulted from economic expansion. In Appalachia, for example, the schools of twenty years earlier were the most underfunded in the state. By 1920, the area had experienced rapid growth in industry and mining and boasted the largest per capita school funding of any nonurban region. But economic growth did not entirely account for the decline in interregional disparities, for even in Virginia's poor regions in 1920 school terms and public financing were not far from the state average.

Perhaps the most important reason for interregional homogenization was the growing role of government, both at the state and local levels, which independently stimulated educational growth. Put another way, early twentieth-century educational expansion was intimately associated with centralization and standardization of rural school governance. Growing from almost nothing, white high schools provide an example by which constructing new schools and expanding public support for them after 1900 usually meant creation of permanent, central facilities under greater state control. The Mann High School Act of 1906, which appropriated $50,000 for new high schools, not only spurred a rapid

growth of high schools but also established central control over them by
making public support contingent on state involvement. To receive state
funds, high schools were required to follow state accreditation standards, including a prescribed curriculum, length of session, and type of
facilities. The act further gave state officials the power to inspect high
schools annually.

In elementary schools, greater funds and more extension facilities
also resulted in greater centralization. Bureaucratic control, in turn, was
aimed at eliminating what officials considered the social blight of ram-
shackle, transient one-room rural schools. The Williams Building Act of
1906, which appropriated funds for elementary education, attached state
directives about school architecture, and the Strode Act of 1908 provided for state financing of school construction and included strict and
specific stipulations about ventilation, lighting, and design. Not only did
it mandate fire exits and suitable outhouses, it also required fifteen
square feet of floor space and two hundred cubic feet of airspace for
each pupil and stipulated that air should move out of the schoolroom at
a rate of thirty feet per minute. Subsequent measures added even more
stringent requirements.[8]

By the end of World War I, the outlines of a new educational system
were coming into focus. The trend of increasingly centralized governance and the augmentation of state power at the expense of private
local power spawned a new degree of statewide standardization. In
1900, the length of school terms and quality of educational facilities
were extremely localized; they varied considerably from school district
to school district, and the effect of socioeconomic variables such as
wealth and population density differed regionally. In some parts of the
state, wealth tended to increase the demand for labor and decrease the
community's desire for schools; in other parts, wealth allowed a greater
amount of time available for education. The passage of twenty years did
not alter these circumstances dramatically. There continued to be a significant regional variation in educational quality, especially between urbanized counties and the rest of the state. Overall, the length of the
school session increased substantially and tended to narrow differences
between the state's regions. Even so, the urbanized counties recorded
an 18 percent longer school session than the state average. Moreover,
factors associated with longer terms in 1900—agricultural wealth and
population density—were still important two decades later.[9]

Change and modernization coexisted with the stubbornly persisting
remnants of the community-controlled school system. The areas in

which growth and expansion occurred in the late nineteenth century—
the extension of the school term, the growth of local tax support, the
profusion of facilities and the availability of schools, and a continued
surge in enrollments and attendance—also saw expansion in the early
twentieth century. Enrollment grew from about three-fifths for whites and
about half for blacks in 1900 to four-fifths and two-thirds twenty years
later, and attendance increased at a similarly rapid rate. The average
length of the school session grew by over a third; district tax support
rose by 784 percent. Substantial expansion in school availability also
occurred.[10]

At the same time, new influences were prominent in 1920, especially
the growing presence of centralized school administration and bureaucratic supervision. School modernization and rapid growth during the
early decades of the twentieth century were complex, interrelated processes. Emanating from above, reform brought an unprecedented stimu-
lus for school improvement under increasingly centralized control.
Growth was tied to modernization; school expansion to a large extent
depended upon the initiative provided by modernizers. Undeniably, the
rapid growth of school facilities at all levels narrowed the regional
differences.

Side by side with the emerging modernized school system, however,
were inescapable vestiges of the past. Although considerable headway
was made in reducing the number of small schools, as late as 1920,
one-room schools constituted a third of all schoolrooms in the state.
Their persistence was vivid evidence of the contradictory character of
educational change; they were reminders of the continuing differences
between "have" and "have not." In 1920, a clear statistical correlation
existed between poverty and sparse population and one-room schools.
And they were in clearest evidence wherever white, yeoman landowners—who traditionally resisted higher school expenditures—composed
a large portion of all farmers.[11]

Educational Change and the Rural Teacher

No single group was more affected by centralization than rural teachers,
long ignored by any outside agencies. They were affected by attempts to
establish statewide educational and professional standards through enlarged educational facilities for teachers, the promotion of professionalism, and effective certification and inspection. Teacher education be-

came a primary vehicle of modernization. In 1905, the University of Virginia created a school of education that became a center for the new science of education and teacher certification. Along with the female normal school established at Farmville in 1887, the state added new normals for white women at Harrisonburg, Fredericksburg, and Radford after 1908. A variety of teachers' institutes and state-sponsored summer normals were also established. Between 1906 and 1912, state officials began a pronounced effort to raise standards for teachers through summer normals, which they sponsored at fourteen different locations for from six to eight weeks.

Closely tied to the education of teachers were new, centrally controlled standards for examination and certification. Teacher certification in nineteenth-century Virginia offered vivid evidence of the power of localism in public education; professional qualifications usually were not the primary consideration in selecting teachers. Imposing outside control through examination and certification—in effect, the power to regulate local hiring and teachers—depended on the power to coerce through a supervisory force attached to the state department of education. Modernizing school officials grasped this reality at an early date. In 1904, they secured the establishment of a five-member State Board of Examiners responsible for five circuits across the state, which reported directly to the state superintendent.[12]

The creation of the State Board of Examiners in 1904 marked a crucial change in the balance of power in Virginia's rural schools. As the first group of state officials charged with extending state authority, they constituted an opening wedge for the future expansions of the supervisory and regulatory powers of the state in public education. The examiners were an advance guard in a process by which they and other state officials increasingly intervened in decisions normally the exclusive preserve of the community. Both prophets and promoters of modernized rural schools, the examiners at first exercised a broad variety of duties. They worked with superintendents, trustees, and patrons to further the "material progress" of the schools by extending the school term, increasing the pay of teachers, and consolidating local schools. In these activities, the examiners—and the other state officials who followed them in the twentieth century—were clearly beginning to usurp powers previously held by localities.[13]

As other supervisory officials were added to the state superintendent's office, however, the examiners focused specifically on extending central control over rural teachers. One examiner recalled that teaching standards were in an "appalling state of affairs," but the examiners and other supervisors made important inroads within a decade. Although in 1911 the State Board of Examiners was replaced by a force of three state inspectors (most of whom were former examiners), the level of state supervision and standardization if anything grew dramatically during the first decades of the twentieth century.[14] Because of the specialization made necessary by age grading and secondary education, teacher certification became increasingly complex and closely connected with state facilities for teacher training. Special certification was required for high school teachers by 1920, including courses in pedagogy and practice teaching; elementary school teachers were subject to less stringent requirements but were also expected to have had exposure to state institutions of teacher training. The combination of expanded teacher education and rigorously enforced state standards contributed to a spectacular rise in the educational levels of rural teachers in Virginia. The proportion of both black and white teachers who by 1916 had training beyond high school—those with collegiate or professional certificates—about doubled in just six years. Meanwhile, the number of less qualified teachers—those with third grade and emergency certificates—declined.[15]

Modernizing officials were determined to extend their success in standardizing rural teaching by changing the attitudes and behavior of teachers. Thus, while they centralized control over teaching through education and supervision, they also consciously fostered new allegiances among teachers and created links—some statewide, some national—extending beyond the locality. Teachers who were exposed to the new statewide bureaucratic apparatus began to exhibit new attitudes toward their work as shown in the formation of teachers' organizations—a black group, founded in 1887, and a white group, formed in 1901—that became visible centers of these new values.[16] Closely connected with state facilities, teachers' associations owed their existence to state-sponsored normals, which provided a setting of self-organization and a forum for the expression of professional attitudes. Professional-minded teachers were also linked to the state educational bureaucracy through schools of education, and they were avid readers of state educational journals such as the *Virginia School Journal*, published until 1906, and the *Virginia Journal of Education*, published thereafter.[17]

Professionally trained and organized teachers were becoming a pervasive influence in the state. As one professional told an audience of white teachers in 1905, Virginia had almost equal proportions of two categories of teachers: permanent and transitory. Teachers' organizations drew support from permanent, career-oriented professionals; transients provided "temporary assistance" before leaving teaching. Female transients usually married; males became merchants, lawyers, or physicians.[18] Although their power and influence did not come from large numbers, professional-minded teachers as a group were nonetheless committed to the cause of reform. The "comprehensive function" of the modern school, stated one educator, required a professional teacher who created "correct ideals" through instruction in every aspect of society. "Bad citizenship," whether a product of illiteracy, inefficiency, immorality, or ill health, was a problem "against which the powers of the school are marshaled."[19]

Supervision and Resistance

Most reformers were satisfied with the new status of rural teachers, but others recognized the difficulty of enforcing central control over rural communities. Eggleston admitted in 1911 that "expert supervision" remained Virginia's "greatest need" and the "only cloud" visible "on the educational skies." He further acknowledged that establishing supervision had encountered some opposition, which he dismissed as the product of a "lack of knowledge" and the "designs" of those with "axes to grind."[20]

Eggleston's candid observations suggest that a crucial part of rural school modernization—changing the status of teachers—was taking place despite the wishes of rural Virginians. They also suggest a tone of caution about the troublesome potential of active local opposition to educational change. Such opposition did not exist simply in the fertile imaginations of modernizers. And although it was rarely unified or articulate, rural resistance to standardization of the teaching force—and to the larger issue of limiting local autonomy—appeared among patrons, teachers, and even trustees.

Despite all-out attempts to encourage local support, there was little evidence of substantial enthusiasm for change and some opposition. In 1906, a teacher criticized the certification process to the secretary of the State Board of Education. His "standing" in the community was well known, he complained. Why was further examination necessary? A northern Piedmont patron was more direct in his opposition to state intervention. It was "altogether wrong" to hire a supervisor, pay him an exorbitantly high salary "out of our school funds," and then allow him to "go around to interfere with our schools." "Some of us poor people can only afford to send our larger children to school a few months during the school term," he wrote. Was it proper to waste their "valuable time" and taxpayers' money?[21]

The clash between traditional community standards for teacher employment and new norms established from above created an unresolved tension. For the most part, the contest between centralization and local power resulted in the loss of community control. Even so, well into the twentieth century localities maintained some veto power over teacher selection. Rural school modernizers themselves frequently recognized the necessity of community approval. In one instance, a modernizing trustee who was confronted with a conflict between qualifications and popularity in 1916 decided to appeal to the state superintendent for help. Could Richmond officials "indulge" the superintendent, the trustee asked, and let him "pass a few who have made good" but who were not "in possession of the required certificate"?[22]

Because modernizers depended upon community financial support as well as approval, increased professionalism among teachers and greater centralized supervision more likely occurred in counties that already possessed ample resources. Statewide, a positive statistical relationship existed between two measures of the extent of modernization in 1920— membership in teachers' associations and number of schools inspected by state officials—and agricultural wealth. The same relationship existed in all but one of Virginia's five regions, confirming the uniform observation of contemporaries: modernization widened educational inequity as much as it narrowed it.[23]

Improving the status of teachers through education and professionalism often made them less willing to teach in backwoods schools, and better-trained teachers preferred to avoid these schools. Teachers exposed to the "new" education had raised expectations and surely found a future in a one-room school unappealing. The reaction of one modernizer to rural Southside Virginia was typical. Complaining about "most abominable" mail schedules and newspapers that were "old before they arrive," he also detected a noticeable gap between professional and unprofessional teachers. He found many "earnest inquiring minds," but much more numerous were those untrained and undeveloped "poor souls" "into whose hands . . . our children should not go."[24]

In short, improvement and standardization raised teachers' expectations and thus widened the gap between town and country schools. The problem was brought home to Jesse H. Binford, executive director of the

CEA, when he traveled with a group of normal school graduates. He reported that normal-trained teachers refused "fine old Virginia dishes" of black-eyed peas and sweet potatoes at a local hotel because they had consumed this fare for a month and were tired of it. But to the reformer, their attitude suggested a larger problem: the greater the teacher's education, the less attractive the rural school. Most attended normal school for three years, where they enjoyed constant activity—basketball, tennis, access to newspapers and magazines—as well as the "delicious fare of the college dining-room with its bi-weekly dessert." A trip to a rural school—and life "in some humble and isolated farm home"—naturally made the teacher feel "like Napoleon on Saint Helena."[25]

Professionalization also encouraged a pedagogical hierarchy among teachers based in part on the growing gulf between town and country schools. Small, isolated schools often had difficulty finding normal school graduates, who usually preferred graded schools and high schools in towns or villages. Trained teachers took jobs in the country as a last resort; in 1916, for example, only about 50 percent of rural teachers had certificates of first grade or above, as compared to 70 percent for the state as a whole.[26] Those who taught in rural schools were frequently eager to leave. In 1915, a teacher in eastern Virginia explained her request for a transfer to a town high school by saying that she had taught "as faithfully" as she could at an "inconvenient distance," and she now deserved a better-located school.[27]

In other respects, modernization also abetted persistent—but to modernizing officials, objectionable—characteristics. The sad reality was that professionalization did little to alter what one observer described as a "constant changing of teachers."[28] As late as 1916, the state inspector of high schools estimated that each year one-half of rural schoolteachers were new to their schools, and another quarter lacked teaching experience. "In school after school in the rural districts," read a comprehensive survey of Virginia education, the same teacher rarely remained more than one year; each year, out of a work force of about fourteen thousand, new teachers numbered between twenty-five hundred and thirty-five hundred. In these circumstances, it was difficult for most rural teachers to become professional or to regard their jobs as anything more than a way station. The response of one teacher who obtained a teaching position in a rural district in 1915 was not atypical. "If I can get a good place to board and come into town on Saturdays and Sundays," the teacher remarked, "I guess I can stand it for six months."[29]

School expansion widened opportunities considerably and simultaneously gave the state greater control over standards. Yet several factors fostered the old problem of transiency among teachers. The continued entrance of large numbers of women into schoolteaching did not alter a basic fact: women teachers, like other women workers before World War II, were overwhelmingly young and single; upon marriage, most of them left the profession. The establishment of widely available teacher-training facilities raised standards, as did the construction of increasingly modernized school plants. But in the process, a new hierarchy of ability among teachers and power among administrators came into existence in which relatively talented, ambitious teachers had attractive incentives and opportunities to leave rural schools for town and city schools.

The Extension of Schooling

For the children and adolescents of early twentieth-century Virginia, the modernization of rural education brought a new intensity to the experience of education. Longer school terms and increased attendance were evidence of a clear tendency for rural schools to occupy a larger and larger share of the time of the rural young. Modernized education, thrusting schools further into rural society while challenging the priorities of children, forced choices between school and country life. It was not always clear that the modern school was the winner in this struggle. As a white teacher in northeastern Virginia confided, she preferred to begin school in mid-September because of conflicts with the harvest season. The "call of the farmer," she wrote, "may be louder and stronger than the call of the school room."[30]

Over time, schools steadily encroached on the time and attention of rural students. The first two decades of the twentieth century witnessed a rapid rise in attendance. In 1900, slightly more than a third of white students and about a quarter of black students attended regularly; twenty years later, more than half of the whites and close to 40 percent of the blacks attended regularly.

Longer terms and increased attendance occurred long before effective compulsory education, which began in Virginia in 1922. Much of school modernization, then, was the result of incentives and opportunities that accompanied early twentieth-century expansion—well before the complete destruction of post-Reconstruction education. One such opportunity was the availability of secondary and graded elementary schools. Actually, the expansion of secondary education and consolidation of rural schools were closely related, for new high schools were often simply slightly expanded consolidated schools. After the passage of the Mann High School Act in 1906, many communities eagerly demanded state-funded secondary education, and by 1920 22,358 students, some 5 percent, were enrolled in high schools. The state department of education attempted to control secondary school development. In accordance with the act's provisions, the department disbursed funds to high schools in matching grants and required strict standards. Each school was obliged to follow a state-mandated course of study, to run for at least eight months, and to observe attendance requirements, and each was subject to annual inspection by the state. From the outset, the state department of education promulgated a classification system for high schools. Between 1906 and 1917, it stipulated that a "first-grade" high school indicated a four-year course, "second-grade" a three-year course, and "third-grade" a one-year course. After 1917, the state department of education accredited only first-grade high schools and designated second- and third-grade schools as "junior high schools."[31]

Still, secondary school expansion and the benefits it brought took place in an incongruent combination of central control and community power. Because the district system remained the basic administrative unit before the 1920s, district boards directed the growth of secondary education under the guidance of state officials. High schools, like post-Reconstruction common schools, came into existence as often at community initiative as they did according to the plans of modernizers. High school enrollment for 1920 suggests that the growth of high schools did not always follow modernization. Enrollment in high schools was above the state average in three nonurban regions; the lowest enrollments occurred in the urbanized counties.

Inevitably, these early high schools, following the pattern of nineteenth-century growth, were isolated, local in orientation, and furiously competitive among themselves for financial support and students. District boards zealously advocated small, local high schools, according to a supervisor in 1916, and created a surplus of "weak" high schools that attempted "more work than can possibly be accomplished." So serious was this problem that high school growth was sapping the district's ability to improve rural elementary schools. Another modernizing official, coming to the same conclusion, complained that the "unwholesome growth" of high schools had "impaired" elementary schools "for lack of funds."[32]

School Consolidation and Pupil Transportation

No better physical symbol of rural school modernization survives today than the consolidated schools constructed during the early decades of the twentieth century. School consolidation in Virginia reversed the major tendency of the post-Reconstruction system to increase the number of schoolhouses, which reached a peak of 7,417 in 1901. Thereafter, through consolidation, the number of schoolhouses steadily declined and the number of schoolrooms steadily rose. Between 1900 and 1915, the number of schoolhouses declined 19 percent, but the number of schoolrooms increased 36 percent. School consolidation most affected one-room schools, which declined in numbers from 5,308 in 1910 to 3,786 ten years later.[33]

State officials considered consolidation a prerequisite for further modernization. The consolidated school, they contended, was more efficient because it made possible economies of scale and provided cheaper instruction for more pupils. Consolidated schools, wrote Eggleston, invariably resulted in increased enrollment and attendance. By fostering an atmosphere of social and intellectual stimulation and gregariousness, consolidated schools also helped children transcend the "depressing and devitalizing" consequences of constant isolation in school and community. Larger schools diminished the potential for a localistic "spirit of truculence" and thereby expanded the power of the organized community.[34] By acting as a beacon of town values, consolidated schools would presumably reinforce the social stability of the countryside. Consolidation enabled rural schools to resemble urban schools, argued one educator, and, in the process, stemmed depopulation. "Persons of means and influence," who otherwise would have left because of superior schools in towns and cities, now could remain in the countryside. Modern consolidated schools, agreed another school official, provided educational opportunities that approximated those "now enjoyed by the children in the representative cities of the State."[35]

Consolidation, in turn, depended upon transporting pupils to these schools—a forceful extension of state authority that would also increase regular attendance. Isolation and bad roads caused "irregular and broken attendance," charged one educator, and created "an aversion in the child for the schoolroom instead of pride in punctual attendance and studious advancement." School consolidation and pupil transportation were central ingredients in rural school modernization, moreover, because they constituted an obvious precondition for further standard-

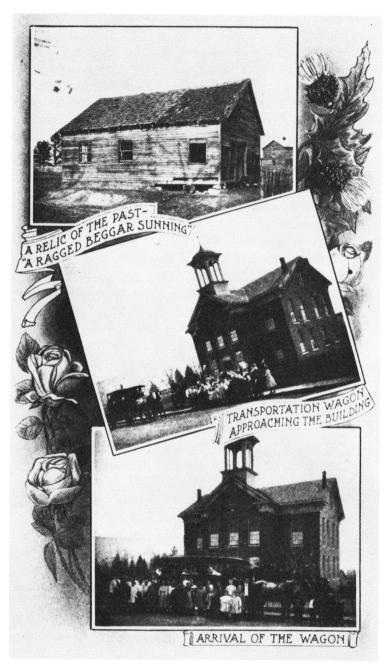

School modernization, Shenandoah County, Virginia, 1907
(courtesy of the Virginia Department of Education)

ization and administrative control and extended control over the socialization of country children.

It was obvious to modernizers that progress was impossible without consolidation. School wagons would stop at every farmhouse where schoolchildren lived, promised one official, and their drivers would assume responsibility for the children during the day; transporting pupils would give the consolidated schools greater authority over rural children. Such transportation would instill order among rural children because they would no longer tramp in the mud and snow and, because the wagons were under the "control of a responsible driver," who would prevent "vicious conversation" or bullying by "tyrannical" boys. It also ensured "better behavior" en route to and from school because the driver assumed responsibility for the pupils' welfare, maintained another official. Discipline in the transportation wagons was strict; boys were forbidden to smoke or chew tobacco, use profane or "unbecoming" language, or bully smaller children.[36]

Modernizing school officials, working before the age of compulsory education, promoted consolidation through both subtle and direct persuasion. Attached to the state department of education, these supervisors consolidated schools by whatever means possible—moral suasion, arm twisting, and the lure of increased revenues. Wherever communities supported consolidation, it was hailed in an age in which "new" usually meant better.[37] Local support tended to reflect the rural community's self-image. If it considered itself modern and forward-looking, it boasted of a new consolidated school as a symbol of a proud and growing community. If convinced of its value to their community, even former opponents of consolidation, according to one observer, petitioned for a modernized school "faster than trustees can build the houses." Parents in another neighborhood reacted similarly when they became "very interested" in school consolidation; "when they got started," people in the community became "hustlers" for school improvement.[38]

As with other forms of school modernization, state officials fostered early consolidations by working within the post-Reconstruction system. They openly cultivated local opinion by forming alliances with parents and trustees. They almost always promoted consolidation by publicizing its visible successes and the advantages that it offered the community. Eastern Shore trustees in one district closed several schools on the advice of an examiner and began transporting students to a consolidated school. As they proudly reported, attendance then rose by about 50 percent. In Middlesex County, in the eastern Tidewater, local officials and a

School wagons, Prince Edward County, Virginia, 1907
(courtesy of the Virginia Department of Education)

visiting state official agreed to replace four "unattractive and unsanitary" schools with a single modern six-room structure.[39] Across the state, in Loudoun County, T. S. Settle, who was state supervisor of rural schools, worked in alliance with local parents and school officials. Settle reported in 1911 that he had "most gratifying" results in school improvement. During the previous winter, in a two-week campaign, he held rallies to generate support for school consolidations with apparently positive results. In one part of Loudoun County, three small schools amalgamated with the consent of the "leading citizens" of the community. There was every reason to believe that reform would in the future proceed harmoniously, Settle reported, for the school wagons that took pupils to the consolidated schools were now "well patronized," and the parents were "highly pleased" with the new arrangement.[40]

Change and Persistence in School Consolidation

In spite of all optimistic predictions, school consolidation encountered nagging obstacles. The most serious was the absence of enthusiastic popular support for, and even open opposition to, educational change among rural Americans. Although it is clear that most of them were dissatisfied with country life in general and with rural schools in particular, such dissatisfaction only rarely translated into support for rural school modernization. Wherever school consolidation was open to public debate by rural Americans, potent opposition emerged.[41] The extent to which rural Americans were able to discuss consolidation—or any other aspect of school modernization—varied regionally and reflected important differences in rural political structures. In midwestern states, the decision to consolidate could be made only after a popular vote, and the debates preceding such votes frequently demonstrated the depth of local suspicions toward drastic educational innovation. The one-room school, wrote the authors of a well-known manual of reform, was "so deeply rooted in the hearts of the people . . . [and] so much a part of their mental constitution, that it will not be given up without a struggle." The result, not infrequently, was a popular vote against consolidation and against modernization in any form.[42]

In Virginia and in most of the South, however, reformers possessed a distinct advantage. For although every state in the Middle West provided for consolidation only after a referendum of propertyholders, every former Confederate state except Arkansas allowed it at the discretion of school officials. There can be little doubt that the rapid pace of administrative centralization and school modernization in the South during the first half of the twentieth century was closely connected to the absence of democratic decision making. Yet in the absence of effective compulsory education before World War I, the modernization of southern rural schools had to rely on a degree of popular approval and at least acquiescence. Modernizers could not openly defy public opinion because the very existence of schools still depended on sufficient enrollments and attendance.

The persistence of post-Reconstruction schools and the limited impact of consolidation before World War I was made clear in other respects. Most amalgamations occurred haphazardly through the cumbersome machinery of the district board; rarely did a master plan exist on the county level, let alone for the entire state. Most consolidations took place as part of general school expansion, without careful distinction between elementary and secondary schools. In 1910, for example, one Valley district board approved a consolidation as part of plans to build a two-room structure that was to serve as both the elementary and high school. Six years later, a trustee in eastern Virginia requested that a superintendent do something for the parents of the lower end of his district. The trustee suggested that, whatever patrons thought, several rooms be added to a local school.[43]

School wagons, Augusta County, Virginia, 1907
(courtesy of the Virginia Department of Education)

Many of these early school consolidations were limited in scope and very much within the structure of the nineteenth-century school system. Before the 1920s, truly effective pupil transportation remained the exception. It awaited the construction of hard-surfaced highways and the rumbling presence of school buses; the reality was frequently rutted dirt roads and horse-drawn wagons. Because most amalgamations were small and local, moreover, mass pupil transportation was not necessary. Of 179 consolidations in 1907, for example, a state official reported that most were within approximate walking distance; the longest walk was about seven miles and the shortest about three miles. Nonetheless, the combination of school amalgamations and a lack of mass pupil transportation prompted some parents to complain. It was her "due," a patron wrote in 1913, to have a wagon because she and other parents in her locality paid taxes that furnished wagons to other localities. The lack of transport meant that eight or ten pupils supplied their own; others had not attended school for two years because they had "too far to make."[44]

This instance was not unusual, for early efforts at consolidation did little to change the problem of inaccessibility. As one superintendent recounted, consolidation was ineffective in his county because mountains and "impassable streams" cut school districts "asunder" and made it impossible to bring "all sections together." The obstacles of geography and rural isolation were not exclusive to any region in rural Virginia, as a northern Piedmont neighborhood discovered when it complained to a district board that its children were "remote" from the nearest school-house and requested pupil transportation. The board demurred, however, maintaining that it was "not practicable at present to incur the necessary expense." Even avid proponents of consolidation admitted that it would have only a limited effect on rural schools. The sad reality, lamented one official, was that a "large proportion" of pupils would attend isolated and ungraded rural schools or will "not be taught at all."[45]

These realities and others made modernizers cautious about attempting school consolidation. Although he advocated consolidation as the most effective instrument of change in Virginia rural education, for example, SEB agent Robert Frazer believed it possible only in the long run. Among the many other problems he cited were dispersed, sparse population and racial tension. In short, he warned in 1905, it was "prudent" to approach the subject with "much circumspection." Despite some subsequent success at consolidation, this cautious attitude persisted. Another modernizer who was otherwise "pretty cheerful" about educational change thus warned of the potential for opposition from "whole regiments of soreheads and 'stone age' people."[46]

The reserve and caution of these men was based on a reality of rural opposition and indifference. Wherever consolidation and pupil transportation occurred, they often met significant opposition from inarticulate but powerful local blocs that traditionally dominated school affairs. Opponents of school reform rarely left a record of their position. What has survived comes from the accounts of reformers, which almost always refer to the opponents of consolidation in muted tones, if at all. It is clear, however, that mere mention of these "soreheads" usually suggested significant problems for reformers. In one such moment of candor in 1903, Frazer told of a superintendent who encountered "serious trouble" when he attempted to establish a consolidated school where the new teacher had a "free hand" in converting the school to modern pedagogy. But the teacher soon confronted extensive opposition that threatened, "on account of withdrawals," the very existence of the school. In still another instance in a Northern Neck county, an attempt to consolidate several popular local schools was greeted by a "storm of protest from one end of the county to the other." Even after consolidation had occurred in some communities, admitted one reformer, the opposition of "the chronic kicker" persisted; trustees should therefore take care to avoid confusing "a large quantity of noise for a high quality of noise."[47]

Nor was it clear that pupil transportation, which was indispensable to rural school consolidation, would prove altogether acceptable. Lacking coercive powers, district boards had to persuade parents to agree to some sort of transportation arrangement; because these arrangements frequently depended on subscriptions by parents, pupil transportation depended on local approval. When the Manassas district board decided to consolidate two schools on a trial basis, it polled patrons about their willingness to provide financial support for school wagons. Frequently, however, parents opposed transportation as much as consolidation. When a trustee in one school district offered to pay parents to transport students, parents complained that the offer was not generous enough. Still more typical was the case of another community which, when asked to support a plan of pupil transportation in 1907, sent a delegation, which declined to "cooperate . . . in the matter of transporting their children."[48]

Still, most characteristic of the opposition to school consolidation was its impotency. More often than not, the desire to preserve the nineteenth-century school was less an example of the coordinated action of all rural Virginians than of isolated, generally ineffective outbursts. Nor was such opposition necessarily aimed at consolidation per se. Instead, it frequently resulted from the location of modern school facilities in one community rather than another. In a northern Piedmont community, the mere circulation of a rumor about consolidation prompted protest delegations from two communities whose schools were imperiled. In another instance, when a district board attempted to persuade two communities to consolidate, both vigorously opposed the idea. One community announced its determination not to "send their children" to a new school, and the other, according to the district board's minutes, "said the same."[49]

Resistance to school consolidation was often fused with the familiar force of parochialism, and modernization raised the old issue of school location but gave it even greater intensity because the stakes—a new, permanent building—were much higher. When, for instance, a Valley district board agreed in principle to a consolidation, it was unable to decide on its location. Two groups of patrons had, in the fashion of the nineteenth century, presented petitions, and when the board expressed its position, "considerable contention" resulted. Other examples abound of the fusion of localism and opposition to reform. In 1903, advocates of a school consolidation in one locality faced difficulties when three neighborhoods were unable to agree "upon anything definite." In another area, a superintendent proposed consolidating two schools but met "obstacles" from objecting patrons.[50]

Although district trustees usually avoided directly confronting localistic pressure, they could ultimately decide to consolidate with or without local approval, and the likelihood was strong that their superiors would support their decision. When a district board decided in favor of a consolidation in Prince William County in 1909, dissenting patrons were able to call a board of appeal headed by the county superintendent. But after hearing their case and declaring that none present could suggest a better location, the board of appeal unanimously upheld the trustees. Another appeal, however, suggested more of the caution that characterized the actions of school officials. When a district board located a consolidated school, a "large number of patrons" protested and demanded a special board of appeal. This time, however, the board avoided a ruling on the technicality that the appeal was "premature" because the schoolhouse was not yet built. A year later, when a building contract had been awarded, the reassembled board of appeal upheld the district trustees but was careful to provide only a weak endorsement of its decision. Because the consolidated school's location would "inconvenience some families," the board resolved, another school should eventually be built in the neighborhood.[51]

This mixture of resistance to change and the physical limitations on modernization meant that, before 1920, school consolidation was in an experimental stage. Indeed, when the Virginia Education Commission conducted the first comprehensive school survey in 1919, it concluded that school amalgamation had proceeded only haltingly. Rural schools posed a staggering challenge in both their physical inaccessibility in many parts of the state and the inability of "groups of communities" to agree on new school locations. Because of convenience, explained the commissioners, localities still clung to the neighborhood school. Because the district system had "interfered seriously" with rural school modernization, the commission recommended the centralization of local districts into countywide systems. Indeed, it saw the only hope for reform in the complete abolition of the nineteenth-century system: the further expansion of the powers of the state department of education, the institution of compulsory education, and the end of local autonomy.[52]

Although by 1920 the consequences of rural school modernization were far from clear, the basic structure of nineteenth-century education had undergone permanent alteration. The operating rules of public education had changed. As school expansion increasingly derived its force from public financing, the power of local, private groups correspondingly decreased. Under the new educational polity, school officials and their local representatives relentlessly exploited the new balance of power to their advantage. They demolished, or attempted to demolish, the visible symbols of nineteenth-century rural education. Shocked at the impermanence of schools, modernizers encouraged the training of teachers in normals and sponsored among them the internalization of professional values, even as they stimulated the extension of the school term and increases in attendance. A more visible symbol of the old country school, the dilapidated one-room school, became an object of further change, as state officials used compulsion and incentives to stimulate the construction of permanent, modern facilities in secondary schools and consolidated elementary schools.

Chapter Seven
The Modern School Experience

The goal of restructuring the relationship between post-Reconstruction rural schools and rural society united school modernizers. That relationship had been rooted in localism and community dominance; how much or how little was learned, who participated in education, and who controlled school governance were all issues in which outsiders took little part. Directly challenging the nature of this relationship, modernizers sought an end to absolute community control over education and the inauguration of an entirely new conception of schooling.

Changing the function of schooling ultimately meant altering the environment of public education in at least three respects. First, rather than simply altering decisions, modernizers sought a wholly new process of decision making through the introduction of bureaucratic governance. Second, rather than simply building new schools or even new facilities, they insisted on school interiors and exteriors that reflected their view of education. Third, modernizers attempted to create an environment of learning in which rural students directly experienced the new relationship between schools and their society.

Rural Schools and the "Sanitary Millennium"

"Of the achievements of the present generation," wrote an early twentieth-century health official, none attracted "less general attention" but had "greater influence upon posterity" than the emergence of what he called "sanitary science." Although sanitation and public health were beginning to influence the rural South profoundly, to this observer the arrival of what he described as a "sanitary millennium" depended on changes in rural education.[1]

The modernization of public health and rural schools were tied together by common leaders, supporters, and objectives. Health and school modernizers were convinced that the social problems of the rural South, environmental in origin, could be solved through institutional change. Health officials hoped to use rural schools to transform popular health practices and to eradicate disease, parasites, and malnutrition among southerners; by effecting attitudinal changes through schools, health officials could also help to build a future-oriented, healthy society. Educational modernizers embraced these objectives for slightly different reasons. They saw sanitizing school interiors and exteriors, acquiring power to inspect schoolchildren, and transforming schools into centers of modern health all as part of a modernized relationship between school and society.

The alliance between health and school officials became possible because of a southern public health campaign that resembled the earlier educational crusade. Drawing on the medical profession's new awareness of microscopic disease and the rapid expansion of public health facilities in the urban North, a group of southern social reformers and northern medical professionals persuaded the Rockefeller philanthropic empire—previously involved in the South only in school reform—to found a comprehensive regional public health organization to eradicate the hookworm parasite.

Founded in 1909, the Rockefeller Sanitary Commission for the Eradication of Hookworm Disease could justifiably claim success after only five years. Combining scientific precision with evangelical fervor, it documented and then publicized the shocking extent of hookworm, which infected close to two-fifths of all southerners and, in heavily infected coastal regions, over two-thirds. By 1914, the commission, in demonstrating a real medical and social problem, also discovered that hookworm and parasitic infection were only part of a regionwide pattern of malnutrition, hunger, and disease. The commission's conclusions seemed irresistible: regional poverty and a host of social problems were consequences of environmental conditions. The formula for change was simple: the use of sanitary privies and the adoption of standard sanitary practices in homes, farms, and public institutions.[2]

The focus on public health and environmentalism united school modernizers and hookworm campaigners into a firm alliance. Included as charter members of the Rockefeller commission were the original leaders of the Conference for Education in the South and then the SEB—Alderman, Page, Murphy, the reforming state superintendent of North

Carolina, James Y. Joyner, and the Tennessee school reformer Philander P. Claxton. Although the Rockefellers appointed the acclaimed "discoverer" of hookworm, Charles Wardell Stiles, as the commission's scientific secretary, they named to the more important position of administrative secretary Wickliffe Rose, a Tennessee native who had achieved regional prominence as a school reformer and as executive secretary of the SEB.[3]

With or without the SEB's blessing, southern "educational people," wrote Rose, became "immensely interested" in public health.[4] Because the interests of health reformers and school modernizers converged, cooperation between the two occurred almost immediately. Soon after the commission was organized in Virginia in 1910, the CEA pledged its support; help was also forthcoming from major black educational organizations. With the enthusiastic backing of the state educational bureaucracy, rural schools in Virginia developed into centers of detection, community education, and preventive public health. At the same time, health reformers quickly grasped the possibilities of an alliance with modernizing school officials. As one Rockefeller agent wrote, rural schools were both the "greatest medium" for the spread of hookworms and the "most important agency" for their prevention.[5]

By the second year of the commission's operation in Virginia, field agents had launched an aggressive program of detection, cure, and prevention through rural schools. Rockefeller officials arrived bringing microscopes, lanterns, and slides for lectures, pamphlets, and photographs—"working tools" of a determined campaign of exposure and publicity. Armed with a letter of introduction from the state superintendent, they first met with teachers' organizations and school officials. Thus officially sanctioned, Rockefeller agents inspected the schools, often giving a public lecture to local physicians and parents, and then distributed literature that explained hookworms and advised the necessity of sanitation. In many instances, the agents took the opportunity to circulate tin boxes among parents, who were encouraged to send a sample of their child's feces to the commission's laboratory in the state capital.[6]

If the state laboratory confirmed hookworm infection, the field men then began treatment through the schools. In most mild cases, infection among schoolchildren was quickly cured with the usual dose of epsom salts, which dislodged the hookworms from the intestinal wall, and the poison thymol, which killed them. Virginia hookworm campaigners reported a high success rate working through the rural schools—even higher than the better-publicized campaigns in other states that were conducted through county dispensaries. The state director of the commission in Virginia, Allen W. Freeman, reported that treating mild cases through the schools had brought "wonderful success," which seemed to suggest that for Virginia more than other states, it was a better approach than working through the dispensary. In rural schools, commission agents enjoyed regular, institutional support. Schoolchildren and their parents provided a representative sample of the rural population, probably more so than those treated at dispensaries; as ever-present public institutions, schools reached cases "which we could not reach by a free dispensary."[7]

But the diagnosis and treatment of hookworm was only one effect of the Rockefeller commission on Virginia rural schools. Although, as John Ettling has shown, the commission failed to eradicate the hookworm parasite,[8] it left an indelible mark on southern society. Spawning the creation of permanent state and local public health agencies, it inaugurated a long era of public health efforts by state agencies. Equally important was its effect on schools. The hookworm campaign gave rural school modernization a scientific justification; modern facilities meant healthy facilities. It also provided support for regular state intervention through rural schools designed to alter patterns of community behavior and remake popular health practices. By focusing attention on a specific, well-documented problem and by establishing a link between modern schools and public health, the hookworm campaign had by 1914 mobilized support for a general, sanitized environment of public education.

The School as Public Health Center

No public institution was more affected by the hookworm campaign than the rural school. Hookworms and parasitic infection were demonstrable social problems linked to educational underdevelopment; bureaucratic intervention, the institution of state standards, and the end of community control offered an end to ill health. Hookworm campaigners claimed that they had discovered the "germ," the single cause of regional stagnation and, in rural schools, of irregular attendance, indifference or hostility toward schools, and the apparent backwardness of southern children. As a result of hookworm infection, wrote one physician in Virginia, many teachers wrongfully assumed that rural schoolchildren were innately "dull and stupid." Hookworm debilitated schooling in other respects because older children found it difficult to progress beyond the early grades and frequently dropped out with only a minimal education.[9] In a directive to rural schoolteachers, the Virginia State Board of Education made the same connection. The "widespread prevalence" of hookworm impaired the bodies and minds of the young; "easily fatigued," infected children were unable to study with interest or enthusiasm. Even with the determined commitment of teachers, hookworm-infected children would probably make "poor progress" and leave school undereducated.[10]

The logic of this analysis—that the responsibility of the modernized school necessarily extended to regulating the health of schoolchildren—led reformers beyond the immediate question of hookworms. Indeed, the intensified focus brought on by the Rockefeller commission convinced them that parasitic infection was only part of a larger pattern of disease and malnutrition. Ill health among rural schoolchildren reflected the social environment of the rural South; rather than models of modernized living, schools helped to transmit sickness and parasites. In 1911, Freeman described rural school conditions as not "even approximately satisfactory." Of buildings constructed before the turn of the twentieth century, "hardly one" was so constructed "as not to seriously impair the physical constitution of the children compelled to remain in it many hours a day for many months of the year." Among other problems, he cited inadequate lighting, causing eye strain; insufficient ventilation, especially in one-room schools; and the use of badly constructed furniture, which caused "unnatural and constrained positions" to be "impressed upon the plastic bones of the growing child." The school was a center of contagion, moreover, because of the absence of privy facilities and the prevalent practice of using a common drinking cup.[11]

A study sponsored jointly by Virginia state school officials and the Rockefeller commission reached similar conclusions. In an examination of the health conditions of the rural schools of Orange County, located in the northern Piedmont region, Dr. Roy K. Flannagan and a group of investigators confirmed the general debilitation of the average Virginian. This region, the survey noted, should have been "as healthful as any locality on the globe"; instead, it was a center of ill health. Flannagan reported that a "large percentage" of schoolchildren were malnourished, some 25 percent of the whites and 38 percent of the blacks; another 86 percent of white children and 82 percent of black children had suffered from major illnesses such as whooping cough, measles, and pneumonia. Along with a high rate of hookworm infection, Flannagan found an "alarming percentage" of children afflicted with a variety of intestinal parasites.[12]

For school and health reformers, the Flannagan survey suggested the presence of the real social problem of ill health; an identifiable cause, insanitary conditions and backward parental attitudes; and an obvious solution, the separation of rural children from their home environment through the increased influence of schooling. Adopting "sanitary science" meant not only uplift but also the abandonment of centuries-old health practices. The modernized school would become a beacon of new health values, a "lighthouse in the community," in the words of one health official, which would spread "the gospel of sanitation abroad in the land."[13]

As a direct result of this new emphasis on school sanitation, Virginia health and school officials introduced sanitary privies to public schools. In 1909, only 3,900 of the 7,000 schools possessed privies, most of which were probably insanitary; of 1,000 farms inspected, only 150 had privies. Stimulating privy construction on two fronts, Rockefeller field men publicized the need for sanitary privies in homes and schools. CEA leagues, working with commission agents, began raising local funds in 1910 to build privies in rural schools either privately or through local authorities.[14] But even more effective was the symbolic and actual intervention of the State Board of Education, which in 1914 stipulated that all schoolhouses provide two outhouses, designated male and female, and further empowered health officials with sweeping powers to enforce this regulation.[15]

Important evidence of the new public health responsibilities of rural schools also came in the introduction of medical inspection of children. Here again, officials from the school bureaucracy and the new health bureaucracy found common ground. To school officials, medical inspection expanded the function of modern public education; to health officials, sanitized schools, no longer places "for the exchange of disease," would exemplify new health practices for the entire rural community, where the means of "preventing disease is taught and the teachings put into practice."[16] Within ten years after the dissolution of the Rockefeller commission, medical inspection of schoolchildren had become a reality in Virginia and most of the South and a visible manifestation of the invigorated power of the progressive state.[17]

The transformation of Virginia rural schools from centers of ill health into centers of public health provides a clear view of the evolving relationship between school and community in modern rural Virginia. In almost every aspect of public education, modernizers regarded the symbiosis between the nineteenth-century school and its social environment as worthy only of destruction. That rural schools appeared to perpetuate the bad health practices provided grist for the modernizers' mill, for here was empirical evidence of the need for educational change. The interrelationship between the success of rural public health and the success of school modernization emphasized the need for changing the environment of public education—most obviously, in the construction of clean and new facilities physically apart from the rural landscape. Introducing modern health practices into rural schools was, however, but one example of this milieu. Still another was a new approach to the stuff of learning, which itself suggested different assumptions and goals.

Shaping the Curriculum

Twentieth-century schoolbooks differed from their post-Reconstruction predecessors in both emphasis and organization. Schoolbooks changed because schools changed—because public education was now becoming a total, integral, and continuous part of childhood and adolescence. Nineteenth-century schoolbooks and pedagogy reflected a localized educational environment; in the twentieth century, they increasingly embodied patterns of standardization and centralization. Previously an assortment of subjects whose purpose was to provide basic literacy and moral instruction, the curriculum now assumed new significance.

After 1900, the State Board of Education, as it had for the previous three decades, continued to publish multiple lists of textbooks from which local boards could choose. Yet unlike nineteenth-century school officials, it made effective progress in standardizing the school curriculum. In secondary education, for example, it tightened curricular control by requiring local compliance with a state-established course of study. State officials similarly pressed communities to follow a standardized elementary school curriculum; they were notably successful whenever schools received some form of state aid. Diversity, moreover, accompanied standardization. Along with the nineteenth-century subjects of spelling, reading, writing, arithmetic, and geography, the State Board of Education added the subjects of physiology and hygiene, civil government, and drawing. High school expansion and age grading in elementary schools stimulated interest in modern languages and the physical sciences, as well as shop for boys and home economics for girls. Especially popular was the introduction of the study of agriculture.[18]

Nothing better illustrates the tendencies of standardization and curricular diversity than the changing nature of schoolbooks. By 1900, popular nineteenth-century texts—Holmes's readers, spellers, and histories, McGuffey's readers and spellers, and Harvey's grammar—had disappeared from schoolrooms. Stories in the new readers that replaced McGuffey—in Virginia, commonly *The Haliburton Reader* and *The Howell Reader*—stressed different messages. Gone were the simple exhortations of rural Victorian values of thrift, work, and self-discipline; stories less frequently attempted to draw moral lessons from real-life situations. Detached from either a social or moral reality, twentieth-century readers no longer portrayed farms and rural society as the primary units of life. Tales set on farms often featured urban children visiting their rural cousins.[19] In a typical story in Logan Douglass Howell's *The Howell Reader* (1910), two children visiting a southern plantation heard a song about metropolitan dominance: "I used to get my living / By wagon and team; / Now I get my living / By railroad and steam."[20]

Popular schoolbooks in early twentieth-century Virginia were also deeply imbued with contemporary cultural values. Nineteenth-century readers avoided the race issue by rarely mentioning blacks; in the new twentieth-century texts they began to surface in obviously subordinate positions. Northern children visiting the rural South in *The Howell Reader* discovered two blacks, "Uncle Daniel" and "Aunt Hannah," both domestic servants. Racial subordination meant, of course, segregation. When Aunt Hannah discovered that the white children had imitated Indians by painting their faces with berry juice, she used the opportunity to teach a valuable lesson about modern society. She recounted the story of a crow, who, after trying to become white by washing the black away, lost only his voice. "You children," she warned, "had better keep to your own color, and leave pokeberry juice alone."[21]

History texts exhibited an even greater cultural imperiousness. Like nineteenth-century histories, they were aggressively ethnocentric; unlike them, they were willing to propose a new view of southern history and its lessons for present-day race relations. Most of them—such as J.L.M. Curry's *The Southern States of the American Union*, Philip Alexander Bruce's *A School History of the United States*, and Royall B. Smithey's *History of Virginia*—were white supremacist in both tone and substance. Not unlike his predecessors in the 1870s, Bruce thus pictured the American Indians in his *School History* as in the "lowest state of barbarism."

But in contrast to post-Reconstruction writers, the twentieth-century historians rallied to the South's defense. Observing that most historians had "grossly misrepresented" the region, Curry promised that his text would restore its "true place" in American history. Reconstruction became a central event in the historical panorama of these texts. It was a complete failure, according to Smithey, because of "sectional prejudice" and the rule of "ignorance, fraud, and robbery." Another failing was corruption, which was fostered by northern carpetbaggers and their southern scalawag allies, who, wrote Bruce, descended on the South like "an ill-omened bird to fatten on the spoil."[22]

The lesson of Reconstruction extended beyond the question of corrupt government; it offered an example of the disastrous consequences of meddling in the racial affairs of the South. Maintaining power by promising freedmen social and political equality, meddling northerners had disrupted the stability of southern race relations. Although southern whites united to overthrow Reconstruction, Curry suggested that it failed precisely because of the attempt to grant blacks full equality. The implications for the present were clear. "The lesson should not be forgotten," he wrote, "that the races, so distinguishable, may meet, side by side, but are far more immiscible than Jew and Gentile, Greek and Moslem."[23]

The Organized Curriculum: Civics and Health

Perhaps the most obvious distinction between the curriculum of the nineteenth-century school and that of the twentieth century was its approach to individual and group behavior. The nineteenth-century school's goal, as espoused by schoolmen as various as Horace Mann and William Henry Ruffner, was to train children in the skills of literacy and, in the process, to inculcate in them a moral framework for future actions. Educators of the early twentieth century were interested in broadening the vistas of the school in every direction, not only by extending its reach over the young but also by broadening the scope of the curriculum. Expansion and diversification also meant training children for organized group behavior in an industrial society.

Civics and health were two significant additions to the twentieth-century curriculum that reflected these objectives. Civics instruction sought to teach students the meaning of government and the significance of responsible citizenship in a cooperative democracy. It communicated "ideas of community life," according to one manual, and served as "a miniature democracy." But civics also served to teach children, especially rural children, about the state's new role in local life. The purpose of his civics textbook, wrote Howard L. McBain in *How We Are Governed in Virginia and the Nation* (1908), was to acquaint pupils with government as "a real, active thing" around them. Government represented the sum total of the cooperative community; it was the "whole people of any community, acting together," and it undertook to do "for us many things which we cannot do for ourselves." Although instruction in civics emphasized obedience to the rules of society, writers of civics textbooks also stressed interaction between individuals and the community and the importance of organized group relations. To another civics writer, William E. Fox, author of *Civil Government in Virginia* (1904), respect for government was as necessary as respect for the authority of the family. As in the family unit, if individuals did as they pleased, chaos would result, and there "would be no peace or happiness." School, store, and factory alike all required discipline and social responsibility, for "disorder and confusion" would result without the direction of "managers or masters."[24]

Curricular innovations—products of the alliance between health and school officials—were designed to establish new bonds of modern community responsibility by increasing pupils' awareness about sanitation and hygiene. As early as 1912, at the urging of Rockefeller officials, rural teachers in Virginia circulated a "hookworm quiz" informing students of the dangers of improper sanitation. The State Board of Education similarly prepared and distributed a "health catechism" in which pupils responded to prepared questions about the germ theory of disease, the nature of specific diseases, and the principles of sanitation. These early experiments, a direct outgrowth of the hookworm campaign, paved the way for permanent changes. Soon knowledge about health and sanitation became a standard part of teacher training at southern normals.[25]

At the same time, health and hygiene textbooks began appearing on state-approved lists. These textbooks stressed the connections between good health and an orderly, modernized society. Health textbooks such as those by John W. Ritchie, William O. Krohn, and Columbus N. Millard, providing a basic outline of human anatomy and physiology, stressed that good habits brought healthy and productive lives. Because good health habits began early, schools should instill a routine of sanitary practices and good nutrition in children. Ritchie's *Primer on Sanitation* (1919) justified an ultimate right of coercive governmental intervention to ensure community safety through public health. School and health officials with "authority over all the people" could properly protect community health; if necessary, the "ignorant and careless" should be forced to "live so that they will not be a source of danger to those about them." In other instances, textbooks employed more imaginative ways to introduce students to the rules of good health. In one text, children participated in an imaginary "health court" where errant but remorseful children confessed to such crimes as spitting on the sidewalk, drinking whiskey, violating a quarantine for measles, or smoking cigarettes.[26]

The introduction of health as part of a modernized curriculum implied a new relationship between public education and leisure and recreation. As both Daniel T. Rodgers and Dominick Cavallo have shown, early twentieth-century American cultural leaders responded to the increasing separation of work and leisure in industrial America by promoting organized recreation through playgrounds, physical education, and team sports.[27] Dangerous consequences could result unless public schools trained students through organized recreation in the productive use of leisure time, warned health textbooks. One textbook cited the case of Bobby, a student in a village high school who was previously "punctual, regular, and reliable in both work and play." Yet by the end of the first year, Bobby had experienced a "marked change": he belonged to a gang so bad that Fred—the "worst" boy in the school—had refused to join it. Worse still, the avowed purpose of this gang was to make swearing "easy." The problem, the author concluded, was that the school had not organized Bobby's work and leisure time; neither the curriculum nor recess play had provided the "needed activity," and the gang became his "more effective school."[28]

These textbooks thus advocated using schools to organize leisure time. It was not proper, maintained Millard, that work should occupy all of the student's time, for "active" recreation and "vigourous exercise" were keys to true success. Games, especially organized team sports, accomplished "something for the growing boy and girl that work alone cannot supply," agreed Krohn, because they trained the mind in judgment, quickness, and determination. He considered organized sports a necessary part of the school experience because of the lessons they provided for group relations. Baseball stimulated judgment, as well as skill, daring, and courage; swimming, "determination and self-reliance"; and football, "will, courage, obedience to orders." Football instructed in socialized behavior by reinforcing attitudes among players that each had a "place to fill," and the "concerted action" of the sport gave it "great value."[29]

The Rise of Agricultural Vocationalism

All of these changes were landmark innovations appearing with modernized schools everywhere in the urban and rural United States. More characteristic of rural schools were attempts to introduce the study of farming into the public school curriculum.[30] The introduction of agriculture soon became the most ambitious of the changes in the modern school environment. It was appealing in part because, by tying schooling to the economic needs of farmers, it sought to overcome the imposing obstacle of rural resistance and indifference to change. Agriculturalists had long lamented the drift of the rural young away from the farm; some of them even charged that public education speeded emigration by projecting urban values and by instructing in subjects irrelevant to country life. How could schools help keep the young "on the farm?" asked one Virginian in 1908. The answer lay in altering "the character of training" in rural public education, which created "ambitions in many a little breast" without providing any chance for their fulfillment. If rural youth were persuaded that there was "no future in agricultural work and no happiness in rural life," was it any wonder that they would flee farms and their "so-called drudgery"?[31]

For Virginia school officials, vocational agriculture would further strengthen rural school modernization in three ways. First, by satisfying agrarian discontent, vocationalism might not only overcome local objections to educational innovation, it would also wed the rural community to school modernization. Second, like urban school officials, modernizers believed that vocational education would remake schools into vital forces by linking education to future development. Third, vocational agriculture would further school modernization by helping to inaugurate modern values and work habits among rural children. Drawing upon nineteenth-century traditions of manual training, vocational agriculture —along with technical education for northerners and "industrial education" for rural blacks—sought to redirect the values and skills of children. Acquiring more than literacy, vocationally educated pupils would internalize values of hard work, thrift, punctuality, and acquisitiveness.

Among the strongest advocates of agricultural education in Virginia and elsewhere were commercial and "scientific" farmers whose views were represented in agricultural journals such as the Richmond *Southern Planter* and the Raleigh *Progressive Farmer*. They received support and additional expertise from a network of scientific agriculturalists sponsored by the Virginia Polytechnic Institute at Blacksburg and the United States Department of Agriculture (USDA). To these men, the problems of rural Virginia could partly be solved in rural schools. Public education did nothing to alter traditional "defective" farming, wrote one scientific farmer to the *Southern Planter*; modernized schools should help foster a transition to commercial agriculture. "Bad farming" meant drudgery and low profits, but it resulted from inadequate knowledge.[32]

Scientific farmers and school officials alike believed that agricultural education would transform schools into active agents of change. Rural Virginians were locked into a debilitating, stagnant home and work atmosphere that spawned a cycle of poverty and inertia. Offering a way out, agricultural education, as one advocate put it, made possible an "ideal" relationship between modernized rural schools and their society. It reached deep into the heart of rural society and intervened directly in familial upbringing by teaching economic skills and imbuing rural children with modern attitudes. The study of agriculture in public schools, claimed a state official, interwove public education into rural society by linking schooling with the economic needs of the community. Thus united, school and society would be connected in such a way that "nothing can pull them apart."[33]

By 1910, modernizing the environment of rural education seemed impossible without introducing this fundamental innovation. It was possible to introduce the study of farming to elementary schools through Liberty Hyde Bailey's "nature study," but even this innovation required that teachers receive some training in agriculture. Given the usual impediments of geography and the resistance of rural communities to change, agricultural education faced formidable obstacles.

The Agricultural High School Experiment

The most ambitious manifestation of the vogue of vocationalism in Virginia rural schools was the establishment of a system of agricultural high schools for whites. The state college of agriculture reached only a small audience; teaching agriculture in elementary schools was simply not practical because of untrained teachers. Maximizing the exposure of scientific farming, agricultural high schools thus served a dual function. Because the typical normal-trained teacher preferred town or village schools, they would serve as makeshift rural normal schools. By fulfilling a second function of training students in modern agriculture, agricultural high schools would foster interest in farming, improve social conditions, and stem rural depopulation. Once Virginia's rural young were "reminded and given a start" through agricultural high schools, claimed one Virginia vocationalist, many of them would choose farming "as their life work."[34]

Supported by scientific farmers and state school officials, Virginia inaugurated an experiment in secondary agricultural education in 1908, when the legislature appropriated $20,000 for the establishment of departments of agriculture and "domestic economy" in at least one high school in each of the state's ten congressional districts. Patterned upon other forms of state involvement in public education, the act stipulated that these agricultural high schools be supported by both state and local resources. The state provided funds for equipment and dormitories, as well as an annual appropriation of $2,500 to each school. Localities were expected to supply land, buildings, and supplemental financial support.[35]

To qualify for the state appropriation, the four-year agricultural high schools were required to demonstrate that at least a quarter of their total instruction was vocational. Going beyond this legal requirement, some of the new high schools followed a model curriculum drawn up by Virginia Polytechnic Institute's president Paul B. Barringer. Under Barringer's plan, the high schools taught a classical curriculum but spent about 40 percent of classroom time on vocational subjects. Male students attended classes entitled "The Plant and the Soil," "Farm Animals and Dairying," and "The Farm Home and Local Agriculture."[36] Female students studied the same subjects during the first two years, but then received instruction during their third and fourth years in domestic science and homemaking—food preparation, cleaning, and household management.[37]

Few schools strictly adhered to Barringer's plan, but the most successful made some attempt to integrate the study of agriculture as a major part of the classical curriculum. In all of the schools, both male and female students spent much of their time in practical field experience either on a school farm site or in a school kitchen. According to Barringer's plan, six out of every ten class sessions in courses in agriculture or domestic science were spent outside the classroom in practical expe-

Driver Agricultural High School, Nansemond County, Virginia, 1912
(courtesy of the Virginia Department of Education)

rience. All students were also encouraged to introduce their parents to modern methods of agriculture and home management.[38]

By 1916, the experiment in state-supported vocational education was well under way. The ten schools supported by the state claimed a combined enrollment in that year of almost three thousand students, or 12 percent of all high school students in the state.[39] Overall, however, agricultural high schools suffered from serious problems. Aside from successful schools in Appomattox (Southside) and Middleton (Valley), the typical school managed only weak offerings in agriculture and domestic science. A "serious handicap" debilitating the entire vocational system, as a state official put it, was a public perception that the agricultural schools were "not functioning properly"—an attitude that brought even successful schools "into disrepute." According to another assessment in 1917, agricultural high schools were "not doing much" and were "unpopular" because they had "done very little work."[40]

Even the strongest agricultural high schools survived only precariously and were, as one observer wrote, in an "unsettled condition."[41] Located in rural areas that possessed few educational facilities, they usually served combined functions as consolidated elementary schools, high schools, normal schools, and vocational schools—and usually in that order. Middleton Agricultural High School, for example, reported 247 students enrolled in 1916, of whom 61, or a quarter, were secondary school students.[42] With a dubious distinction dividing high schools and agricultural high schools, moreover, vocational training did not automatically establish its popularity. Lacking a secure identity, agricultural high schools sometimes suffered from intense competition with other high schools for students and local resources. In one southwestern Appalachian county, nine high schools and one agricultural high school bitterly competed for enrollments; "every one of the nine" apparently exerted itself to prevent pupils from attending the vocational school.[43]

Competition between the academic and vocational curricula sometimes occurred inside agricultural high schools. Within three years of its founding in 1908, the Manassas Agricultural High School was affected by squabbling between its regular and vocational components. When the district board applied for and received state recognition and funds in 1908, it had transformed an existing high school into an agricultural high school simply by hiring Herbert F. Button, a graduate of Cornell University's College of Agriculture, and by constructing a new agricultural building. The board granted Button control of the entire high school and appointed him director, but two women, Fannie O. Metz and Mary S. Moffett, continued to operate autonomously the regular high school and normal training department, both of which were located physically apart from the agricultural building.[44]

Tensions between the regular and vocational wings of the Manassas Agricultural High School soon erupted into conflict. Both Metz and Moffett undermined Button's authority while they expanded their own. Opponents of Button and agricultural vocationalism took their case to the Manassas district board, which in January 1912 divided bitterly over the issue. Two of the three trustees voted to dismiss Button; a third trustee then paralyzed the board over the issue. The question was not resolved until the county superintendent restored Button's authority and forced the resignation of all three trustees.[45]

The intensity of these divisions suggests a larger problem for vocationalists elsewhere in the state: agricultural education never became extensively available to, nor particularly popular among, rural Virginians. As was the case in urban vocational schools, the community response to agricultural education fell well short of the expectations of its popularizers. Because the district schools served large areas, it was virtually impossible to make them accessible to all Virginians. Most made almost no effort to serve more than a single county; if they did, they boarded students at prices few could afford. At Appomattox, boarding students from six outlying counties paid $12.50 per month, a price that would disqualify most potential pupils. Remoteness and inaccessibility restricted access even for those who lived nearby, and although students made a long commute by horse-drawn wagon, for most the obstacles of distance and cost made agricultural education fanciful and unrealistic.[46]

Agricultural high schools sometimes also suffered from the persisting strength of localism in public education. School location posed a troublesome decision that invariably alienated some neighborhoods even though it pleased others.[47] If the schools were too intrusive or openly flouted local opinion, moreover, they risked potentially disastrous community opposition. When a southwestern Virginia agricultural high school attempted to begin an "aggressive policy" of recruitment and to introduce an innovative curriculum, local opposition surfaced and eventually succeeded in ending local financial support. In another Southside school, local parents, revolting at what they claimed was excessive outside intervention in the organization of the school, demanded that educational policy making "be left to the discretion of the [local] School Authorities."[48]

At the same time, the agricultural schools could not bend completely to the local will—or even appear to be under community domination—without risking the loss of state financial support. When the Elk Creek Agricultural High School, in southwestern Virginia, decided to build a new dormitory in the summer of 1916, it confronted the thorny problem of location. The school's governing board submitted the question to local opinion, promising to honor the community consensus. Although the board's sensitivity doubtless strengthened local support, it was criticized by state officials as "somewhat surprising" because the community lacked "full authority" in the decision.[49]

The most important reason for the precariousness of the agricultural schools was a shortage of money. Without steady state or local funds, the schools led a hand-to-mouth existence during the decade after their founding. How could the advocates of agricultural vocationalism expect anything but failure, argued the principal of an agricultural school, with a miserly annual state appropriation and even less local support? Despite meager support, agricultural high schools were expected to have dormitories, a well-paid faculty of college- and university-trained educators, expert supervision, and ample land to house experimental and demonstration farms. All of these advantages required much more money than either the state or the local community was willing to spend. Seriously underfunded, the agricultural high schools had succeeded about "as far as could have been expected."[50]

Agricultural high schools' desperate need for money was made clear in 1916, when a state appropriation of $50,000 prompted an avalanche of requests from the long-starved schools.[51] Yet neither this appropriation nor the beginning of federal support for vocational education in the Smith-Hughes Act, enacted by Congress in 1917, forestalled the decline of independent agricultural high schools. If anything, the first federal intervention in public education since Reconstruction hastened the end of independent vocational high schools while it stimulated the spread of vocationalism as part of the general high school curriculum. Under the supervision of a state-run vocational education board, Smith-Hughes support was given only if high schools satisfied rigorously defined criteria. After 1917, as a result, most of the older agricultural high schools did not survive the transition to federal control; those that did lost their former identities and became high schools with departments of vocational agriculture. To qualify for federal funds, numerous other high schools added vocational programs. In 1920, the state counted a total of forty-three high schools with separate departments financed at least in part by Smith-Hughes money.[52]

County Extension and Rural Schools

Vocational agricultural high schools were one example of the broad effort to diffuse scientific agriculture and modernize rural society in Virginia. Another was the spread of knowledge and expertise outside the classroom through adult education, a concept in existence in rural America since the Civil War. As a way to promote knowledge about commercial and scientific farming, the USDA and land-grant colleges of agriculture sponsored adult education through farmers' institutes and experiment stations during the last decades of the nineteenth century. Yet these efforts were limited to a small minority of "alert and progressive" farmers, as one adult educator wrote, already converted to scientific agriculture methods. A more effective way to inform and instruct the mass of farmers about the advantages of commercial agriculture and modern living existed in a new agency of expertise, the county extension service.[53]

Seaman A. Knapp, a professor of agriculture and later president of the Iowa State College of Agriculture, pioneered what became the county extension service. At the close of the nineteenth century, he began a highly successful program in Louisiana and Texas to persuade farmers to adopt modern methods of crop rotation, fertilization, and scientific agriculture. This project attracted the attention of Rockefeller manager Wallace Buttrick, who in 1906 persuaded the GEB to finance the expansion of Knapp's project—known as "co-operative demonstration work"—to other states. Financed jointly by the GEB and the USDA, the program was so successful that, with the passage of the Smith-Lever Act in 1914, its main features were incorporated into a federally funded system of county agents.[54]

Aggressive salesmen of a modernized rural America, county agents proceeded only after laying careful groundwork. Soliciting support from town or village bankers, merchants, and newspapermen and the county's largest farmers, they then persuaded one farmer to adopt modern agricultural methods on an experimental "demonstration" basis and to follow the program of the extension service. Usually able to show greater productivity on the demonstration farm, the county agent publicized it as evidence of the superiority of scientific agriculture.

Adult education through county extension, argues David Danbom, sought to increase farm productivity through the diffusion of scientific commercial agriculture.[55] But this was not its main goal. Like vocational agricultural education, adult education proposed detaching rural southerners from a devitalizing home and work environment by training them in values of work, punctuality, and thrift. Going beyond the goal of industrializing American agriculture, the county agent's primary objective was in leading what Knapp characterized as a "revolution" in attitudes that would alter "home conditions" and establish a new "standard of excellence for farming and for living." Teaching productive agriculture was a way of motivating farmers toward business acumen and acquisitive values; county agents also promoted rural modernization through schools, sanitation, roads, telephones, and even phonographs.[56]

County agents first came to Virginia in 1907 under the direction of T. O. Sandy, a Southside scientific farmer and agricultural high school enthusiast.[57] Eager to publicize success and to minimize failure, Sandy and his agents reported a story of steady progress in which benighted farmers willingly relinquished traditional farming practices. Virginia farmers were "*stirred up* & wisely so," wrote one agent. Among the "most noticeable effects" of county extension, the same agent later wrote, was "greater interest" and "increased contentment" on the part of farmers.[58]

Other evidence suggests that enthusiasm was not their only response.

The message of commercial agriculture had little relevance for poor farmers who lacked good lands and capital resources. A "majority of the farmers of our county," complained one Appalachian farmer, derived little benefit from county extension expertise. Poor farmers realized that more fertilizer and better tools brought higher yields; the real issue was how they could afford them. Did "soft handed" county agents, knowing practically nothing about local conditions and coming from a comfortable "steam heated office of an official whom the people are taxed to maintain," really have the answer for the impoverished majority of farmers?[59]

Facing a wall of caution, independence, and reserve among rural Virginians, county agents found natural allies in rural school modernizers. The "best place" to promote the gospel of scientific agriculture, said one experienced agent, was the home; the "next best place," the school.[60] In a typical experience, an agent in 1914 first visited thirty-five of the county's thirty-six schools, describing the support of school officials as "absolutely necessary" to beginning extension. Not long afterward, agents were advised that an "undissenting unanimity of opinion" existed that the proper place for agents to begin their work was the schools.[61]

Strongly supported by the state department of education and the state agricultural college at Blacksburg, county agents in 1910 organized corn clubs for boys and tomato and canning clubs for girls in the rural schools. Under the direction of an agent, corn club boys learned productive agriculture and competed for the highest per-acre yields. Sons and fathers alike learned through the corn clubs. "I could not interest the fathers," explained an agent, "except through the boys"; some fathers who had resisted scientific agriculture thus became converted. By teaching rural boys modern agriculture and entrepreneurial skills, boys' clubs sought to stem emigration.[62]

County agents were careful to respect southern mores about race and gender. Strictly segregated, separate black extension agents worked with the South's black farmers. By 1912, authority for extension activities among Virginia blacks was transferred to J. B. Pierce, who worked under both state agent Sandy and Hampton Institute.[63] Modeling their work upon that of the white county agents, black extension workers organized through schools and formed black corn clubs which they called "Negro Boys Farm Makers' Clubs." Fully under way by 1914, the black clubs, less ambitious than the white clubs, claimed only limited success in a total of twenty-one clubs and only 340 members. Established through black rural schools, the clubs encountered problems of poverty among the state's black farmers that were so staggering that their efforts were limited.[64]

Rural Women and Home Demonstration

Adult education was directed at altering the rural home as well as the farm. In 1914, the extension service began hiring white women, known as home demonstration agents, who worked for "better living" and modernized homes among Virginia women. Home demonstration was based on the assumption that adult education applied equally to women as to men. "We hear a great deal about chivalry towards the women," wrote the head of Virginia home demonstration, yet farm women still worked "hardest." Men had livestock, land, and crops; rural women, in contrast, had "nothing at home to keep them."[65]

Instructing women and girls in modern home management provided such a stake. Just as boys needed instruction in the science of agriculture, so girls, through up-to-date education in modern home management, would acquire a "definite place" "socially, economically, and spiritually." Women agents provided expertise about nutritious cooking and sanitary food preparation and preservation. Like county extension, home demonstration was also explicitly directed at instilling attitudes of thrift and hard work among rural women. By instructing girls and women in the value of work and savings and by introducing them to the commercial market economy, home demonstration would instill not only pride in home life but also, as one agent claimed, "good business training."[66]

Home demonstration agents found entrance into rural homes facilitated by school clubs, which taught girls expertise in domestic science, poultry raising, and vegetable canning and sponsored demonstration projects and areawide competitions.[67] Representing "all phases" of rural Virginia, according to one agent, canning and poultry clubs had three purposes: to introduce labor-saving methods into the rural home; to improve its diet and sanitation; and to develop leadership for modernization among rural women.[68]

Canning and poultry clubs offered additional evidence of the alliance between rural modernizers and public school officials. School officials sometimes suspended school to allow the organization of the clubs. State agent Ella Agnew observed that home modernization followed a

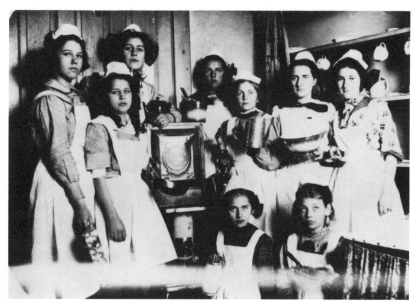

Domestic science class, Virginia, 1914
(courtesy of the Southern Historical Collection)

path of least resistance through the schools; by comparison, organizing clubs was a "far superior" method to reach the rural home. She believed that home demonstration and rural school change marched hand in hand. The "leading girls" in rural schools were also leaders in the canning clubs, a conclusion apparently confirmed by a school inspector visiting a one-room school, who was impressed by the "wide awake" and "alert" gazes of teacher and pupils. "On inquiry," recounted Agnew, the inspector found the teacher a "canning club girl."[69]

Canning clubs not only brought "greater efficiency" to the schools, but also resulted in improvements in home, community, and even county. Their advocates sought a larger objective: a close association with the cosmopolitan market economy and all the benefits accompanying rural modernization. The successful home demonstration agent and canning club organizer could show "a closet with a supply of food for winter," a farm wife "who sees a faint dawn appearing over the hill of life," and "greater efficiency" for the next generation of rural women and their homes.[70]

Extending this expertise would transform the rural home. "The tomato can," as one agent put it, was the "key to open the kitchen door . . . to get into a woman's pantry." Canning club girls learned the use of new mechanized conveniences such as jelly makers, "fireless" cookers, and "iceless" refrigerators, which aided in food preparation and preservation. They were also carefully instructed about home sanitation through the installation of window screens and the use of fly traps. Not least important, by growing vegetables and livestock for market, club girls were taught the values of association with the outside economy. They were shown how to package canned goods attractively for market, to distribute them to local merchants, and even to begin a statewide marketing system.[71]

Still, club organizers and home demonstration agents did not always find rural women as accommodating as their optimistic rhetoric might suggest. Although 1,149 members were enrolled in twenty of Virginia's counties in 1915, the clubs typically experienced steadily declining attendance. Despite claims of expertise, home demonstration and the clubs were plagued by inadequate training—a problem that was made obvious in a public dispute in 1916. In an unusual display of candor, Rhea C. Scott, second in command in the state home demonstration apparatus, charged in a report to her superior, Agnew, that home demonstration was weakly run and had little impact on rural women. Most of the twenty local agents, she claimed, were "weak in knowledge." Even more serious was Scott's suggestion that these agents were ineffectively supervised and generally indifferent toward rural modernization. Scott cited the case of an agent who exerted herself only to reach those homes "most convenient" to her. Although Agnew's response to the report was to prevent it from reaching USDA authorities because of the "wrong impression" that it might create, Scott's charges of ineffectiveness and lack of expertise rang true.[72]

Home demonstration also encountered another familiar obstacle—rural resistance to innovation. Modernizing rural homes and beginning girls' clubs required a greater initial cash outlay for cans and canners than most girls or women could afford. A canning club in a mountainous community grew forty-three bushels of tomatoes which it allowed to rot because it could not afford cans or canners. Agents also reported a strong reluctance on the part of rural women to admit that their households needed modernizing. Rural girls "as a rule" were "interested," wrote an agent about a mountain community outside Lynchburg, but their parents "won't let them join." Nor was suspicion of outsiders confined to Appalachia. Agnew herself described a "great deal of opposition" in a Southside community in early 1916, and she reported that a northern Piedmont school principal was "not at all interested in the development of the Canning Club."[73]

Like the male extension service, the home demonstration program was strictly segregated. After July 1913, a black woman agent, Elizabeth Jenkins, coordinated a club movement for black women through the public schools and through Hampton and the Petersburg normal. Beginning in 1914, Jenkins enlisted the aid of local agents, who worked nine months of the year as supervising teachers of industrial education and the three summer months as organizers of black "home makers" clubs. Even more than the white women agents, black women agents concentrated most of their energies on combating staggering problems that accompanied rural poverty. Although also organized to foster commercial vegetable preservation and livestock raising for market, the home makers clubs were instructed "to do anything in their power" to make rural homes "more attractive and comfortable."[74] Through home and school, the black clubs' attention was directed toward a "cleanliness of persons and homes" through basic sanitation, screening against flies, and whitewashing of buildings.[75]

The black home makers clubs' emphasis on qualitative improvements was enthusiastically greeted in the black community, a response stark in comparison with the tepid reception encountered by the white home demonstration agents. Organized in the heavily black Tidewater and Southside, the black home makers clubs claimed a total membership in 1915 of 2,155—greater than that of the white poultry and canning clubs.[76] Not unusual was the report of one agent in Charlotte County, the heart of the Southside tobacco district. "Homes are better kept," a direct result of club activities, and the "gospel of the whitewash has been obeyed." Screens had been fitted, yards cleaned and landscaped, and homes improved for ventilation and general sanitation.[77]

Chapter Eight
The Ambiguity of Race

A perplexing problem for most students of the early twentieth-century South has been the reconciliation of school and social reformers' confidence in progress with their support for racial subordination. Not only did southern reformers avoid challenging racism and racial subordination, they also worked hard to extend legally sanctioned racism. Considering the disfranchisement of southern black voters as among their most lasting accomplishments, they strongly favored applying segregation to almost all areas of public life. Early twentieth-century social reformers were not racial liberals—at least by late twentieth-century standards—for very good reasons. As political realists, most of them approached the volatile issue of race cautiously, reluctant to sacrifice political support for social reform. More important, as prisoners of contemporary attitudes, they believed in the innate inferiority of blacks and assumed the necessity of preserving the caste system.[1]

The policy consequences of these attitudes—and of a deliberate decision reached by SEB reformers not to include black education as part of their agenda—soon became clear for southern public schools. At least before 1910, rural school reform and modernization were for whites only; modernizers carefully avoided the politically sensitive issue of black education. In a trickle-down approach to school modernization, officials believed that improving white schools would, in the long run, also effect improvement in black schools. In the short run, however, the results were clear: qualitative differences between black and white schools widened rather than narrowed. Even those blacks who urged compromise and conciliation, such as Booker T. Washington, were conceding by 1910 that black schools had experienced little improvement, and they were becoming increasingly alarmed at future prospects. Occurring at the "expense of Negro education," Washington wrote, white

173

school modernization effectively took from black schools "to advance the education of white people."[2]

The whites-only approach of school reformers and the resulting inequities, however, present only one side of the Janus face of school modernization. At least nominally, reformers and modernizers were united by a belief in progress and change. Although supporters of segregation, few advocated a static system of apartheid in which the status of blacks would remain permanently inferior. School officials favored black educational progress for another, more concrete reason: they perceived that southern educational uplift was impossible without it. The welfare of the South and of the nation—"its prosperity, its sanitation, its morale"—depended on black uplift, argued one white modernizer. To deny blacks the advantages of modern schools ultimately affected white uplift; as another reformer wrote, oppressing blacks suppressed the general quality of rural life and held "down our average to a lower level."[3]

The contradiction between a belief in black progress and an acceptance of a system that denied it created an unresolved tension in the relationship between rural school modernization and black education. Operating on an assumption of innate racial inferiority, modernizers attempted to segregate the school pedagogy by adapting learning to the different, and supposedly unequal, abilities of black and white children. A belief in innate differences also justified glaring disparities in facilities and funding; common features of white school modernization, such as elementary school consolidation and the establishment of high schools, rarely were available for blacks. All the while, however, school officials found themselves increasingly drawn to a contrary conclusion. They discovered that black rural schools functioned under essentially similar conditions of poverty and isolation that insulated white schools from change. But they also found that instituting any change—even the introduction of a segregated pedagogy—depended on basic qualitative improvements.

Race and Reform in the Modern South

Antebellum southern slavery, according to the well-known observation of historian Ulrich Bonnell Phillips, served the same function as a modern settlement house. By training blacks in "orderly, well bred conduct" and a "vigor of discipline," the slave system civilized semibarbaric Africans and exposed them to white social and political institutions. Plantations, he concluded, were "the best schools yet invented for the mass training of that sort of inert and backward people which the bulk of American negroes represented."[4]

Phillips's conclusions about the role of blacks in American life were common intellectual fare in the early twentieth-century South. Social reformers affirmed their belief that social cohesion, economic growth, and political stability—all prerequisites of their vision of change in the South—depended upon racial harmony. They were acutely aware of the need to reconcile subordination and progress—a problem of global importance, affecting relations between the developed and underdeveloped worlds. The southern experiment in race relations was of "world significance," wrote Samuel C. Mitchell, in which the South lay at the "bloody angle" of a worldwide battle line.[5]

Accepting innate racial differences, modernizing educators came to the conclusion that black underdevelopment was rooted not in the social environment but in an inferior level of socioanthropological development. According to this view, nationalities and races developed from infancy to mature adulthood. Some, primarily those of western Europe, were "adult"; others, like those of Africa and Asia, remained in a stage of underdeveloped childhood. American blacks were a "child race," asserted an educational reformer, which would achieve the "essential of modern civilization" only through time and racial evolution; blacks were, according to a similar assessment, "at least two thousand years behind the Anglo-Saxon" in racial development.[6]

Through constant training in and exposure to the ways of modern civilization, reformers believed, blacks would acquire necessary habits of thrift, industry, and energy. Slavery furthered these desirable habits among blacks; the master-slave relationship hastened the civilizing process. Slavery, according to a white educator, served as a "great elevator" bringing blacks under the civilizing influences of religion, language, and work discipline and protecting them from their "lower" selves. While inhibiting the "terrible temptation" of vagrancy, slavery also forestalled laziness and drunkenness. It accelerated racial advancement by inculcating "regular habits of industry" and the knowledge of white religion, language, and civilization.[7]

Although to reformers slavery's civilizing influence was moral, it also provided blacks with concrete skills. "If a Southern white man wanted a house, or a bridge built," observed Booker T. Washington, "he consulted a Negro mechanic about the plan, about the building of the house, or the bridge." Slavery not only developed civilized modes of behavior, according to Frissell, it also "trained the hand." As the railroad magnate and philanthropist William H. Baldwin expressed it, the black slave learned "to work and was made to work" on the plantation. Slavery thus provided an ideal civilizing school, a vast "industrial" system of training—without factories or industrialization. Rather, slavery was "industrial" in another sense: it implanted a work ethic, a habit of industry among blacks, which, in turn, hastened their socioanthropological development.[8]

Although reformers characterized antebellum slavery as benevolent and socially harmonious, they also believed that it had left a dangerous legacy. Slavery stunted the South's social and economic development, Walter Hines Page declared on several occasions, making it a region bound and constricted by its past. Although elevating the racial development of blacks, slavery had deleterious effects. Its most obvious deficiency, according to Hampton educator Samuel C. Armstrong, was that it encouraged the "vices" of "improvidence, low ideas of honor and morality, and a general lack of directive energy, judgment and foresight"—more serious deficiencies than ignorance.[9] Nor did slavery prepare blacks for survival in a free society, for upon emancipation, blacks remained ill equipped to function in a modern society.

Stripped of the educative functions of the master-slave relationship and sorely dependent on whites for leadership, energy, and economic advancement, freedmen were in some respects in a worse condition than under slavery. The peculiar institution had at least provided them with habits of obedience, industry, and civilization, observed Mitchell; emancipation left them without moral or economic independence, "the two essentials for citizenship in a democracy." Children and "child" races "kept under careful restraint" and then "turned suddenly out into the world" lacked "self-control" as adults, wrote Baldwin. Freed from the shackles of slavery, blacks suffered in the absence of "outside control."[10]

The reformers' solution to the problem of modern race relations therefore partly lay in recreating the harmony and hierarchy of the slave regime. Jim Crow provided such a solution by defining the status of the races and by clearly establishing the principle of white supremacy. By ending overt racial competition and eliminating black political power, reformers also believed that de jure segregation allowed blacks to develop as junior citizens in a modernized, cooperative political system. Particularly instrumental were black public schools, which reformers and modernizers believed had failed—as white schools had failed—because they were too closely linked to their social milieu. Post-Reconstruction black schools, reformers charged, misguidedly attempted to give the black community what it most wanted: the same education received by white children. Yet, to modernizers, this pedagogical similarity between rural white and rural black schools meant that the latter made little attempt to address the needs of blacks, who were a childlike, essentially "imitative" race. Blacks were not required to "see what poor children they were in the ways of civilization," wrote a white educator, "and how they must start in the very kindergarten of racial development." Applying white pedagogy to black education encouraged aspirations for "social equality"; more properly, black education should establish a "moral substratum" for "desirable" citizenship.[11] At least among white reformers and educational modernizers, there seemed to be a clear disjuncture between black schools and socioanthropological realities. An important lesson about post-Reconstruction white education was that it was "too academic" and "too much unrelated to practical life," wrote Edgar Gardner Murphy. Who, he asked, "will measure the folly of that scholastic traditionalism which would persist in applying this system to the children of the negro?"[12]

Industrial Education and the Black Public School

Assuming an inferiority of ability among nonwhites, modernizers concluded that a pedagogy which disregarded racial differences failed to serve the needs of the black community. In the name of progress and educational change, reformers, under the rubric of "industrial" education, advocated inaugurating a segregated pedagogy that sanctioned substantial inequalities. Industrial education, hardly the invention of early twentieth-century reformers, had long enjoyed popularity among educators, who had applied it to "underdeveloped" groups as varied as northern laborers, Hawaiian islanders, and colonized Filipinos. In the South, industrial education achieved its most important post-Civil War successes at Hampton Institute, under the leadership of Samuel C. Armstrong, and at Tuskegee Institute in Alabama, which was founded by Armstrong's protégé, Booker T. Washington.

The vogue of industrial education paralleled the rise of various forms of vocational education in nineteenth-century America. Like agricultural education for whites, it was based on the assumption that students could internalize new habits of thrift, energy, and acquisitiveness only outside of normal channels of youth socialization. Schooled only by a classical curriculum, industrial educators contended, blacks would remain trapped by a vicious cycle of inertia, stagnation, and underdevelopment. Drawing upon the same Pestalozzian tradition of "learning by doing" that underlay all of the American experiments in manual training and vocational education, industrial education would therefore provide marketable skills as well as the moral advantages of classical schooling. At Hampton and Tuskegee and at similar, mostly private, schools such as the Penn School in South Carolina, the Calhoun School in Alabama, and the Manassas Industrial Institute in Virginia, black pupils learned carpentry, joinery, and blacksmithing skills.

For most of its advocates, however, the value of industrial education extended beyond the acquisition of skills. A more valuable result was the acceleration of individual moral development and the training in habits of work and self-discipline which blacks as a race allegedly lacked. A common characteristic of industrial education was therefore instruction in the discipline of hard work and rigorous routine, and not unusual was the requirement of participation in organized military units stressing order and punctuality as day-to-day values.[13]

Although modeled on similar principles, industrial education and other forms of vocationalism such as agricultural education for whites served distinctly different purposes. Whereas agricultural education sought to correct an environmental problem—the rural white home— industrial education was intended to change racial characteristics and accelerate the process of racial evolution. Because it also attempted to reconcile the conflict between a belief in racial progress and an assumption of innate racial differences, industrial education had a special appeal for white educators. Industrial education, wrote Murphy, was designed to provide "under conditions of freedom, those elements of skill, those conditions of industrial peace, which our fathers supplied under the conditions of slavery." Industrial education instructed blacks in independence and self-sufficiency—a "matter of the first importance," as Washington declared, in which rural blacks came to recognize labor as "dignified" and "idleness" as the "disgrace of any race." Through "regular routine," religious instruction, and military drill, industrial education, wrote another of its advocates, produced economic independence and a "self-directing" and "useful" citizen.[14]

Ultimately, however, most definitions of industrial education were shrouded in a hazy imprecision, which, in the final analysis, worked to its advantage. Vague parameters made industrial education simultaneously attractive to white and black educators—but for very different reasons. Conservative blacks such as Washington embraced it because it served the dual purpose of securing white cooperation and support for black schools and providing for continued educational progress. Industrial education, Washington wrote, killed "two birds with one stone": it secured the "co-operation of the white man" and did the "best possible thing for the black man." Although the price blacks paid for that support was a dual and unequal system of schooling, industrial education was nonetheless the common denominator for moderate white and black educators. As one black educator in Virginia expressed it, the whites-only southern education campaign benefited blacks; ultimately, it was impossible "for the white man to make any progress without at the same time helping us."[15]

The vagueness of industrial education masked its most important characteristic—its conservative orientation. Washington, Frissell, and its other promoters steadfastly maintained that its purpose was to keep southern rural blacks on the farm. The task of reform, as Ogden wrote, was to "attach the Negro to the soil and prevent his exodus from the country to the city." The rural black, wrote another reformer, was the "hope of the race, and the training of his hand and eye will reach in due time his head."[16]

Industrial education served as a bulwark of a new vertical system in which separate but stratified black and white societies coexisted. Better race relations, the *Richmond Times*, a white newspaper, advised Virginia blacks, depended on the creation of a society "for themselves, among themselves," in which a sharp line distinguished the "coarse and unclean" from their social betters. During slavery, added Frissell, the "best element" of blacks led the race; industrial education expanded class development and stratification without challenging the caste system. Southern whites should therefore encourage educated blacks to exert authority over the "lower element of their own race." According to Murphy, racial segregation furthered the growth of "abler minds" among blacks; it stimulated "differentiations" of talent that then gave the race a "sane and instructed leadership from within." He continued: "The true and permanent way to lead the negro race to keep wisely to itself is to make it sufficient within itself. The race which is to be forever forced to go outside of itself to touch the broadest and richest life of its generation will never be consciously and finally anchored in the doctrine of race integrity."[17]

"A Mere Pretense": Blacks and Industrial Education

The conceptual vagueness of industrial education allowed blacks considerable leeway. On the one hand, they were able to reject any assumption of racial inferiority and the need for a segregated pedagogy; on the other, they could accept it as a vehicle of autonomy and improvement. For both black leaders and rural blacks, a built-in contradiction existed in their simultaneous enthusiasm for and rejection of industrial education.[18] The ambiguity of this response is nowhere better exemplified than in the position of industrial education's chief advocate, Booker T. Washington, although his advocacy was accompanied by limitations. Never accepting the position that industrial education meant institutionalized, permanent racial inferiority in education, Washington skillfully cast different poses for different audiences, preaching for whites a message of accommodation and, for blacks, autonomy through self-help and education. Before white philanthropists and southern reformers, he appeared to accept their assumptions—even perhaps encouraging them —in exchange for further support for black education. Yet before southern blacks—who well understood the power realities in the South—he stressed the pragmatism of industrial education as a short-term solution to the long-term problem of better schools.[19]

Not all blacks, of course, agreed with Washington's approach. The most famous opponent of industrial education was W.E.B. Du Bois, who in 1903 published a searing attack on Washington in *The Souls of Black Folk*. A graduate of Fisk University with a Ph.D. from Harvard University, Du Bois criticized the abdication under the Washingtonian program of full civil and political equality for blacks, a goal possible only through the development of a college-educated black elite. In a speech three years later before an astonished audience at the Hampton Negro Conference, Du Bois denounced industrial education as "fundamentally false" because it denied the full potential of black development. "Never in God's world," he said, would blacks assert themselves unless they demonstrated "fully developed and carefully trained power." He was "particularly sorry" that the leaders of the Hampton conference had "never found courage to say in this matter what they really believe." Predictably, Du Bois's speech outraged his audience. So complete was his alienation from Washington and the citadels of industrial education that he was not invited back to Hampton for thirty years.[20]

Du Bois's critique was based on both educational elitism and an integrationist approach to race relations; other black leaders, however, rejected the assumptions and approach of industrial education for different reasons. When a black visitor to a Hampton commencement during the 1870s discovered that the ceremony was segregated, he concluded that blacks were better without a high school or college education "if our youth are to be brought up under such influences." Even Alexander Crummell, black rector of St. Luke's Church in Washington and a leading advocate of vocational education, criticized industrial education in 1898 as the creation of "a lot of white men" who pitied blacks "but who have never learned" to love them, who took up a "miserable fad." Crummell saw industrial education as another example of white efforts to limit "our brains and culture."[21]

The most forceful and effective critics of industrial education were the students at black industrial institutes. As early as the 1870s, Hampton students objected not only to the work routine but also to the underlying assumption of black inferiority. Many of them complained bitterly that the emphasis on routine and moral instruction imparted few useful skills. One student claimed in 1878 that he was "not learning anything" and that the school was "greatly over-rated." The newly created Hampton Alumni Association charged during the same year that graduates and other black visitors were not accorded the "courtesies and hospitalities due them as a race."[22]

An even more telling reflection of the unpopularity of industrial education was its rapid decline at Hampton during the 1920s. During that decade, largely because of pressure from the state department of education to improve its facilities for teacher education, Hampton began a transition to a liberal arts curriculum. In the process, students there began to object vociferously to the strict regime of military discipline and moral instruction. In October 1927, a student-led protest erupted against the entire "Hampton idea" and the dominance of the white faculty and administration. Students' demands grew so intense that the administration dismissed or suspended forty-three students and closed the school for two weeks.[23]

Although the options were limited for the great mass of black southerners who lacked these powers of articulation, they objected nonetheless. Few rural blacks enjoyed the luxury of refusing any school improvement out of hand. They thus rejected the assumptions of innate inferiority on which industrial education was based but accepted the possibility of a general improvement in facilities, school terms, and teachers' salaries that it offered. The subtlety of the black response—acceptance of white support coupled with rejection of the assumptions

Industrial education in a Virginia school
(courtesy of the U.S. Department of Education)

behind it—was not lost upon so avid a supporter of industrial education
as Hollis B. Frissell. He admitted that as early as 1898, a "vast number"
of black schools had "taken the name industrial, because it is thought to
be popular in the North." All the while, however, these schools surrepti-
tiously adhered to a classical curriculum and subscribed to the tenets of
industrial education only as "a mere pretense."[24]

Reform and the Black Elementary School

The impact of modernization upon rural black elementary education
was thus shaped by two influences: the modernizers' desire to segregate
the pedagogy and blacks' determination to reject racial inequality. The
convergence of these contradictory influences had several important
consequences. It made possible the modernization of rural black
schools in Virginia outside of better-publicized campaigns for white
schools—but did so in a way that was acceptable to both southern
whites and blacks. It meant that industrial education, previously confined to black private schools, would be incorporated into public
schools as the major vehicle of black rural school modernization. Most

important, the ambiguity of industrial education, and its deliberately vague definition, meant that its application in rural black schools brought results not envisioned by its creators.

The most effective advocate of extending industrial education to rural blacks was the General Education Board, which since its inception in 1902 remained committed to black education. For primarily strategic reasons, however, its leaders concentrated on white uplift and refrained from active involvement with black schools until about 1910. The growth of other northern philanthropies, particularly the Jeanes Fund, spurred the GEB into a more active role. In 1904, the Philadelphia Quaker philanthropist Anna T. Jeanes gave Frissell and Washington $10,000 each to stimulate the improvement of rural black elementary schools through Hampton and Tuskegee; a year later, she donated $200,000 to the GEB to initiate a campaign on a larger scale. In 1907, at the urging of George Foster Peabody, Frissell, and Washington, Jeanes added $1 million to be used for the "rudimentary education" of southern blacks. Closely tied to the SEB and GEB, the Jeanes Fund stressed a close partnership between southern governmental agencies and northern philanthropy. Nonetheless, it evolved into a unique organization. Its president, James Hardy Dillard, dean of the College of Arts and Sciences at Tulane University, enjoyed a reputation as a racial moderate who possessed strong educational credentials and, as a man of tact, was equally at ease with northern philanthropists, southern whites, and southern blacks.[25]

The history of the Jeanes Fund demonstrates subtle changes in reformers' attitudes toward black education. In the face of pervasive and overwhelming poverty, industrial education became a nearly meaningless concept that was impossible to implement without substantial qualitative improvements. Inherently unequal, industrial education required equal facilities to become effective: controlling rural black schools depended upon a minimum of educational modernization. In time, this larger problem of uplift, transcending racial differences, began to attenuate the reformers' ambitions for a segregated pedagogy and curriculum and made industrial education more rhetorical than actual.

The leaders of the Jeanes Fund quickly discovered these realities in Virginia. Soon after Frissell received the initial grant from Jeanes in 1904, he began to send Hampton students into Virginia's hinterlands to organize improvement leagues that attempted "to do for the colored people what the Co-Operative Educational Association" did for whites. The Petersburg black normal, led by its president, James Hugo Johnston, also initiated a campaign to establish school leagues. By early

James Hardy Dillard
(from Charles William Dabney, Universal Education in the South *[Chapel Hill: University of North Carolina Press, 1936], 2:435)*

1911, the Hampton and Petersburg campaigns had united, with the blessing of the Jeanes Fund, into a new organization known as the Negro Teachers' and School Improvement League of Virginia. League organizers—Hampton graduates such as Thomas C. Walker and W.T.B. Williams—encouraged local blacks to increase school funds to train blacks in self-sacrifice and self-help.[26]

League organizers carefully stressed that these groups promised racial cooperation between the better elements of white and black society. Offering an opportunity for responsible, middle-class black leadership, the leagues sought out thrifty persons in rural black communities.[27] These networks also served as forums for black-white cooperation, and organizers made an attempt to consult with and secure the support of leading whites. Although one black leader characterized gaining white support as a "difficult undertaking," whites who dared "brave the difficulties" eventually found or created the "necessary public sentiment." A leading result of black school improvement, commented Hampton's *Southern Workman*, was a "more effective co-operation between the races."[28]

By 1908, the leaders of black school improvement had begun to alter their approach. Taking their cue from the white school campaign, they turned to institutional solutions and began to rely less on the school leagues. The most prominent feature of the Jeanes Fund program was supervising industrial teachers, later known as "Jeanes teachers," who combined the approaches of the early teacher-organizers in Virginia after 1904 and the "extension teachers" who appeared in Louisiana in 1908.[29] But the future shape of the Jeanes teacher was above all determined by its earliest advocate, Jackson Davis, superintendent of Henrico County, Virginia, schools. He fashioned his notion of supervision from a black teacher, Virginia Estelle Randolph, who had transformed her school from a run-down, ill-attended, "little wayside school" to a model progressive rural school. Randolph was instrumental in organizing a school league and soon whitewashed and cleaned the building; she also improved its physical appearance by planting shrubs and vines and by building a pathway to the school's door. When Davis visited Randolph's school in 1905, he concluded that he had found a teacher "who thought of her work in terms of the welfare of the whole community, and of the schools as an agency to help the people to live better, to do their work with more skill and intelligence and to do it in the spirit of neighborliness." Encouraged to propose a wide-ranging plan to Dillard, Davis suggested that the Jeanes board support industrial training in Henrico

County by paying the salary of two black supervisors. Enthusiastically endorsing the proposal, Dillard and the Jeanes Fund sponsored Randolph as the first Jeanes teacher supervisor of the rural black schools of Henrico County.[30]

Virginia Randolph's success established a pattern throughout the South, and by 1920, there were 272 Jeanes teachers in the region. All were black women, and a significant portion—half, by one estimate— were educated at Hampton, Tuskegee, or some other normal or industrial school.[31] These Jeanes teachers were required to work with discretion and energy; as Dillard wrote, they should be both "self-effacing" and hardworking.[32] Randolph and other Jeanes teachers also became, in essence, the black representatives of the state educational bureaucracy. In 1910, when the Peabody Fund created the position of white rural school supervisor attached to the state department of education, the GEB established a similar office for rural black schools. The first such official was Jackson Davis, appointed in 1910 to supervise rural black schools in Virginia; within a year, six other southern states had followed suit. The state supervisor served as a coordinator of all philanthropic efforts to improve black schools. In consultation with state officials, he appointed the Jeanes teachers and directed their work. The supervisor, always a white male, sent monthly reports to the GEB on educational progress; he was responsible for stimulating local interest among school officials and other whites. Most important, the black school supervisor served as the liaison among state educational officials, northern philanthropy, and the black community.[33]

But in its implementation through the Jeanes Fund, industrial education underwent a transfiguration. The original goal of the Jeanes teachers—at least as presented to their white benefactors—was the inauguration of a segregated pedagogy, and Randolph and others were instructed to begin industrial training in rural elementary schools.[34] In the impoverished environment of rural black schools, however, Jeanes teachers frequently discovered more pressing needs, which assumed greater priority. Jeanes officials granted teachers considerable leeway without, as Dillard put it, "cut-and-dried rules." The supervisors were required to "introduce and supervise simpler forms of industrial work," but they often followed "any line of neighborhood improvement which opened up."[35]

Randolph and other Jeanes teachers interpreted this mandate broadly. As she indicated in her first annual report in 1909, the emphasis of Jeanes teachers was on modernization of facilities, fund raising, and the

Virginia Estelle Randolph
(from Charles William Dabney, Universal Education in the South *[Chapel Hill: University of*
North Carolina Press, 1936], 2:445)

introduction of hygiene in the black school and home.[36] Even white officials found improvement of facilities more important than curricular change. Reporting on the activities of Virginia Jeanes teachers, Davis said less about industrial education than about the extension of the school term, the construction of new buildings and the enlargement of old ones, and the establishment of privies for black schoolchildren. On another occasion, Davis stressed improvement as the chief goal and admitted that these results were beginning to bear a similarity to white school improvement. A major consequence of the Jeanes program was the "new interest" among blacks in making their homes "more comfortable and beautiful." Jeanes officials avoided curricular change partly because of a perceptible tendency among local blacks to accept school improvement but to reject an industrial curriculum. As one GEB official complained, Jeanes teachers often instituted industrial education only to discover soon thereafter that "no work of this kind has been done by pupils during their absence."[37]

That the concerns of modernization obscured the rhetoric of a segregated school curriculum was also the experience of two subsequent philanthropic foundations, the Julius Rosenwald Fund and the Phelps Stokes Fund. Julius Rosenwald, a partner in Sears, Roebuck and Company, first gave money to Tuskegee in 1912 to finance offshoot industrial institutes in Alabama. Two years later, he gave Washington $30,000 to finance one hundred model rural black schools designed to set a high standard for new construction in school buildings. In 1915, Rosenwald paid the salary of an agent to supervise the construction of these schoolhouses—the first Rosenwald "building agent"—and two years later he formally incorporated the Rosenwald Fund and expanded its work throughout the South.[38]

The Rosenwald Fund was singularly successful in the modernization of black schools, especially during the 1920s. It followed a plan of action similar to that of the Jeanes Fund. Although a northern-based board controlled general policy and worked through black institutions such as Tuskegee, the fund quickly allied itself with southern educational bureaucracies. As with the Jeanes teachers, the state agent for rural black schools administered the Rosenwald program, and the fund worked closely with local officials and superintendents. It was also successful in stimulating local and state support for the construction of black schools. The fund was directly responsible for the expenditure of about $28 million during the 1920s, most of it public revenues; the fund also claimed credit for the construction of 5,357 new schools in fifteen states.[39]

Unlike either the Jeanes or Rosenwald funds, the Phelps Stokes Fund eschewed direct involvement. Instead, it concentrated on research and exposure of the conditions of rural blacks in the South. The fund also paid the salaries and expenses of workers in the United States Bureau of Education's Division of Racial Groups, the only early twentieth-century federal agency that investigated the condition of blacks.[40] By far the most significant product of the Phelps Stokes Fund was Thomas Jesse Jones's *Negro Education in the United States*, published in 1917. A Welsh immigrant, Jones had long been associated with the study of black education, both as a graduate student at Columbia University, where he completed a dissertation in sociology under Franklin H. Giddings, and as director of social research at Hampton Institute.[41] *Negro Education in the United States* presented, with unusual candor, the stark inequalities that existed between private and public black and white schools in length of term, teacher training, and facilities.[42]

Beginnings of Black High Schools

The clearest indicator of the baneful consequences of Jim Crow was access for whites and blacks to secondary education. For whites, the high school became an obvious measure of educational change; for blacks, it was a symbol of discrimination. Whereas all but three Virginia counties had high school facilities in 1920, only sixteen had black high schools. Even more striking, although 22,061 white students in rural Virginia in 1920 attended high schools, only 297 black pupils did so.[43] The absence of black high schools reflected a hard political reality of the early twentieth-century South: no legislature or governor was willing to risk public support for improving black schools. White educational reformers provided a rationalization of this dual, and inherently unequal, system; blacks, they explained, did not require the sophisticated education offered by a high school.[44]

Events soon demonstrated, however, that reform in black elementary education depended upon high schools to train black teachers and provide them with instruction in industrial education. Soon, as a result, the advocates of industrial education endorsed the establishment of rudimentary black secondary schools, euphemistically known as "training" schools. The first such school was the Tanyiphra Parish Training School in Louisiana, established in 1911 as an enlarged elementary school that also trained teachers. In part in response to a need for industrially trained teachers—which, reformers foresaw, the black normal in Petersburg could not alleviate—similar training schools began in Virginia in 1914. As a stopgap measure, Davis proposed in that year that some of the strongest graded black schools expand their facilities to include teacher training. Most white educators concerned about black education, moreover, began to advocate the establishment of a rudimentary secondary education for blacks. Known as "county training schools," these were first financed by the Slater Fund (whose director was Dillard) and later by the GEB. Thus began the first effort to provide rural black secondary schools in the South.[45]

The sponsors of county training schools made certain that they would be firmly under the control of the state department of education. The Slater Fund contributed $500 toward the construction of each school; the GEB also donated funds for both maintenance and teachers' salaries. Within five years, these schools would become the property of the county school board, and the local boards were expected to contribute no less than $750 annually for salaries and upkeep. The county training schools were also connected with the existing programs for rural black elementary education—primarily the supervising teachers, who often used the schools as bases of operations.[46] Although the schools were under the immediate direction of county school officials, they were also responsible to state officials, who supervised the curriculum and the selection of teachers.[47]

The same assumption that guided the operation of the Jeanes Fund —that blacks needed a rudimentary, "industrial" education—also dominated the approach of county training schools. The way of life among most rural blacks, observed Davis in 1919, was "very simple and crude." The schools should therefore also be "simple," but should be "far enough ahead to lead the people and the younger generation to higher standards and better practices."[48] County training schools began industrial education early in the primary grades. Younger children were encouraged to develop "manual dexterity," particularly in "handling and utilizing native materials"; they were also instructed in the "common industries" of the home and farm. During the two or three years of secondary schooling which these schools provided, students usually learned more specific skills: for the girls, sewing, cooking, and housekeeping; for the boys, cobbling, harness making, soldering, setting window glass, simple joinery, and basic carpentry. Both boys and girls received instruction in agricultural subjects and were encouraged to organize—often in cooperation with the black county extension agents—corn and poultry clubs. In addition, the county training schools emphasized instruction in those "academic" subjects—mathematics, English, grammar, science, and history—necessary to provide normal training for elementary schoolteachers.[49] Each of these schools—in theory, at least—included five black teachers. The principal, always a man, led the school, and he was required to be "well qualified educationally" and capable of working "harmoniously" with local whites and blacks. The school also included two "industrial" instructors: one woman who specialized in "home industries" and taught academic subjects in the upper grades and a man who taught industrial and agricultural subjects. Two other women taught the primary grades.[50]

By 1920, nine years after they began, it was clear that the training schools were a pale imitation of the white high schools. Although their creators had envisioned them as models for future expansion, the concrete results were meager: by 1920, only seventy-five of the schools existed in the entire South, twenty of them in Virginia.[51] Many of the training schools encountered the same obstacles that were confronting Jeanes teachers—the resistance of black patrons and the overwhelming problems of rural poverty. In 1914, one official visiting a training school found to his horror that its teachers were neglecting the industrial curriculum in favor of instruction in Latin. Especially in their early years, many county training schools ignored the official course of study, and most probably did well to provide a basic course in teacher education. A GEB official who visited some of these schools wrote in 1915 that although county training schools would eventually render a "valuable service to the local community," several years would probably elapse before they produced "any considerable number of teachers." To regard them as teacher-training schools was "fallacious," for most pupils never advanced to the upper grades and the teachers were "not qualified to be teachers of teachers."[52]

The Negro Organization Society

For southern reformers, the term "cooperation" came to have a special significance, not only for the general transformation of their region's social and political system but also for its race relations. In the context of race relations, cooperation for reformers meant the improvement of the status of blacks under a segregated system. The attempts during the early twentieth century to better black education did not challenge segregation or inequality; reformers fostered only contacts between the races that respected the color line. The Jeanes Fund was an example of a form of uplift that linked better blacks and better whites, according to one of its supporters, on a basis of "common brotherhood, common needs, and common sympathy." The Jeanes teachers, as Davis added, represented the "best leadership" of blacks in alliance with the "best" whites. Such was "cooperation" as applied to the problem of race.[53]

In Virginia, an active representative of interracialism was the Negro Organization Society (NOS), founded in 1909. The NOS grew out of the Hampton Negro Conference, a series of meetings held at Hampton Institute each year from 1897 to 1912. After the meeting of 1909, Frissell proposed that the conference organize a committee to foster a "unity of purpose and effectiveness" among all black organizations in Virginia.[54] Later that year, the new organization held its first meeting in Richmond. Robert Russa Moton, who was then commandant of cadets at Hampton Institute and later became principal of Tuskegee after Washington's death in 1915, was elected as the organization's first president; as secretary, the group chose W.T.B. Williams, a black reformer and Hampton graduate. The NOS acted as an umbrella organization on the assumption that Virginia blacks belonged to "some organization"—a church, Sunday school, or lodge—and, within only a few years, the group, as Williams remembered, had incorporated all black reform organizations that existed in the state.[55]

Like the Jeanes Fund, the NOS promoted an interracial approach. It offered a common platform for the expression of black leadership and promised to confederate the state's black organizations. Representing a variety of church organizations and reform groups, the NOS became the mouthpiece of black school leagues and teachers' groups.[56] The reform group also professed to advance self-improvement as had the CEA among whites; indeed, it consciously modeled itself on the white organization. As Williams maintained, just as the CEA propagandized the cause of white rural education, so it was essential that the NOS agitate for "some special training" for blacks. Like the CEA, the NOS promised to mold diverse black groups into "one unit" to improve morals, health, and education.[57]

The Hampton Negro Conference and the NOS endorsed accommodation with de jure segregation as a realistic way to foster racial independence and development. Under segregation, an extended degree of class hierarchy among blacks, and, ultimately, cooperation between the "better" elements of each race would become possible. Self-help and self-improvement would also lead to better race relations, NOS organizers declared. "In any community where Negroes will work together," wrote the Reverend A. A. Graham, the "white people will understand them, and wherever they are divided the white people will not work with them." Racial independence for blacks depended upon convincing whites that they were "industrious, honest, and truthful," that they would pay their debts, and that they would live an "upright" life. As a result of these efforts, better-behaved blacks would have white friends. Racial pride led to cooperative race relations, according to Washington, who praised the NOS in 1914. The organization, he said, taught blacks "how we can be and are separate in strictly social matters, but one in all that concerns the fundamental things of life in the South." The true purpose of the NOS, according to Graham, was to effect "co-operation" between the races. "We want," he declared, to "bring the colored people into closer contact with the white people who are charged with the responsibility of the work of public education and health."[58]

The most significant black organization in pre-World War I Virginia, the NOS later became an aggressive opponent of the Jim Crow system. It established a pattern and precedent for interracial cooperation between white reformers and blacks which stopped short of violating southern strictures against social contact among the races. The NOS represented a culmination of what Jack Temple Kirby has described as "black progressivism" in Virginia and the beginning, in Virginia and the South, of the liberal, interracial approach to the problem of racial tension. Like the Jeanes Fund, the NOS included in its councils both blacks and whites; unlike the Jeanes Fund, the NOS evolved as an organization dominated by blacks but acceptable to white reformers. Moreover, the organization's first president, Moton, was instrumental in the founding in 1919 of the Commission on Interracial Cooperation, the most important interracial group in the South.[59]

But the direction the NOS had taken by 1920 revealed the central ambiguities of the reform approach to race. White reformers, assuming black inferiority, believed that a separate and carefully differentiated approach to black education was necessary. Reformed black schools should emphasize, through industrial education, the acquisition of basic economic as well as moral skills which blacks lacked as a race. Some black leaders, most notably Booker T. Washington, accommodated and accepted—or appeared to accept—the positions of white re- formers. But in practice, industrial education had a distinct meaning for blacks, who reshaped a concept of unequal public schools into a vehi- cle for school improvement. Yet, for reformers, who faced the over- whelming backwardness of rural black schools, industrial education soon proved an impractical concept, and its implementation depended on the same improvement in teachers' standards, facilities, and supervi- sion that reformers had deemed essential for white schools.

Afterword
A Century After

The changes affecting rural schools and society in the century after Reconstruction were sweeping, even revolutionary. Post-Reconstruction Virginia was a land of isolated farms and dusty villages; the late twentieth-century Old Dominion is a predominantly modern and urban society. A century ago, with the Civil War etched in their psyches, Virginians were southern and rural—probably in that order; today, with suburban extensions of metropolitan Washington dominating northern Virginia, a large part of the commonwealth is allied with a placeless, highly mobile urban nation. In 1880, about three-quarters of the state's population lived outside towns and cities; a century later, about two-thirds reside in urban areas. This massive demographic relocation was part of a larger historical process in which the American population, 72 percent rural in 1880, became 74 percent urban a hundred years later.[1]

Schools experienced equally convulsive changes. In the 1880s, every dimension of rural education in Virginia was profoundly shaped by localism and community control; in the 1980s, outside standards and decision making are the norm. As community institutions, rural schools in the 1880s mirrored local mores, attitudes, and social and racial structures; in the 1980s, rural schools serve as a main instrument of the public policy objectives of upward mobility, desegregation, and racial equality. The contrasting images of past and present in rural education are perhaps most evident in the physical presence of rural education. In the 1880s, its architectural symbol was the one-room school, typically as poor and shabby as the buildings surrounding it but rarely standing apart from the landscape of rural society. A century later, rural schools immediately strike the eye as permanent physical symbols of their different role in society.

These changes resulted from the sustained and pervasive growth of public education in Virginia and the United States. Between the 1920s and the 1980s, expansion nationwide affected almost every educational category. Expenditures for public schools, adjusted for inflation, increased by about five times during this period, and the numbers of rural Americans who graduated from high school rose from 33 percent to over 80 percent. The explosive growth of elementary and secondary public schools affected urban and rural areas alike; a major consequence was the narrowing of educational disparities between city and country. Growth also largely ended another historical disparity—the wide gap between the schools of the post-Reconstruction rural South and the rest of the country. In the 1880s, schools symbolized the huge gap in income and wealth between the rural South and the rest of the nation; in the 1980s, they offer positive proof that the South is becoming incorporated into the national economic and social mainstream. Nationally, per capita income in 1980 was $9,480; in Virginia, it was only slightly less, $9,380.²

The twentieth-century nationalization of the South—and the accompanying changes—resulted in the disappearance of the educational disparities prevalent in the nineteenth century. In 1930, Virginia spent, per capita, about half the national average; by 1958, that proportion stood at 72 percent; and in 1981, it was about 98 percent. In another important category—the length of school session—Virginia schools were closely abreast of national norms. In 1981, the average length of session for Virginia schools was 180.3 days, as compared with 178.2 days for the United States as a whole, 177.0 days for Oregon, 180.3 days for Connecticut, and 182.9 days for Kansas.³

The end of undereducation was a direct product not only of economic growth but also of the extension of central state control over rural education. Central control followed school consolidation, which was possible on a large scale because of hard-surfaced roads and school buses; school consolidation meant the beginning of the end of the one-room school. On the eve of World War I, there were close to a quarter of a million one-room schools in the United States. By the end of the Great Depression, that figure had declined to about 114,000; and by 1960, it had fallen to about 20,000. In 1981, there were only 921 one-room schools across the country.⁴

An even more obvious symbol of state supremacy was the inauguration of effective compulsory education in Virginia in 1922 and in rural America during that decade. Along with school consolidation, compulsory education tipped the balance of power in favor of centralizers and made possible extensive changes in the structure of rural education. In Virginia, the establishment of a county system of educational adminis- tration and the abolition of district control soon followed compulsory education.

Despite school consolidation and compulsory education, persistence as well as change characterize late twentieth-century rural schools. For the nation as a whole, community-controlled education demonstrated a remarkable ability to resist centralization. From the Committee of Twelve's report on rural education in 1897, a full half century passed before rural school officials could claim real control over local power. Nationally and regionally, the pace of change varied. In general, modern- ization occurred earlier and more rapidly in the South, and strong oppo- sition persisted during the 1950s in the upper Middle West and prairie states. Even within the South, however, local communities resisted cen- tralization with varying degrees of success and continued to exert con- siderable power in public education.

Nor has one hundred years of educational change eliminated social and racial injustice in rural public schools. For the nation as a whole, increasing access for students to elementary, secondary, and higher edu- cation had become a prime public policy objective by the middle of the twentieth century. Although remarkable increases followed in enroll- ments—especially in secondary schools—inequality in education, as Diane Ravitch has concluded, persists in public education.[5] Despite post-World War II attempts by Virginia and other southern states to equalize school expenditures, significant differences are apparent, not only in rural-urban comparisons, but also in rural-rural and urban-urban comparisons. Growth and centralization improved public schooling, ex- tended its availability to a wider spectrum of students, and spread the net of education forward into adolescence and backward into child- hood, but it also fostered qualitative differences that continue to our own time.

The continuing impact of societal inequality on public education is nowhere more evident than in the relationship between race and school- ing. As a product of centuries of public policy that first prohibited slave education and then fostered a wide educational gap between the races, public schools in Virginia, the South, and the nation came to bear the special burden of the problem of racial inequality. Almost fifty years after the May Campaign and the conscious choice by school reformers to tolerate substantial racial inequality, the Supreme Court ruled that the principle of equality and de jure racial segregation were incompatible in

Prince Edward County, Virginia; despite all-out white resistance, by the early 1970s desegregation became a reality of rural education. Yet it is indisputable that a cycle of poverty and undereducation has persisted. In the early 1980s, rural blacks nationwide earned 58 percent of the per capita median family income earned by rural whites; in Virginia, the proportion was 71 percent. In the twenty to twenty-four age cohort, 71 percent of rural white Virginians were high school graduates in 1980, but for rural blacks the proportion was 62 percent.[6]

Characterized by both continuity and change, the evolution of schools in rural Virginia suggests several insights about the process of social and cultural change over the past century. In their relationship to a fundamentally conservative, rural society, the evolution of country schools in Virginia demonstrated the slow pace of change and the strength of localism in social and political life. At least two generations of reformers proposed a centralized educational polity for rural Virginians before it was adopted. What is striking about the response to these public policy initiatives is that, until the end of World War I, the balance of power lay with local communities, and modernizers effected change only by accommodation.

In part a product of and in part an active agent in economic change, modernized rural schools occupied a central position in a profound social transformation. Only in a resolution of the local-central conflict—a concrete accomplishment of World War I era reformers and modernizers—did real educational change become possible after 1920. Modernized rural schools were advance agents in a sweeping series of changes in the social landscape of rural Virginia. They pioneered the end of ignorance, isolation, and provincialism so typical of the late nineteenth-century South. They led and were the first public institutions actively working to transform health practices and eradicate rural disease, parasitic infection, and malnutrition. And they were active promoters and prophets of economic change and a general increase in the rural southern standard of living.

In all of these respects, the transformation of rural education fulfilled the vision of early twentieth-century reformers and confirmed their diagnosis that localism in education and society was the major reason for southern underdevelopment, poverty, and ignorance. Far from ushering in a new millennium, however, educational change brought costs as well as benefits. Old problems have persisted; the indicators of inequality that have disappeared have been replaced by new ones. As the main vehicle for modernization, change was accompanied by bureaucratic governance in schools that had never before experienced bureau-cracy. Along with qualitative improvement, bureaucratic education brought impersonal education at least partly detached from its roots in the community. The slow but steady progress of bureaucracy meant the erosion of community control over schools—a hallmark of post-Recon-struction education—and the end of extensive parental participation in almost every area of public education.

Appendixes

Note on Method

The following tables are derived from county-level data published in the reports of the Virginia Superintendent of Public Instruction, appearing annually and biennially after 1871, and in the United States censuses of population and agriculture for 1900 and 1920. Different measures of educational, economic, and social status were compiled for the one hundred counties of Virginia; cities were excluded when possible. Some of these measures, such as those on enrollment and attendance or length of school session, could be immediately employed as variables; others, such as the proportions of female teachers, one-room schools, and landownership, were calculated into some other variable that could be standardized for all counties. The raw data files were then processed by the Statistical Package for the Social Sciences (X), Release 2.1.

To provide a clearer statistical portrait of a state in which geography was all-important, I have coded each county into one of six regional groups—Appalachia, the Shenandoah Valley, the Southside, the northern Piedmont, the Tidewater, and the five counties contiguous to Virginia's major urban areas. Each of these regions is defined by the geographical boundaries discussed in Chapter 1: the James River, which separates Southside from northern Piedmont and Tidewater; the Blue Ridge, which surrounds the Valley and separates Appalachia from the rest of the state. These regions include the following counties:

Appalachia (N = 22)
Alleghany, Bath, Bland, Botetourt, Buchanan, Carroll, Craig, Dickenson, Floyd, Giles, Grayson, Highland, Lee, Montgomery, Pulaski, Russell, Scott, Smyth, Tazewell, Washington, Wise, Wythe.

Valley (N = 8)
Augusta, Clarke, Frederick, Page, Rockbridge, Rockingham, Shenandoah, Warren.

Southside (N = 26)
Amelia, Appomattox, Bedford, Brunswick, Buckingham, Campbell, Charlotte, Chesterfield, Cumberland, Dinwiddie, Franklin, Greensville, Halifax, Henry, Isle

of Wight, Lunenburg, Mecklenburg, Nansemond, Nottoway, Patrick, Pittsylvania, Powhatan, Prince George, Southampton, Surry, Sussex.

Northern Piedmont (N = 18)
Albemarle, Amherst, Caroline, Culpeper, Fairfax, Fauquier, Fluvanna, Goochland, Greene, Hanover, Loudoun, Louisa, Madison, Nelson, Orange, Prince William, Rappahannock, Spotsylvania.

Tidewater (N = 21)
Accomac, Charles City, Elizabeth City, Essex, Gloucester, James City, King George, King and Queen, King William, Lancaster, Mathews, Middlesex, New Kent, Northampton, Northumberland, Prince Edward, Richmond, Stafford, Warwick, Westmoreland, York.

Urban (N = 5)
Alexandria (later Arlington), Henrico, Norfolk, Princess Anne, Roanoke.

Like other statistical evidence of nineteenth- and early twentieth-century social experiences, these data have clear limitations. Although I have tried to observe trends over time, nineteenth- and early twentieth-century data-gatherers recorded some variables only erratically. Data for some counties were unreported and were coded as missing. Because the data are county-level, it is impossible to observe important subtleties and differences presented on the district, neighborhood, or individual levels. Some of the data are imperfect—certainly as suspect as most of the available data on American society before the twentieth century. Figures on school expenditures are probably the most reliable, followed by those on county superintendents, teachers, and school session. The least reliable data are probably those on enrollment and attendance.

The shortcomings of these data require their use in conjunction with other historical evidence; educational statistics are just one part of the record. They do not answer all of the questions about the historical world of rural Virginia; in many cases, they raise more questions than they answer. And they present a picture of public education that is imperfect in still another sense: they measure only a part of the diverse impulses—personal, societal, economic, and cultural—that went into educational decisions.

Partly because of these imperfections, I have attempted to remain close to the data through simple and accessible statistical manipulations. The following appendixes are divided into two general parts. The first part (1.0 through 4.4) provides descriptive statistics, by region, on Virginia schools and society between 1870 and 1920. The averages for these variables are means for counties. The second part (5.0 through 6.9) contains, also by region and state, a select group of Pearson product moment correlation coefficients for these variables. The possible combinations for all the variables in this data base are staggering;

reproducing all possible coefficients would serve no useful purpose. I have therefore included only coefficients for wealth, farm ownership (by race), population density, and race with school variables such as attendance, enrollment, school session, and district expenditures for 1900 and 1920. Having run all possible combinations of variables from the same year, when possible I have referred to additional relevant coefficients in the notes.

The Pearson r is not a completely clear statistic, but it does provide a simple measure of linearity, and thus of association, between any two variables. By themselves, these correlation coefficients tell us only part of a very complex story. Moreover, as these are county-level data, the Pearson r measures only relationships at that level and does not provide conclusive proof of individual decisions. Nonetheless, the Pearson r is useful in testing assertions about broad relationships between social phenomena and educational experiences. In general, the closer the Pearson r is to $+1.0$ or -1.0, the stronger the statistical association between those two variables. If, for example, for any two variables x and y, the Pearson r were $+1.0$, then x would increase at the same rate as y; if the Pearson r were -1.0, then x would decrease at the same rate as y increased, or vice versa.

Along with the Pearson r, I have included the N of cases and a two-tailed significance test. Determining the significance tests the reliability of a statistic by measuring the probability of any relationship occurring randomly. If p equals .01, therefore, the probability that the correlation could have occurred randomly is one out of one hundred. Put another way, because one would assume that the relationship between school and society was not random, the level of confidence in the strength of the association measured by r is, in this instance, 99 percent. Using both the r and p, it is possible to test the strength of association between educational variables and social and economic conditions. As a test of reliability, I have assumed that p should be no greater than .05 and that r should be no less than .25.

Tables

1.0: County Superintendents, 1900

	Days employed	Miles traveled
Region		
Appalachia	149	748
Valley	208	1144
Southside	198	824
Northern Piedmont	153	783
Tidewater	148	679
Urban	170	1500
State	168	830

1.1: Length of School Session, 1900

	Days
Region	
Appalachia	95
Valley	108
Southside	110
Northern Piedmont	111
Tidewater	116
Urban	147
State	110

1.2: Percentage Enrollment and Attendance, by Race, 1870

	White enrolled	Black enrolled	White attending	Black attending
Region				
Appalachia	45	18	23	11
Valley	40	26	23	17
Southside	32	20	21	13

1.2: continued

	White enrolled	Black enrolled	White attending	Black attending
Northern Piedmont	37	26	23	15
Tidewater	37	23	23	13
Urban	33	31	19	16
State	37	23	22	14

1.3: Percentage Enrollment and Attendance, by Race, 1900

	White enrolled	Black enrolled	White attending	Black attending
Region				
Appalachia	71	47	43	25
Valley	63	49	38	30
Southside	59	45	35	26
Northern Piedmont	56	42	33	22
Tidewater	59	45	35	23
Urban	63	45	40	22
State	61	45	37	25

1.4: Percentage Female Teachers, by Race, 1870 and 1900

	Whites 1870	Blacks 1870	Whites 1900	Blacks 1900
Region				
Appalachia	21.83	27.80	50.24	23.65
Valley	26.33	39.25	50.63	58.13
Southside	37.42	17.17	77.29	61.81
Northern Piedmont	40.22	32.54	75.67	58.06
Tidewater	41.50	8.44	79.35	62.71
Urban	25.00	44.00	80.20	55.50
State	34.39	24.47	68.83	53.76

1.5: Square Miles per School, 1870–1920

	1870	1900	1920
Region			
Appalachia	16.31	5.77	3.57
Valley	10.39	4.14	3.56
Southside	18.22	5.95	3.78
Northern Piedmont	11.32	5.05	3.89
Tidewater	12.91	4.99	3.55
Urban	13.66	3.65	2.09
State	14.80	5.27	3.61

1.6: Per Capita School Expenditures, in Cents, 1900

	District	County	State	Other
Region				
Appalachia	18	17	51	0
Valley	31	27	54	10
Southside	14	12	58	1
Northern Piedmont	18	20	58	2
Tidewater	16	12	57	3
Urban	56	37	45	19
State	19	17	55	3

1.7: Monthly Salaries for Teachers, in Dollars, 1900

	Males	Females	Percent difference
Region			
Appalachia	25.68	22.95	12
Valley	26.56	23.34	14
Southside	26.29	24.09	9
Northern Piedmont	24.35	22.69	8

1.7: continued

	Males	Females	Percent difference
Tidewater	26.60	24.44	8
Urban	36.28	32.50	12
State	26.40	24.03	10

1.8: Percentage Schools Having Outhouses, 1900

Region	
Appalachia	31.11
Valley	71.88
Southside	23.81
Northern Piedmont	45.28
Tidewater	30.52
Urban	70.80
State	37.06

2.0: Percentage Farms Owned, by Race, 1900

	White	Black
Region		
Appalachia	75.76	55.73
Valley	78.25	77.33
Southside	64.42	45.54
Northern Piedmont	73.28	74.88
Tidewater	73.86	68.50
Urban	68.00	57.00
State	71.74	60.45

2.1: Agricultural Wealth, per Acre, in Dollars, 1900

	Total wealth	Land	Crop	Labor
Region				
Appalachia	14.56	11.47	2.90	.19
Valley	24.61	18.75	5.29	.57
Southside	8.87	5.17	3.34	.36
Northern Piedmont	13.61	9.79	3.40	.42
Tidewater	16.20	11.32	4.40	.49
Urban	68.50	55.79	10.81	1.90
State	16.78	12.30	4.02	.46

2.2: Volume Produced, Selected Crops, 1900

	Tobacco (pounds)	Cotton (bales)	Peanuts (bushels)
Region			
Appalachia	72,576	0	13
Valley	659,424	0	8
Southside	3,599,695	369	141,535
Northern Piedmont	946,824	0	6
Tidewater	249,837	0	1,430
Urban	23,982	147	322
State	1,228,734	103	37,120

2.3: Percentage of Total Population Black, 1900

Region	
Appalachia	11.38
Valley	12.34
Southside	47.81
Northern Piedmont	33.81
Tidewater	48.65
Urban	42.32
State	35.05

2.4: Percentage Literate, by Race, 1900

	Whites	Blacks
Region		
Appalachia	82.15	48.48
Valley	90.22	49.62
Southside	86.79	36.96
Northern Piedmont	87.94	41.30
Tidewater	87.66	44.12
Urban	91.14	52.55
State	86.69	43.42

3.0: Employment of County Superintendents, 1920

	Days employed	Percent time inspecting
Region		
Appalachia	249.92	31.51
Valley	200.75	37.62
Southside	212.47	33.53
Northern Piedmont	230.77	35.35
Tidewater	167.91	32.78
Urban	300.00	15.67
State	216.98	33.33

3.1: Length of School Session (Days), by Race, 1920

	All schools	White schools	Black schools
Region			
Appalachia	152	147	131
Valley	147	152	125
Southside	145	157	127
Northern Piedmont	144	155	123

3.1: continued

	All schools	White schools	Black schools
Tidewater	151	164	137
Urban	175	181	168
State	149	157	131

3.2: Percentage Enrollment and Attendance, by Race, 1920

	Whites enrolled	Blacks enrolled	Whites attending	Blacks attending
Region				
Appalachia	83.83	61.13	59.27	43.50
Valley	82.19	66.23	56.14	44.47
Southside	84.00	66.29	60.05	39.21
Northern Piedmont	74.16	63.83	52.38	41.86
Tidewater	76.29	66.44	58.61	43.48
Urban	73.18	61.28	57.08	41.22
State	79.89	64.52	57.73	42.03

3.3: Per Capita School Expenditures, in Dollars, 1920

	District	County	State	Other
Region				
Appalachia	1.73	1.36	2.97	1.52
Valley	1.60	1.37	2.18	2.07
Southside	1.29	.87	2.31	2.03
Northern Piedmont	1.13	1.05	2.19	1.38
Tidewater	1.28	.92	2.28	1.69
Urban	1.88	1.38	2.07	2.64
State	1.41	1.08	2.40	1.77

3.4: School Expansion, Selected Areas, 1900–1920

	Percent expansion in school term	Percent expansion in district expenditures
Region		
Appalachia	59.54	1,160.47
Valley	36.76	411.28
Southside	31.80	839.31
Northern Piedmont	30.63	605.09
Tidewater	30.83	705.35
Urban	20.64	488.51
State	37.10	784.13

3.5: Percentage One-Room Schools, by Race, 1920

	All	White	Black
Region			
Appalachia	35.61	38.46	73.49
Valley	34.80	33.58	63.13
Southside	31.55	19.40	64.21
Northern Piedmont	42.49	32.06	74.87
Tidewater	29.70	20.81	49.33
Urban	18.49	10.19	41.23
State	33.47	26.77	62.92

3.6: Percentage High School Enrollment, by Race, 1920

	White	Black
Region		
Appalachia	5.81	.70
Valley	7.13	0
Southside	6.12	.39
Northern Piedmont	7.10	.42

3.6: continued

	White	Black
Tidewater	8.44	.72
Urban	5.49	1.72
State	6.75	.57

3.7: Percentage Schools Inspected by State Officials, 1920

	Special inspector	State inspector
Region		
Appalachia	25.28	6.57
Valley	54.91	6.95
Southside	42.94	9.25
Northern Piedmont	28.61	10.61
Tidewater	278.04	22.34
Urban	328.35	7.82
State	102.62	11.60

3.8: Percentage of Membership in Teachers' Associations

Region	
Appalachia	81.60
Valley	67.20
Southside	65.03
Northern Piedmont	58.15
Tidewater	69.78
Urban	93.22
State	69.62

4.0: Percentage of All Farms Owned, by Race, 1920

	White	Black
Region		
Appalachia	79.11	2.31
Valley	74.03	2.36
Southside	39.76	23.86
Northern Piedmont	57.63	22.17
Tidewater	46.53	31.95
Urban	53.78	11.85
State	56.50	18.19

4.1: Agricultural Wealth, per Acre, in Dollars, 1920

	Total wealth	Value land	Value crop
Region			
Appalachia	53.95	43.89	9.64
Valley	79.20	58.59	19.73
Southside	46.85	30.30	16.27
Northern Piedmont	46.17	32.95	12.28
Tidewater	71.59	45.42	25.27
Urban	167.34	134.89	28.06
State	62.18	44.44	16.92

4.2: Volume Produced, Selected Crops, 1920

	Tobacco (pounds)	Cotton (bales)	Peanuts (bushels)
Region			
Appalachia	81,510	0	8
Valley	15,713	0	15
Southside	3,478,272	2,001	254,377
Northern Piedmont	528,077	3	97

4.2: continued

	Tobacco (pounds)	Cotton (bales)	Peanuts (bushels)
Tidewater	314,005	0	495
Urban	12,929	437	1,370
State	1,190,570	1,659	99,392

4.3: Percentage of Total Population Black, 1920

Region	
Appalachia	7
Valley	10
Southside	46
Northern Piedmont	33
Tidewater	46
Urban	29
State	32

4.4: Percentage Literate, by Race, 1920

	Whites	Blacks
Region		
Appalachia	89.73	76.82
Valley	93.38	75.25
Southside	94.58	71.73
Northern Piedmont	93.39	75.67
Tidewater	94.62	73.95
Urban	96.40	79.40
State	93.30	74.69

5.0: Pearson Correlation Coefficients, White Attendance and Selected Variables, 1900

Variable	Total farm wealth, per acre, 1900			Percent farm owners, whites, 1900			Percent farm owners, blacks, 1900			Population density, 1900			Percent black, 1900		
Region	*r*	*N*	*p*	*r*	*N*	*p*	*r*	*N*	*p*	*r*	*N*	*p*	*r*	*N*	*p*
Appalachia	.25	21	.28	.12	21	.62	.01	11	.97	.35	21	.13	.32	19	.18
Valley	−.25	8	.55	.77	8	.03	.62	3	.57	−.22	8	.60	−.62	8	.10
Southside	−.04	26	.83	−.18	26	.38	−.38	26	.06	.01	26	.96	−.06	26	.77
Northern Piedmont	−.07	18	.78	.42	18	.09	.41	17	.11	−.40	18	.10	.10	18	.69
Tidewater	.76	21	.00	−.13	21	.58	−.47	20	.04	.71	21	.00	.09	21	.69
Urban	−.28	5	.65	.49	5	.44	.70	5	.19	−.14	5	.83	−.41	5	.50
Statewide	.10	99	.33	.17	99	.09	−.11	82	.33	.20	99	.05	−.33	97	.00

r Pearson coefficient of correlation   *N* number of cases   *p* level of significance, two-tailed test

5.1: Pearson Correlation Coefficients, Black Attendance and Selected Variables, 1900

Variable	Total farm wealth, per acre, 1900			Percent farm owners, whites, 1900			Percent farm owners, blacks, 1900			Population density, 1900			Percent black, 1900		
Region	*r*	*N*	*p*	*r*	*N*	*p*	*r*	*N*	*p*	*r*	*N*	*p*	*r*	*N*	*p*
Appalachia	.59	21	.01	−.16	21	.50	.38	11	.25	.50	21	.02	.14	19	.57
Valley	−.07	8	.86	.49	8	.22	.84	3	.37	−.08	8	.85	.29	8	.49
Southside	.27	26	.19	−.12	26	.56	−.24	26	.24	.23	26	.26	.03	26	.91
Northern Piedmont	.28	18	.26	.17	18	.50	.20	17	.45	.20	18	.43	.09	18	.71
Tidewater	.25	21	.28	.17	21	.45	−.07	20	.76	.43	21	.05	−.31	21	.17
Urban	−.12	5	.84	.87	6	.05	.95	5	.01	−.08	5	.90	−.79	5	.12
Statewide	.02	99	.84	.01	99	.94	.01	82	.95	.12	99	.24	−.20	97	.05

5.2: Pearson Correlation Coefficients, White Enrollment and Selected Variables, 1900

Variable	Total farm wealth, per acre, 1900			Percent farm owners, whites, 1900			Percent farm owners, blacks, 1900			Population density, 1900			Percent black, 1900		
Region	r	N	p	r	N	p	r	N	p	r	N	p	r	N	p
Appalachia	−.34	21	.13	−.45	21	.90	−.16	11	.33	−.08	21	.74	−.46	19	.05
Valley	−.00	8	.99	.54	8	.16	.52	3	.65	.02	8	.96	−.57	8	.14
Southside	−.19	26	.35	−.18	26	.37	−.28	26	.16	−.01	26	.96	−.19	26	.36
Northern Piedmont	.31	18	.20	.29	18	.24	.24	17	.35	.10	18	.69	−.31	18	.21
Tidewater	.51	21	.02	.08	21	.74	−.35	20	.13	.42	21	.06	.38	21	.09
Urban	−.10	5	.87	.81	5	.09	.74	5	.15	−.21	5	.73	−.89	5	.04
Statewide	.07	99	.49	.16	99	.12	−.19	82	.09	.10	99	.31	−.39	97	.00

5.3: Pearson Correlation Coefficients, Black Enrollment and Selected Variables, 1900

Variable	Total farm wealth, per acre, 1900			Percent farm owners, whites, 1900			Percent farm owners, blacks, 1900			Population density, 1900			Percent black, 1900		
Region	r	N	p	r	N	p	r	N	p	r	N	p	r	N	p
Appalachia	.26	19	.28	−.32	19	.19	−.56	10	.09	.60	19	.01	.10	19	.67
Valley	.25	8	.55	.45	8	.26	.02	3	.99	.30	8	.48	.25	8	.55
Southside	.26	26	.21	−.07	26	.73	−.24	26	.25	.21	26	.30	.06	26	.77
Northern Piedmont	−.04	18	.86	−.07	18	.79	−.14	17	.59	.22	18	.37	.25	18	.31
Tidewater	−.04	21	.86	.05	21	.82	−.14	20	.57	.03	21	.89	−.52	21	.02
Urban	−.10	5	.88	.87	5	.06	.73	5	.17	−.28	5	.65	−.98	6	.01
Statewide	.01	97	.95	.03	97	.77	−.09	81	.41	.03	97	.76	.16	97	.13

5.4: Pearson Correlation Coefficients, Length of School Session and Selected Variables, 1900

Variable	Total farm wealth, per acre, 1900			Percent farm owners, whites, 1900			Percent farm owners, blacks, 1900			Population density, 1900			Percent black, 1900		
Region	r	N	p	r	N	p	r	N	p	r	N	p	r	N	p
Appalachia	.40	21	.07	−.42	21	.06	.59	11	.06	.61	21	.00	.41	19	.09
Valley	.30	8	.47	−.73	8	.04	−.54	3	.63	.34	8	.42	.90	8	.00
Southside	.18	26	.38	.25	26	.21	.44	26	.03	−.14	26	.48	.57	26	.00
Northern Piedmont	.82	18	.00	−.07	18	.79	.15	17	.57	.43	18	.08	−.45	18	.06
Tidewater	.54	21	.01	−.44	21	.05	−.45	20	.05	.59	21	.01	.09	21	.69
Urban	.47	5	.42	−.21	5	.73	−.14	5	.82	.75	5	.15	.51	5	.37
Statewide	.51	99	.00	−.25	99	.01	.07	82	.55	.52	99	.00	.44	97	.00

5.5: Pearson Correlation Coefficients, District Funding and Selected Variables, 1900

Variable	Total farm wealth, per acre, 1900			Percent farm owners, whites, 1900			Percent farm owners, blacks, 1900			Population density, 1900			Percent black, 1900		
Region	r	N	p	r	N	p	r	N	p	r	N	p	r	N	p
Appalachia	.36	21	.11	.21	21	.36	.50	11	.12	.15	21	.52	.50	19	.03
Valley	.10	8	.82	−.08	8	.86	.78	3	.43	−.84	8	.01	−.07	8	.85
Southside	.05	26	.81	.09	26	.66	.31	26	.12	.10	26	.62	.31	26	.13
Northern Piedmont	.84	18	.00	−.05	18	.86	.17	17	.53	.57	18	.01	−.42	18	.08
Tidewater	.66	21	.00	−.40	21	.07	−.55	20	.01	.53	21	.01	.35	21	.11
Urban	.86	5	.06	.69	5	.20	.21	5	.73	.72	5	.15	−.60	5	.29
Statewide	.84	99	.00	.11	99	.29	.12	82	.28	.52	99	.00	−.15	97	.14

5.6: Pearson Correlation Coefficients, Teachers' Salaries, Females, and Selected Variables, 1900

Variable	Total farm wealth, per acre, 1900			Percent farm owners, whites, 1900			Percent farm owners, blacks, 1900			Population density, 1900			Percent black, 1900		
Region	*r*	*N*	*p*	*r*	*N*	*p*	*r*	*N*	*p*	*r*	*N*	*p*	*r*	*N*	*p*
Appalachia	.22	21	.33	−.45	21	.04	.16	11	.64	.27	21	.24	.48	19	.04
Valley	.46	8	.25	−.69	8	.06	−.97	3	.16	.32	8	.43	.48	8	.23
Southside	.42	26	.03	.07	26	.75	.25	26	.23	.36	26	.07	.40	26	.04
Northern Piedmont	.65	18	.00	−.17	18	.50	−.11	17	.69	.59	18	.01	−.37	18	.13
Tidewater	.73	21	.00	−.08	21	.73	−.31	20	.19	.65	21	.00	−.30	21	.18
Urban	.50	5	.39	.64	5	.25	.52	5	.38	.58	5	.30	−.47	5	.42
Statewide	.53	99	.00	−.22	99	.03	−.05	82	.64	.50	99	.00	.25	97	.02

5.7: Pearson Correlation Coefficients, Teachers' Salaries, Males, and Selected Variables, 1900

Variable	Total farm wealth, per acre, 1900			Percent farm owners, whites, 1900			Percent farm owners, blacks, 1900			Population density, 1900			Percent black, 1900		
Region	*r*	*N*	*p*	*r*	*N*	*p*	*r*	*N*	*p*	*r*	*N*	*p*	*r*	*N*	*p*
Appalachia	.32	21	.11	−.41	21	.07	.01	11	.97	.27	21	.23	.51	19	.03
Valley	.10	8	.81	−.29	8	.49	−.74	3	.47	.20	8	.64	.61	8	.11
Southside	.54	26	.00	.14	26	.51	.18	26	.39	.48	26	.01	.29	26	.15
Northern Piedmont	.86	18	.00	.04	18	.89	.22	17	.40	.61	18	.01	−.42	18	.08
Tidewater	.82	21	.00	−.14	21	.54	−.35	20	.14	.88	21	.00	.04	21	.87
Urban	.64	5	.24	.09	5	.88	.07	5	.92	.88	5	.05	.20	5	.74
Statewide	.53	99	.00	−.19	99	.06	−.10	82	.38	.66	99	.00	.14	97	.17

6.0: Pearson Correlation Coefficients, White Attendance and Selected Variables, 1920

Variable	Total farm wealth, per acre, 1920			Percent farm owners, whites, 1920			Percent farm owners, blacks, 1920			Population density, 1920			Percent black, 1920		
Region	r	N	p	r	N	p	r	N	p	r	N	p	r	N	p
Appalachia	−.12	21	.61	.34	22	.12	−.24	22	.10	−.23	21	.32	−.37	21	.10
Valley	.68	8	.06	.49	8	.21	.41	8	.32	.02	8	.97	−.51	8	.20
Southside	.07	21	.73	−.39	26	.05	−.01	26	.97	.12	26	.56	.13	26	.52
Northern Piedmont	−.21	18	.41	−.42	18	.08	.07	18	.80	.23	18	.35	.17	18	.49
Tidewater	.59	21	.01	−.30	21	.19	−.19	21	.40	.37	21	.10	.07	21	.77
Urban	−.68	5	.20	−.15	5	.81	.58	5	.31	−.71	5	.18	.84	5	.07
Statewide	.10	99	.35	−.15	100	.13	−.04	100	.73	.04	99	.69	.07	99	.52

6.1: Pearson Correlation Coefficients, Black Attendance and Selected Variables, 1920

Variable	Total farm wealth, per acre, 1920			Percent farm owners, whites, 1920			Percent farm owners, blacks, 1920			Population density, 1920			Percent black, 1920		
Region	r	N	p	r	N	p	r	N	p	r	N	p	r	N	p
Appalachia	.11	20	.66	.20	21	.39	−.01	21	.96	.35	20	.13	.13	20	.60
Valley	−.41	8	.32	.75	8	.03	−.49	8	.22	.56	8	.15	−.72	8	.05
Southside	.06	26	.77	.38	26	.05	−.56	26	.00	.36	26	.08	−.51	26	.01
Northern Piedmont	−.15	18	.55	−.31	18	.22	−.07	18	.79	.22	18	.37	.02	18	.93
Tidewater	.05	21	.83	−.25	21	.28	−.06	21	.78	−.02	21	.95	.06	21	.81
Urban	−.57	5	.31	.13	5	.83	.57	5	.31	−.58	5	.31	−.05	5	.94
Statewide	−.03	98	.81	.12	99	.24	−.12	98	.23	−.01	98	.91	−.12	99	.22

6.2: Pearson Correlation Coefficients, White Enrollment and Selected Variables, 1920

Variable	Total farm wealth, per acre, 1920			Percent farm owners, whites, 1920			Percent farm owners, blacks, 1920			Population density, 1920			Percent black, 1920		
Region	r	N	p	r	N	p	r	N	p	r	N	p	r	N	p
Appalachia	−.15	21	.51	.31	22	.17	−.34	22	.12	−.02	21	.92	−.50	21	.02
Valley	.90	8	.03	.08	8	.85	−.49	8	.22	−.25	8	.56	−.30	8	.47
Southside	−.28	26	.16	−.37	26	.07	.03	26	.86	−.01	26	.98	−.00	26	.99
Northern Piedmont	−.21	18	.41	−.45	18	.06	.17	18	.51	−.11	18	.67	.29	18	.25
Tidewater	.50	21	.02	−.29	21	.21	−.23	21	.32	.29	21	.20	.04	21	.87
Urban	−.83	5	.08	−.05	5	.94	.44	5	.46	−.85	5	.07	.54	5	.35
Statewide	.08	99	.50	.04	100	.67	.19	100	.06	.11	99	.29	.10	99	.32

6.3: Pearson Correlation Coefficients, Black Enrollment and Selected Variables, 1920

Variable	Total farm wealth, per acre, 1920			Percent farm owners, whites, 1920			Percent farm owners, blacks, 1920			Population density, 1920			Percent black, 1920		
Region	r	N	p	r	N	p	r	N	p	r	N	p	r	N	p
Appalachia	.03	20	.89	.14	21	.54	.02	21	.93	.26	20	.27	.17	20	.47
Valley	−.04	8	.93	−.35	8	.39	−.32	8	.44	.43	8	.29	.18	8	.67
Southside	.16	26	.44	.20	26	.33	−.40	26	.05	.35	26	.08	−.30	26	.13
Northern Piedmont	−.32	18	.19	−.37	18	.13	.15	18	.55	−.17	18	.50	.21	18	.41
Tidewater	.00	21	.99	−.47	21	.03	.18	21	.43	−.19	21	.40	.36	21	.11
Urban	−.63	5	.25	.07	5	.91	.45	5	.45	−.64	5	.25	.01	5	.99
Statewide	−.07	99	.35	−.12	99	.25	.07	99	.53	−.08	98	.43	.12	98	.24

**6.4: Pearson Correlation Coefficients, Length of School Session
and Selected Variables, 1920**

Variable	Total farm wealth, per acre, 1920			Percent farm owners, whites, 1920			Percent farm owners, blacks, 1920			Population density, 1920			Percent black, 1920		
Region	r	N	p	r	N	p	r	N	p	r	N	p	r	N	p
Appalachia	.12	21	.60	−.52	21	.02	−.12	21	.60	.32	21	.16	−.08	21	.72
Valley	.22	8	.60	−.04	8	.92	.78	8	.02	.24	8	.57	.43	8	.29
Southside	−.03	26	.89	−.30	26	.14	.38	26	.06	−.12	26	.57	.25	26	.33
Northern Piedmont	.65	18	.00	.30	18	.23	−.22	18	.23	.12	18	.65	−.22	18	.39
Tidewater	.45	21	.04	−.18	21	.43	−.01	21	.95	.62	21	.00	.16	21	.49
Urban	.79	5	.11	−.39	5	.51	−.13	5	.83	.76	5	.14	−.29	5	.64
Statewide	.31	99	.00	−.05	99	.62	−.04	99	.67	.33	99	.00	−.04	99	.67

**6.5: Pearson Correlation Coefficients, District Funding
and Selected Variables, 1920**

Variable	Total farm wealth, per acre, 1920			Percent farm owners, whites, 1920			Percent farm owners, blacks, 1920			Population density, 1920			Percent black, 1920		
Region	r	N	p	r	N	p	r	N	p	r	N	p	r	N	p
Appalachia	−.01	21	.97	−.45	21	.04	−.05	21	.83	.02	21	.92	−.07	21	.76
Valley	−.38	8	.36	−.26	8	.53	.53	8	.18	−.48	8	.23	.32	8	.43
Southside	.34	26	.09	−.33	26	.10	.14	26	.50	.24	26	.24	.20	26	.34
Northern Piedmont	.68	18	.00	.26	18	.29	−.33	18	.19	.17	18	.50	−.20	18	.43
Tidewater	.48	21	.03	−.07	21	.78	−.31	21	.17	.16	21	.50	−.08	21	.74
Urban	−.19	5	.76	.03	5	.96	.45	5	.45	−.20	5	.75	−.23	5	.72
Statewide	.15	99	.15	.02	99	.81	−.15	99	.13	.05	99	.59	−.12	99	.23

6.6: Pearson Correlation Coefficients, White One-Room Schools and Selected Variables, 1920

Variable	Total farm wealth, per acre, 1920			Percent farm owners, whites, 1920			Percent farm owners, blacks, 1920			Population density, 1920			Percent black, 1920		
Region	r	N	p	r	N	p	r	N	p	r	N	p	r	N	p
Appalachia	−.53	21	.01	.55	21	.01	−.28	21	22	−.57	21	.01	−.46	21	.04
Valley	−.16	8	.71	−.35	8	.39	−.31	8	.45	−.05	8	.90	.07	8	.88
Southside	−.48	24	.02	.34	24	.10	.03	24	.89	−.33	24	.11	−.23	24	.29
Northern Piedmont	−.27	16	.30	.25	16	.35	−.22	16	.42	−.16	16	.55	−.38	16	.14
Tidewater	−.54	21	.01	−.03	21	.90	.32	21	.16	−.42	21	.06	.30	21	.18
Urban	−.49	5	.40	.66	5	.22	−.16	5	.80	−.43	5	.47	.02	5	.98
Statewide	−.40	95	.00	.48	95	.00	−.25	95	.02	−.35	95	.00	−.41	95	.00

6.7: Pearson Correlation Coefficients, Black One-Room Schools and Selected Variables, 1920

Variable	Total farm wealth, per acre, 1920			Percent farm owners, whites, 1920			Percent farm owners, blacks, 1920			Population density, 1920			Percent black, 1920		
Region	r	N	p	r	N	p	r	N	p	r	N	p	r	N	p
Appalachia	−.48	14	.08	.09	14	.77	−.58	14	.03	−.07	14	.82	−.67	14	.01
Valley	−.00	8	.99	.42	8	.30	−.36	8	.38	−.20	8	.64	−.63	8	.09
Southside	−.52	24	.01	.52	24	.01	−.18	24	.39	−.47	24	.02	−.55	24	.01
Northern Piedmont	−.20	16	.48	.17	16	.54	−.09	16	.74	−.07	16	.79	−.07	16	.81
Tidewater	−.41	21	.07	.05	21	.83	.08	21	.75	−.33	21	.15	.07	21	.77
Urban	−.83	4	.18	.51	4	.49	−.08	4	.92	−.85	4	.15	.11	4	.90
Statewide	−.41	87	.00	.30	87	.01	−.22	87	.00	−.31	87	.00	−.32	87	.00

6.8: Pearson Correlation Coefficients, White High School Enrollment and Selected Variables, 1920

Variable	Total farm wealth, per acre, 1920			Percent farm owners, whites, 1920			Percent farm owners, blacks, 1920			Population density, 1920			Percent black, 1920		
Region	r	N	p	r	N	p	r	N	p	r	N	p	r	N	p
Appalachia	.37	21	.10	−.18	21	.45	.57	21	.01	−.25	21	.28	.53	21	.01
Valley	−.41	8	.32	−.15	8	.73	.61	8	.11	.15	8	.72	.44	8	.27
Southside	.33	26	.10	−.54	26	.00	.50	26	.01	−.05	26	.83	.67	26	.00
Northern Piedmont	.09	18	.72	.02	18	.95	−.09	18	.72	.05	18	.85	−.02	18	.94
Tidewater	.32	18	.20	−.07	18	.78	−.27	18	.28	.03	18	.92	−.13	18	.60
Urban	−.82	5	.09	−.06	5	.93	.89	5	.04	−.85	5	.07	.46	5	.44
Statewide	.08	96	.43	−.45	96	.00	.46	96	.00	−.03	96	.77	.53	96	.00

6.9: Pearson Correlation Coefficients, Black High School Enrollment and Selected Variables, 1920

Variable	Total farm wealth, per acre, 1920			Percent farm owners, whites, 1920			Percent farm owners, blacks, 1920			Population density, 1920			Percent black, 1920		
Region	r	N	p	r	N	p	r	N	p	r	N	p	r	N	p
Appalachia	−.09	18	.73	.03	18	.92	−.39	18	.12	−.11	18	.65	−.53	18	.02
Valley	.18	8	.67	.49	8	.22	−.65	8	.09	.32	8	.44	−.60	8	.12
Southside	−.24	26	.25	.33	26	.10	−.20	26	.34	−.03	26	.89	−.44	26	.03
Northern Piedmont	.54	18	.02	.68	18	.00	−.77	18	.00	.54	18	.02	−.75	18	.00
Tidewater	.41	18	.09	.61	18	.01	−.72	18	.00	.48	18	.05	−.85	18	.00
Urban	−.44	5	.45	.87	5	.06	−.12	5	.85	−.37	5	.55	−.63	5	.26
Statewide	−.00	93	.97	.50	93	.00	−.44	93	.00	−.07	93	.56	−.54	93	.00

Notes

Chapter 1

1. For a provocative discussion of the rise of mass education, see John E. Craig, "The Expansion of Education," *Reviews of Research on Education* 9 (1981):151–213.

2. On the early development of common schools, consult Ellwood P. Cubberley, *Public Education in the United States* (Boston, 1934), pp. 12–40; Patricia Cline Cohen, *A Calculating People: The Spread of Numeracy in Early America* (Chicago, 1982); and Carl F. Kaestle, *Pillars of the Republic: Common Schools and American Society, 1780–1860* (New York, 1983).

3. For general discussions, see Frederick M. Binder, *The Age of the Common School, 1830–1865* (New York, 1974); Kaestle, *Pillars of the Republic*; and David B. Tyack, *The One Best System: A History of Urban Education* (Cambridge, Mass., 1974). For local studies of urban school systems, see Stanley Schultz, *The Culture Factory: Boston Schools, 1789–1860* (New York, 1973), pp. 38–100; Selwyn K. Troen, *The Public and the Schools: Shaping the St. Louis System, 1838–1920* (Columbia, Mo., 1975); and Carl F. Kaestle, *The Evolution of an Urban School System: New York City, 1750–1850* (Cambridge, Mass., 1973).

4. Jonathan Messerli, *Horace Mann: A Biography* (New York, 1972), and Kaestle, *Pillars of the Republic*.

5. Urban schools have, in general, occupied a preeminent position in the discussion of the historical evolution of American public education, from early twentieth-century treatments by Cubberley and Edgar Wallace Knight to more recent "revisionist" accounts. Three correctives are David B. Tyack, "The Spread of Public Schooling in Victorian America: In Search of a Reinterpretation," *History of Education* 7 (1978):591–613; William A. Link, "Making the 'Inarticulate' Speak: A Reassessment of Public Education in the Rural South, 1870–1920," *Journal of Thought* 18 (1983):63–75; and Wayne Fuller, *The Old Country School: The Story of Rural Education in the Middle West* (Chicago, 1982).

6. Carl F. Kaestle and Maris V. Vinovskis, *Education and Social Change in Nineteenth-Century Massachusetts* (Cambridge, Eng., 1980), Tables 2.1 and 2.2, pp. 12, 15; Lee Soltow and Edward Stevens, "Economic Aspects of School: Participation in Mid-Nineteenth-Century United States," *Journal of Interdisciplinary History* 8 (1977):Table 3, p. 231. In the same vein, see Lee Soltow and Edward Stevens, *The Rise of Literacy and the Common School in the United States: A Socioeconomic Analysis to 1870* (Chicago, 1981). On the impact of localism, see Binder, *Age of the Common School*, pp. 93–94; and Kaestle, *Pillars of the Republic*, pp. 136–81.

225

226 · *Notes to Pages 6–8*

7. A. C. Monahan, *The Status of Rural Education in the United States*, U.S. Bureau of Education Bulletin 8 (Washington, D.C., 1913), Tables ii and viii, pp. 18, 23. For other discussions of the history of American rural education, see David Tyack, "The Tribe and the Common School: Community Control in Rural Education," *American Quarterly* 24 (1972):3–19; Patricia Albjerg Graham, *Community and Class in American Education, 1865–1914* (New York, 1974), pp. 58–60, 95–99, 101–41.

8. See, for example, the following autobiographical or semiautobiographical accounts: Millard Fillmore Kennedy, *Schoolmaster of Yesterday: A Three-Generation Story* (New York, 1940); A. H. Nelson, "The Little Red Schoolhouse," *Educational Review* 23 (Mar. 1902):304–15; Edward F. Dale, "Teaching on the Prairie Plains, 1890–1900," *Mississippi Valley Historical Review* 33 (1946–47):293–307.

9. Monahan, *Status of Rural Education* and U.S. Department of Interior, *Census of Agriculture, 1900* (Washington, D.C., 1902), Table 13, pp. 158–71.

10. Guion Griffis Johnson, *Ante-Bellum North Carolina: A Social History* (Chapel Hill, 1937), pp. 257–62. On southern undereducation, see Soltow and Stevens, "School Participation," Tables 1 and 2, pp. 226, 230.

11. Quoted in Johnson, *Ante-Bellum North Carolina*, p. 262. On slave education, see Thomas L. Webber, *Deep Like the River: Education in the Slave Quarter Community, 1831–1865* (New York, 1978); Betty Mansfield, " 'That Fateful Class': Black Teachers of Virginia's Freedmen, 1861–1882" (Ph.D. dissertation, Catholic University of America, 1980), pp. 4, 18–44. But compare these views with the interpretations of early twentieth-century historians of southern education, especially that of Edgar Wallace Knight, who argued that there was a strong continuity between antebellum and postbellum schools.

12. On postrevolutionary and antebellum southern education, consult Merrill D. Peterson, *Thomas Jefferson and the New Nation: A Biography* (New York, 1970); Dumas Malone, *Jefferson and His Time*, 6 vols. (Boston, 1948–81), 1:280–83; James D. Conant, *Thomas Jefferson and the Development of American Public Education* (Berkeley, 1962); Edgar W. Knight, *Public Education in the South* (New York, 1922), pp. 160–268; William Arthur Maddox, *The Free School Idea in Virginia before the Civil War: A Phase of Political and Social Evolution* (New York, 1918), pp. 126–53; Knight, *Public School Education in North Carolina* (Boston, 1916), pp. 113–91; and Johnson, *Ante-Bellum North Carolina*, pp. 259–82.

13. Quoted by Lester Lamon, "Black Public Education in the South: By Whom, for Whom and under Whose Control?" *Journal of Thought* 18 (1983):76–90. On the impact of the Civil War, see Cornelius J. Heatwole, *A History of Education in Virginia* (New York, 1916), p. 103; Maddox, *Free School Idea*, pp. 154–69; and Knight, *Public Education in the South*, pp. 198–215, 246–50, 258–61. On Reconstruction and black education, see James D. Anderson, "Ex-Slaves and the Rise of Universal Education in the South, 1860–1880," in Ronald K. Goodenow and Arthur O. White, eds., *Education and the Rise of the New South* (Boston, 1981), pp. 1–25.

14. On northern educational efforts during and after the Civil War, see Henry L. Swint, *The Northern Teacher in the South, 1862–1870* (Nashville, 1941); Jacqueline Jones, *Soldiers of Light and Love: Northern Teachers and Georgia Blacks,*

1865–1873 (Chapel Hill, 1980); Robert Morris, *Reading, 'Riting, and Reconstruction: The Education of Freedmen in the South, 1861–1870* (Chicago, 1981); Willie Lee Rose, *Rehearsal for Reconstruction: The Port Royal Experiment* (New York, 1964); Ronald E. Butchart, *Northern Schools, Southern Blacks, and Reconstruction* (Westport, Conn., 1980); and Alrutheus A. Taylor, *The Negro in the Reconstruction of Virginia* (Washington, D.C., 1926), pp. 137–73.

15. Heatwole, *History of Education in Virginia*, p. 214.

16. For discussions of southern public education and the Reconstruction constitutions, see Knight, *Public Education in the South*, pp. 337–82, and *The Influence of Reconstruction on Education in the South* (New York, 1913). For more detailed treatments, see Daniel J. Whitener, "The Republican Party and Public Education in North Carolina," *North Carolina Historical Review* 38 (1960):372–86; Thomas E. Cochran, *History of Public-School Education in Florida* (Lancaster, Pa., 1922), pp. 49–50; Richard Andrew Meade, "A History of the Constitutional Provisions for Education in Virginia" (Ph.D. dissertation, University of Virginia, 1941); and Jack Maddex, *The Virginia Conservatives, 1867–1879: A Study in Reconstruction Politics* (Chapel Hill, 1970), pp. 204–17.

17. *Annual Report of the School Board of Richmond, 1902* (Richmond, 1902), Table 10, pp. 34–35.

18. For divergent approaches to postwar Virginia, see Allen W. Moger, *Virginia: Bourbonism to Byrd, 1870–1925* (Charlottesville, 1968); and Crandall Shiftlett, *Patronage and Poverty in the Tobacco South: Louisa County, Virginia, 1860–1900* (Knoxville, 1982).

19. *Richmond Dispatch*, 23 July 1884, 9 Jan. 1885.

20. Thomas Nelson Page, *The Old Dominion: Her Making and Her Manners* (New York, 1908), p. 298.

21. Edward A. Freeman, *Some Impressions of the United States* (London, 1883), p. 222.

22. This and the following discussion is drawn partly from published census data discussed in the Appendix. For an interesting treatment of the significance of topography in Virginia, see Rhys Isaac, *The Transformation of Virginia, 1740–1790* (Chapel Hill, 1982).

23. These and other percentages are compiled from published census data in William A. Link, "Public Schools and Social Change in Rural Virginia, 1870–1920" (Ph.D. dissertation, University of Virginia, 1981), Tables 2.4 and 2.5, p. 44.

24. *Richmond Dispatch*, 29 July 1871; see also *Richmond Exchange Reporter*, 28 Jan. 1892, and Edward A. Pollard, *The Virginia Tourist Sketches of the Springs and Mountains of Virginia* (Philadelphia, 1870), pp. 264–65.

25. Ellen Glasgow, *Barren Ground* (New York, 1925), pp. 31, 48.

26. "Report of Robert Frazer, Field Agent of the Southern Education Board for Virginia," typed MS, 24 Dec. 1902, Papers of Hollis Burke Frissell, Hampton University Archives, Hampton, Va.

27. Peter Saunders to Fleming Saunders, 20 Mar. 1874, Papers of the Irvine and Saunders Families, University of Virginia Library, Charlottesville.

28. Page, *Old Dominion*, pp. 332–33, 335.

29. Freeman, *Some Impressions of the United States*, p. 98.

30. Wilbur J. Cash, *The Mind of the South* (New York, 1941), p. 68.

31. For early portraits of Ruffner, see Heatwole, *History of Education in Virginia*, p. 241; Charles C. Pearson, "William Henry Ruffner, Reconstruction Statesman of Virginia," *South Atlantic Quarterly* 20 (1921):25–32, 137–51; Early Lee Fox, "William Henry Ruffner and the Rise of the Public Free School System," *John P. Branch Papers of Randolph-Macon College* 3 (1912):123–44. For a more recent view, see Walter J. Fraser, Jr., "William Henry Ruffner: A Liberal in the Old and New South" (Ph.D. dissertation, University of Tennessee, 1970), and Fraser, "William Henry Ruffner and the Establishment of Virginia's Public School System," *Virginia Magazine of History and Biography* 89 (1971):259–79.

32. *Richmond Evening State Journal*, quoted by Fraser, "Ruffner," p. 275.

33. Quoted in Pearson, "Ruffner," pp. 31–32.

34. Fraser, "Ruffner," p. 262.

35. For examples of such opposition, see *Second Annual Report of the Superintendent of Public Instruction of Virginia* (Richmond, 1872), p. 48; *Sixth Annual Report of the Superintendent of Public Instruction of Virginia* (Richmond, 1876); John B. Minor to Ruffner, 2, 3 May 1870, Papers of William Henry Ruffner, Historical Foundation of the Presbyterian and Reformed Churches, Montreat, N.C.

36. Fraser, "Ruffner," p. 263; James Tice Moore, *Two Paths to the New South: The Virginia Debt Controversy, 1870–1883* (Lexington, Ky., 1974), provides the most complete and lucid account of this tangled controversy.

37. The following discussion is based on the account in Charles William Dabney, *Universal Education in the South*, 2 vols. (Chapel Hill, 1936), 1:154–58, and on the scrapbooks of newspaper clippings in the Ruffner Papers.

38. Dabney, *Universal Education*, 1:159–60.

39. Pearson, "Ruffner," p. 138.

40. *Educational Journal of Virginia* 2 (Sept. 1871):438–39; *Fifth Annual Report of the Superintendent of Public Instruction of Virginia* (Richmond, 1875), pp. 114–15. See also William H. Ruffner, "Concluding Remarks: Chiefly Personal," 1881, MS in Ruffner Papers.

41. In 1870, there were 2,158 white and 706 black schools; by 1900, these numbers had risen to 6,587 and 2,335, respectively. The absolute numbers of enrolled and attending pupils tripled during the same period—from 128,288 enrolled and 75,722 attending to 370,595 enrolled and 216,264 attending—and the numbers of teachers grew from 3,014 to 8,954. See *First Annual Report of the Superintendent of Public Instruction* (Richmond, 1871), Table 2, pp. 156–73; *Biennial Report of the Superintendent of Public Instruction . . . 1899–1900 and 1900–1901* (Richmond, 1901), Tables 1 and 2, pp. 104–10.

42. Statewide and regionally, state involvement either did not correlate significantly or did so negatively with school expansion. Thus statewide the Pearson correlation coefficient for the number of days county superintendents were employed in 1900 and the average school session for the same year was .06 (N = 97, p = .59)—a coefficient and significance level that indicate the absence of any relationship. In no region were the Pearson coefficients any clearer or more significant. Another measure of state involvement was per capita expenditure of state funds. In this instance, state involvement, if anything, tended to have an inverse relationship with school expansion—that is, lower state funds tended to correspond with longer school terms, and vice versa. Thus statewide the Pear-

son correlation coefficient for per capita state funds in 1900 and school session in the same year was − .19 (N = 99, p = .06). The relationship was more clearly inverse in the Tidewater, where the coefficient was − .51 (N = 21, p = .02), and in the urbanized counties, where the coefficient was − .91 (N = 5, p = .03). For further discussion of the calculation of and data for these statistics, see Appendix, note on method.

43. For a discussion of the importance of enrollments in understanding nine-teenth-century rural education, see John W. Meyer, David B. Tyack, Joane Nagel, and Audri Gordon, "Public Education as Nation-Building in America: Enroll-ments and Bureaucratization in the American States, 1870–1930," *American Jour-nal of Sociology* 85 (1979):591–613.

44. For both races, enrollment west of the Blue Ridge was higher than the state average. See Appendix 1.3.

45. If anything there was a striking alinearity or unrelatedness between enroll-ments and the local economy at the state level. The coefficients for wealth and enrollments for both races statewide were very low, and those for land tenure were no clearer. Enrollments appear to be only slightly more related to the type of crop. For whites, lower enrollment corresponded weakly but at a significant level (p = .04) with a county's tobacco production but was statistically unrelated to the production of the other major crops of cotton and peanuts. For blacks, enrollments did not correspond to either cotton or tobacco production, but the coefficient (.31) for peanuts and its significance level (.00) suggest a relationship. See Appendixes 5.2 and 5.3.

46. Statewide, population density was not a significant factor; regionally, it was a factor in black enrollments in Appalachia and white enrollments in the Tidewater. In contrast, race—especially for black enrollments—corresponded with depressed community involvement in schools. The coefficients for enroll-ments and type of crop indicate the absence of a relationship. Yet the Pearson *r* for tobacco production and white enrollment suggests an inverse relationship—that is, the higher a county's tobacco production, the lower its enrollment—while that for peanut production and black enrollment (statewide and especially in the Southside) suggests a positive relationship—that is, black enrollment tended to increase with peanut production. The role of literacy was similarly ambiguous. Statewide, adult black literacy associated with higher white enroll-ment but appeared to have no correspondence with black enrollment. Adult white literacy corresponded with higher white enrollment in the Tidewater but negatively with black enrollment in the same region.

47. Frank A. Magruder, *Recent Administration in Virginia* (Baltimore, 1912), p. 19.

48. See Appendix 1.6. This intraregional gap also existed in county level school funds. The Southside and Tidewater, both spending 12 cents per capita in county funds for schools, expended only about a third as much as did the five urbanized counties.

49. See Appendix 1.1. The major intraregional difference in school term ap-peared to be mainly between rural and urban areas. With the exception of Appa-lachia, the four other regions were only slightly above or slightly below the state average.

50. See Appendixes 5.4 and 5.5.

51. Broken down by region, it is clear that diverse factors affected educational quality as measured by school session and district expenditures. In western Virginia, the most important factors were wealth, race, population density, and landownership; type of crop and literacy seemed to play a small role. In these counties, one can only speculate about the importance of race. It may reflect discrimination, although this would be a factor only in the case of school session and not of district funding. Particularly because race was a less important variable in eastern Virginia—and associated negatively with district funding in the northern Piedmont (although at a significance level of .06)—race may more closely express the fact that economic opportunity and wealth generally meant, in western Virginia, a larger black population. In some instances, moreover, the statistical correlations in the regions were at variance with statewide tendencies. Thus black landownership corresponded with longer terms in Appalachia and the Southside but with shorter ones in the Tidewater; population density associated with longer terms in Appalachia and the Tidewater and higher expenditures in the northern Piedmont but with lower expenditures in the Valley. Literacy correlated with school session and expenditures in regions with low black and white literacy—Appalachia and the Southside. In Appalachia, white and black literacy thus corresponded with higher expenditures; in the Southside, black and white literacy corresponded at high levels with both school term and district expenditures. Type of crop was a significant variable only in correlations between tobacco production and school expansion in the Southside and northern Piedmont—but there it correlated in opposite directions. In the Southside, tobacco production associated with shorter terms, but in the northern Piedmont, it corresponded with higher district outlays.

Chapter 2

1. Richard L. McCormick, "The Party Period and Public Policy," *Journal of American History* 66 (1979):279–98, provides a fresh look at the nature of nineteenth-century distributive governance.

2. Nancy Lucile Cox, "The History and Development of the Office of the Virginia State Department of Education" (M.A. thesis, University of Virginia, 1943), p. 100. See also Ruffner's description in his MS history of the Virginia public school system, Papers of William Henry Ruffner, Historical Foundation of the Presbyterian and Reformed Churches, Montreat, N.C.

3. Diary of Benjamin Mosby Smith, 3 Jan. 1832, Records of the Lexington Presbytery, Synod of Virginia, Presbyterian and Reformed Churches of America, Union Theological Seminary Library, Richmond, Va., microfilm copy. The figure for length of employment of county superintendents is an average for the period 1870 to 1900. There was considerable regional variation in the employment and activities of county superintendents. Measured by both days employed and miles traveled, the county superintendents were busier in 1900 in the Valley and Southside and below average in Appalachia, the northern Piedmont, and the Tidewater. See Appendix 1.0.

4. Mrs. J. K. Campbell to Ruffner, 25 Jan. 1882, Ruffner Papers. Also see J. C. Speer to Andrew Jackson Montague, 12 Feb. 1901, Papers of Andrew Jackson Montague, Virginia State Library, Richmond; J. William Jones to Thomas White Sydnor, 10 June 1870; Sydnor to Blanch Sydnor, 15 Mar. 1871; T. W. Beckham to Sydnor, 8 Feb. 1872, Papers of Thomas White Sydnor, University of Virginia Library, Charlottesville.

5. Robert Frazer, report to the Southern Education Board, 30 May 1903, Papers of Charles Duncan McIver, University of North Carolina at Greensboro Library.

6. *Educational Journal of Virginia* 1 (May 1870):211; Burnette N. Bell to Andrew J. Montague, 9 Mar. 1901, Montague Papers; George H. Southall to Sydnor, 3 May 1870, Sydnor Papers; F. M. Gates to Montague, 9 Mar. 1901, Montague Papers.

7. William A. Link, "Public Schools and Social Change in Rural Virginia, 1870–1920" (Ph.D. dissertation, University of Virginia, 1981), Table 5.1, p. 152.

8. Richard T. McIlwaine, "Some Essentials in the Improvement of Our Public Schools," *Addresses and Papers Bearing Chiefly on Education* (Richmond, 1908), pp. 93–94.

9. Ruffner to the county superintendents, circular, 1 Oct. 1870, printed in *Educational Journal of Virginia* 1 (Oct. 1870):397.

10. J. B. McInturff to Henry H. Coffman, 25 Nov., 8 Dec. 1886, Papers of the Ashby District School Board (Shenandoah County), University of Virginia Library, Charlottesville. For another example of the reluctance of county superintendents to intervene in local decisions, see the Minutebook of the Gainesville District School Board, 22 Sept. 1877, Prince William County School Board Records, Prince William County School Board Records Center, Manassas, Va.

11. Ruffner to the county superintendents, 1 Oct. 1870, p. 398. For other descriptions of local school governance, see Frank A. Magruder, *Recent Administration in Virginia* (Baltimore, 1912), pp. 18–19, 15; Albert O. Porter, *County Government in Virginia: A Legislative History, 1607–1904* (New York, 1947), pp. 243–46, 259–60, 270–71.

12. Sydnor, written report to the state superintendent, 12 Sept. 1872, Sydnor Papers. See also George B. Keezell's comment, 19 Nov. 1901, in the *Report of the Proceedings and Debates of the Constitutional Convention of the State of Virginia Held in the City of Richmond June 12, 1901 to June 26, 1902*, 2 vols. (Richmond, 1906), 1:1135.

13. Porter, *County Government in Virginia*, pp. 256–57.

14. A. F. Morgan to Sydnor, 27 Jan. 1872, Sydnor Papers.

15. Porter, *County Government in Virginia*, p. 286.

16. See, for example, Minutes of the School Board of Nelson County, Virginia, 7 Sept. 1874; Ruffner to Sydnor, 7 July, 6 Oct. 1873, Sydnor Papers.

17. William Burton, Jr., warrant summoning Sydnor, 19 Apr. 1873, Sydnor Papers; G. W. Koontz to Henry H. Coffman, 8 Dec. 1883, Ashby School Board Papers.

18. Wyatt H. Walker et al. to W. C. Tate, 21 Oct. 1871, Papers of W. C. Tate, University of Virginia Library, Charlottesville; Gainesville School Board Minutebook, 4 Oct. 1884. See also H. H. Coffman to Joseph Perry, 18 Nov. 1881, Ashby School Board Papers.

19. M. Frankhouser to M. H. Hefner, handwritten copy, 15 Mar. 1873, Ashby School Board Papers; Gainesville School Board Minutebook, 1 Sept. 1883. For a similar situation in a black school, see ibid., 19 Jan. 1878. Over time, the tendency was for district boards to own schoolhouses. In 1870, they owned only 7 percent of all schoolhouses; by 1900, this figure had increased to about 87 percent (*Annual Report of the Superintendent of Public Instruction . . . 1911–1912* [Richmond, 1914], p. 45).

20. Ashby School Board Minutebook, 24 Sept. 1884; see also ibid., 16 Oct. 1876; "A Country Teacher" to the editor, 11 Mar. 1902, *Richmond Times*, 16 Mar. 1902.

21. Charles G. Maphis, "State Board of Examiners," *Virginia Journal of Education* 4 (Oct. 1910):12.

22. Sussex County, Virginia, School Board, *Sussex County: A Tale of Three Centuries* (Richmond, 1942), pp. 140–41; Affidavit of John S. Hale, 24 Jan. 1886, Papers of the Saunders Family, Virginia Historical Society, Richmond. See also Major William H. Johnson, "Autobiography," typed MS transcript, Papers of William H. Johnson, Virginia State University Library, Petersburg, Va.

23. George W. Dame to W. C. Tate, 25 Feb. 1872, Tate Papers; Colonel W. G. Jeffries to Sydnor, 29 Aug. 1874, Sydnor Papers; Nelson County School Board Minutebook, 4, 5 Aug. 1886; the Reverend S. H. Thompson, "Present Condition of Our Public Schools," *Richmond Times*, 2 Mar. 1902; Robert J. Jeffries to William Gregory Rennolds, 28 Aug. 1912, Papers of William Gregory Rennolds, Virginia State Library, Richmond.

24. For examples of teachers' contracts and how they were drawn up, see *Sixteenth Annual Report of the Superintendent of Public Instruction of Virginia* (Richmond, 1886), p. 19; and Records of the Madison School District, Charlotte County, Virginia, 1874, University of Virginia Library, Charlottesville.

25. T.B. to the editor, 8 July 1875, *Southern Workman* 4 (Sept. 1875):71. For other examples of irregular school sessions, see J. L. Will to Perry, 15 Oct. 1880, Ashby School Board Papers; Nelson County School Board Minutebook, 7 Aug. 1881.

26. T. W. Smith to Sydnor, 7 July 1873, Sydnor Papers; J. to the editor, *Southern Workman* 3 (June 1876):49; S. W. Dickinson to Judge Addison L. Holladay, 8 Mar. 1901, Montague Papers; A. J. Myers to H. H. Coffman, 26 Feb. 1884, Ashby School Board Papers.

27. E. to the editor, 29 Oct. 1875, *Southern Workman* 4 (Dec. 1875):95.

28. Ruffner to Sydnor, 18 Aug. 1874, Sydnor Papers.

29. Gainesville School Board Minutebook, 20 Oct. 1877, 24 Oct. 1891; patrons of Bellefonte School District (Nottoway Co.) to Sydnor, 15 July 1874, Sydnor Papers; C. L. Proctor to W. J. Gibert, 25 Sept. 1881, Ashby School Board Papers.

30. S. M. Bowman to Perry, 3 Oct. 1881; W. J. Gibert to Perry, 2 Oct. 1881; see also B. J. Staunton to Perry, 18 Feb. 1878; Coffman to Perry, 26 Oct. 1878; and E. S. Calvert to Perry, 6 Oct. 1881, all in Ashby School Board Papers.

31. Ashby School Board Minutebook, 14 Sept., 2 Oct. 1884; G. J. Jones to Reamur Coleman Stearnes, 24 Aug. 1915, Papers of Reamur Coleman Stearnes, University of Virginia Library, Charlottesville; see also Gainesville School Board Minutebook, 27 July 1895.

32. S. H. Thompson, "Present Condition of Our Public Schools," *Richmond Times*, 2 Mar. 1902; John H. Grabill to Perry, 11 Feb. 1880, and W. J. Gibert to Perry, 20 Sept. 1881, Ashby School Board Papers. See also Jeffries to Rennolds, 16 Mar. 1917, Rennolds Papers.

33. The patrons of Old School to David P. Powers, 1 Oct. 1886, and James W. Calhoun to Powers, 25 Oct. 1886, Papers of David P. Powers, University of Virginia Library, Charlottesville.

34. W. H. Johnson, speech, ca. 1899, handwritten copy, W. H. Johnson Papers; McIlwaine, "Some Essentials," pp. 93–94.

35. *Nineteenth Annual Report of the Superintendent of Public Instruction of Virginia* (Richmond, 1889), pp. 34–35.

36. Ruffner to Sydnor, Aug. 1874, Sydnor Papers; George E. Caskie to Alexander J. Bondurant, 7 Aug. 1891, Papers of the Bondurant and Morrison Families, University of Virginia Library, Charlottesville.

37. Fauton Ruiker to the Ashby School Board, 28 Sept. 1881, Ashby School Board Papers; Francis Simmons to the editor, *Virginia Journal of Education* 9 (Nov. 1915):142. For other examples, see Col. B. M. Jones to Sydnor, 21 Aug. 1875, Sydnor Papers; Jessie M. Jones to Bondurant, 2 Feb. 1891, and E. R. Evans to Bondurant, 22 Oct. 1891, Bondurant-Morrison Family Papers.

38. A. W. Barksdale to Sydnor, 26 June 1875, Sydnor Papers; W. to the editor, 8 Dec. 1880, *Southern Workman* 10 (Feb. 1881):18.

39. Carl F. Kaestle, "Social Change, Discipline, and the Common School in Early Nineteenth-Century America," *Journal of Interdisciplinary History* 9 (1978): 1–17.

40. W. H. Johnson, "Autobiography"; Edward Eggleston, *The Hoosier School-Master* (New York, 1871); James Luther Kibler, "Autobiography, 1867–1950," MS, Virginia State Library, Richmond.

41. *Second Annual Report of the Superintendent of Public Instruction of Virginia* (Richmond, 1872), pp. 28–29.

42. Grabill to Perry, 11 Feb. 1880, Ashby School Board Papers; see also Fauton Ruiker to the Ashby School Board, 28 Sept. 1881, ibid.; J.R.S. to the editor, 30 Nov. 1884, *Southern Workman* 14 (Aug. 1885):88; Claude A. Swanson, address, Nov. 1906, printed copy, in Papers of James Gibson Johnson, University of Virginia Library, Charlottesville.

43. Ashby School Board Minutebook, 26 Dec. 1884; James W. Calhoun to Powers, 25 Oct. 1886, Powers Papers; see also Gainesville School Board Minutebook, 13 Sept. 1884; Ashby School Board Minutebook, 29 Nov. 1886.

44. Ashby School Board Minutebook, 3 Dec. 1883; W. W. Logan to Coffman, 28 Jan. 1884, Ashby School Board Papers.

45. Walter A. Watson, 19 Nov. 1901, *Virginia Constitutional Convention Debates, 1901–1902*, 1:1133. See also Virginia Randolph, in Lance George Edward Jones, *The Jeanes Teacher in the United States, 1908–1933: An Account of Twenty-Five Years' Experience in the Supervision of Negro Rural Schools* (Chapel Hill, 1933), pp. 29–30; Helen V. Babyok to Rennolds, 15 Feb. 1923, Rennolds Papers. For other examples of teacher-student conflict over discipline, see Gainesville School Board Minutebook, 23 Nov. 1889, 27 Feb. 1892; and Minutebook of the Brentsville District School Board, 1 Sept. 1908, Prince William

County School Board Records Center, Manassas, Va.

46. W. G. Cooke to Rennolds, 24 Oct. 1916; Hilda M. Davis to Rennolds, 26 Feb. 1917; Jeffries to Rennolds, 5 Feb. 1917, Rennolds Papers; see also Brentsville School Board Minutebook, 16 Mar. 1915.

47. James T. Taylor, "A Historical Sketch of the Free Schools of Bland County," *Fifteenth Annual Report of the Superintendent of Public Instruction of Virginia* (Richmond, 1885), p. 55.

48. Sydnor, handwritten report, 12 Sept. 1872, Sydnor Papers.

49. See Coffman to Perry, 28 Sept. 1878, 8 Oct. 1881, Ashby School Board Papers.

50. Inventory of Prince William County schools, ca. 1921; Thomas Jones, statement, 10 Aug. 1874, Prince William County School Board Records.

51. J. B. Whitehead to the Staunton District School Board (Pittsylvania County), 12 Aug. 1872, Tate Papers; Ashby School Board Minutebook, 19 Mar. 1879; J. W. Ruby, J. E. Cooper, and George Maphis to A. J. Meyers, 3 Mar. 1879; Coffman to Perry, 4 Mar. 1881, Ashby School Board Papers.

52. Taylor, "Historical Sketch," p. 55; Coffman to Perry, 7 Nov. 1879, Ashby School Board Papers; John D. Maupin et al. to Powers, 23 Sept. 1886, Powers Papers; see also N. B. Painter to Perry and Myers, 20 Sept. 1899, Ashby School Board Papers.

53. Gainesville School Board Minutebook, 14 Aug. 1880.

54. Virginia was no exception in this regard. See C. Vann Woodward, *The Strange Career of Jim Crow*, 3d ed., rev. (New York, 1974), p. 24.

55. *Educational Journal of Virginia* 1 (Oct. 1870):400. I have come across no references to black trustees during this period.

56. Louis R. Harlan, *Separate and Unequal: Public School Campaigns and Racism in the Southern Seaboard States, 1901–1915* (Chapel Hill, 1958), p. 140.

57. Gainesville School Board Minutebook, 27 Feb. 1892; J. D. Eggleston to Hollis B. Frissell, 19 Feb. 1902, Papers of Hollis B. Frissell, Hampton University Archives, Hampton, Va.

58. *Biennial Report of the Superintendent of Public Instruction... 1907–1908 and 1908–1909* (Richmond, 1910), Table 4, pp. 442–45.

59. See the comments of one black teacher, Mary C. Taylor, in the proceedings of the Triennial Reunion of Hampton Alumni Association, 28 May 1893, in Louis R. Harlan et al., eds., *The Booker T. Washington Papers*, 13 vols. (Urbana, 1972–84), 3:331–32.

60. Edward P. Buford to Montague, 7 Sept. 1904, Papers of the Virginia State Board of Education, Virginia State Library, Richmond.

61. Henry Williams et al., petition, 5 May 1875, W. H. Johnson Papers.

62. Overall, the ratio of black teachers to black schools increased from .63 in 1880 to .94 in 1900 (*Tenth Annual Report of the Superintendent of Public Instruction of Virginia* [Richmond, 1880], Table 3, pp. 29–31; *Biennial Report of the Superintendent of Public Instruction... 1899–1900 and 1900–1901* [Richmond, 1901], Table 2, pp. 108–10).

63. Two letters quoted in the *Southern Workman* 3 (Mar. 1876):19.

64. M. to the editor, 13 Oct. 1885, ibid. 15 (Jan. 1886):6; W. B. Weaver to the editor, 9 Apr. 1881, ibid. 10 (May 1881):51; Hollis B. Frissell, "A Horse-Back Trip

through Tidewater Virginia," ibid. 12 (July 1883):81; Frissell, "A Horseback Trip through Gloucester Co., Va.," ibid. 12 (Oct. 1883):101.

65. George T. Taylor to the editor, 15 Mar. 1875, ibid. 4 (May 1875):39.

Chapter 3

1. *Educational Journal of Virginia* 3 (Nov. 1871):33. Ruffner established the minimum average daily attendance as twenty in 1871, but he made exceptions "where providential hindrances prevent the legal average." He also ruled that the legal average could be lowered to fifteen with the approval of the district board and the county superintendent. See Ruffner to Thomas White Sydnor, 25 Jan., 12 Feb. 1873, Papers of Thomas White Sydnor, University of Virginia Library, Charlottesville.

2. Minutebook of the Gainesville School Board, 24 Nov. 1894, Prince William County School Board Records, Prince William County School Board Records Center, Manassas, Va.; *Educational Journal of Virginia* 14 (Nov. 1883):343.

3. Gainesville School Board Minutebook, 23 Aug. 1890; *Second Annual Report of the Superintendent of Public Instruction of Virginia* (Richmond, 1872), p. 57.

4. *Educational Journal of Virginia* 14 (Sept. 1883):278.

5. Henry H. Coffman to Joseph Perry, 20 Oct. 1880, Papers of the Ashby District School Board (Shenandoah County, Virginia); Ashby School Board Minutebook, 20 Nov. 1883, University of Virginia Library, Charlottesville.

6. Coffman to Perry, 9 Oct. 1881, ibid.; Gainesville School Board Minutebook, 27 Jan. 1894; George E. Caskie, "Needful School Legislation," *Virginia School Journal* 1 (Jan. 1892):11.

7. See C. Wirt Trainham to William G. Rennolds, 17 Oct. 1916, Papers of William Gregory Rennolds, Virginia State Library, Richmond; *Educational Journal of Virginia* 14 (Nov. 1883):345.

8. The Reverend S. H. Thompson, "Present Condition of Our Public Schools," *Richmond Times*, 2 Mar. 1902; Roy K. Flannagan, *Sanitary Survey of the Schools of Orange County, Va.*, U.S. Bureau of Education Bulletin 17 (Washington, D.C., 1914), p. 22; S. to the editor, 11 Nov. 1877, *Southern Workman* 7 (Jan. 1878):4; W. to the editor, 1 Dec. 1877, ibid.

9. D. to the editor, Thanksgiving Day 1878, *Southern Workman* 8 (Jan. 1879):6; girl quoted in Sue Childs Cleaton, "How We Secured a Library in Every Rural School in Our Counties," undated, Papers of Albert J. Bourland, Southern Education Board Papers, Southern Historical Collection, University of North Carolina, Chapel Hill; Irene Goodman to Alexander J. Bondurant, 25 Aug. 1891, Papers of the Bondurant and Morrison Families, University of Virginia Library, Charlottesville; interview with George E. Caskie, 1 Feb. 1902, *Richmond Times*, 5 Feb. 1902.

10. James T. Taylor, "A Historical Sketch of the Free Schools of Bland County," *Fifteenth Annual Report of the Superintendent of Public Instruction of Virginia* (Richmond, 1885), p. 55; M. to the editor, 21 Mar. 1879, *Southern Workman* 8 (June 1879):66; T. to the editor, 5 Feb. 1883, ibid. 12 (Sept. 1883):96; unsigned letter to R. R. Farr, 25 June 1882, *Educational Journal of Virginia* 13 (Aug.

1882):305. Between 1870 and 1900, the frame schoolhouse came to replace the log cabin as typical for Virginia. Thus, in 1870 59 percent of all schoolhouses were log cabins and 34 percent frame, whereas in 1900 16 percent were log and 81 percent frame (*Annual Report of the Superintendent of Public Instruction... 1911–1912* [Richmond, 1914], p. 45).

11. Rhea C. Scott, "How a Rural School was Remade," undated, Bourland Papers; Mrs. Willis Johnson, term report for black school No. 9, Blendon School District, Nottoway County, Virginia, 5 Dec. 1877, Sydnor Papers.

12. James Gibson Johnson, "Autobiography, 1871–1909," MS, Papers of James Gibson Johnson, University of Virginia Library, Charlottesville.

13. T. to the editor, *Southern Workman* 12 (Sept. 1883):96.

14. James H. Dillard, "Statement I," memorandum for the Jeanes Fund, ca. June 1908, enclosed in Dillard to Samuel Chiles Mitchell, 3 June 1908, Papers of Samuel Chiles Mitchell, Library of Congress, Washington, D.C. The document is also available in the Papers of James Hardy Dillard, University of Virginia Library, Charlottesville. For whites, the student-teacher ratio increased from 20.7 in 1870 to 22.2 in 1900; for blacks it decreased from 47.6 to 30.4 during the same period. This figure was derived from the *First Annual Report of the Superintendent of Public Instruction of Virginia* (Richmond, 1871), and the *Biennial Report of the Superintendent of Public Instruction... 1899–1900 and 1900–1901*(Richmond, 1901), and is based on the number of students in average daily attendance divided by the total number of teachers.

15. For the data on the choice between public and private education, see *Twentieth Annual Report of the Superintendent of Public Instruction of Virginia* (Richmond, 1890), Table 11, pp. 84–87. For data on school session and enrollments and attendance, see Appendixes 1.1, 1.2, and 1.3. Statewide, mean white enrollment increased from 37 percent in 1870 to 61 percent in 1900, and black enrollment grew from 23 to 45 percent. Similarly, attendance increased for whites from 22 percent in 1870 to 37 percent in 1900 and for blacks from 14 to 25 percent. Obvious regional differences existed for enrollments and school sessions, with the Valley and Appalachia having higher enrollments and the Southside, northern Piedmont, and Tidewater having longer school sessions.

16. A. E. White to the editor, 8 Jan. 1877, *Southern Workman* 6 (Apr. 1877):31. On rural school participation, see Lee Soltow and Edward Stevens, "Economic Aspects of School Participation in Mid-Nineteenth Century United States," *Journal of Interdisciplinary History* 8 (1977); Soltow and Stevens, *The Rise of Literacy and the Common School in the United States: A Socioeconomic Analysis to 1870* (Chicago, 1981); and Wayne Fuller, *The Old Country School: The Story of Rural Education in the Middle West* (Chicago, 1982).

17. See, for example, Sallie H. Fitzgerald to Sydnor, 8 Feb. 1881, and Beulah Smithson to Sydnor, 4 Oct. 1888, Sydnor Papers.

18. Charles R. Pepper, "A Country School Problem," *Virginia School Journal* 12 (Jan. 1903):5; Superintendent's Annual Report, Rockingham County, Virginia, *Virginia Journal of Education* 4 (Oct. 1910):34.

19. Mary C. Robinson to the editor, 10 Jan. 1873, *Southern Workman* 2 (Feb. 1873):n.p.; S. to the editor, 30 Jan. 1878, ibid. 7 (Apr. 1878):28; Superintendent of King George and Stafford counties, quoted in *Second Annual Report*, p. 59.

20. J. G. Johnson, "Autobiography"; P. to the editor, 13 Nov. 1878, *Southern Workman* 8 (Jan. 1879):6; W.T.B. Williams, "Studies of Public Schools for Negroes in Virginia," Jan. 1905, MS in Papers of Mary Cooke Branch Munford, Virginia State Library, Richmond. For a recent discussion of school participation, see Soltow and Stevens, *Rise of Literacy*, p. 145.

21. J. Austin, report of a teachers' institute held at Hampton Institute, 1881, *Southern Workman* 10 (Aug. 1881):81; J. W. Borum, monthly report for black school No. 11, Haytokah School District, Nottoway County, Virginia, 27 June 1881, Sydnor Papers; Mc. to the editor, Apr. 1885, *Southern Workman* 14 (Aug. 1885):88.

22. This discussion is based upon the same data base used in the Appendix.

23. Race was a more important variable in attendance among both whites and blacks at the state level. Both of the correlation coefficients (− .33 for white attendance and − .20 for black attendance) were matched by significance levels of .00 for white attendance and .05 for black attendance. The documentary record confirms, moreover, the assertion that the injection of race tended to depress support for public education. See Appendixes 5.0 and 5.1.

24. Although tobacco correlated at a high and significant level with black attendance in urbanized counties, it recorded an abysmally low coefficient statewide (r = .00, N = 99, p = .97).

25. Population density correlated with white attendance statewide; the correlation was strong in the Tidewater. Although population density did not associate statewide with black attendance, it corresponded with higher black attendance in Appalachia and the Tidewater. Statewide adult black literacy associated with higher white attendance; in the Tidewater, literacy among both races was a factor. In contrast, only in the northern Piedmont did higher black attendance correspond with higher black literacy.

26. Soltow and Stevens, *Rise of Literacy*, pp. 121–25.

27. On national trends in the feminization of teaching, see Carl N. Degler, *At Odds: Women and the Family in America from the Revolution to the Present* (New York, 1980), pp. 379–80; and David B. Tyack, *The One Best System: A History of Urban Education* (Cambridge, Mass., 1974), p. 61. In Virginia, the trend toward feminization was more apparent in eastern and urban counties, especially for white teachers. Only about 50 percent of white teachers were females in Appalachia and the Valley in 1900, but the proportion was above three-quarters for eastern Virginia. Feminization among black teachers occurred at the slowest rate in Appalachia and at the fastest rate in the Tidewater. See Appendix 1.4.

28. Gainesville School Board Minutebook, 7 Jan. 1882. Although there was an appreciable difference between teachers' salaries in the urbanized counties and the rest of rural Virginia, there was not a major difference among the state's regions. Nor was the difference in salaries paid to males and females great—at least at the county level—as the region with the greatest disparity, the Valley, paid only 14 percent more for male teachers than it did for female teachers. See Appendix 1.7.

29. Ruffner to Sydnor, 26 Nov. 1873, Sydnor Papers; *Twentieth Annual Report*, Table 10, p. 47.

30. Wealth correlated strongly with teachers' pay, both for males and females, in Southside, Tidewater, and northern Piedmont counties; population density associated with higher pay in these regions and in the urbanized counties. See Appendixes 5.6 and 5.7.

31. Statewide, the proportion of blacks in a county's population associated with female teachers' salaries at a weak level; it appeared to be most important in Appalachia and the Southside. For both male and female teachers, literacy corresponded with higher pay; in all of the four possible combinations of white and black literacy and male and female teachers' salaries, the significance level was .00. In no instance was literacy an important variable in western Virginia, but in most of the regions of eastern Virginia it corresponded with higher salaries.

32. James Luther Kibler, "Autobiography, 1867–1950," MS, Virginia State Library, Richmond.

33. *Nineteenth Annual Report of the Superintendent of Public Instruction of Virginia* (Richmond, 1889), Table 11, p. 164.

34. George S. Funkhouser to superintendent of schools, Tyler, Texas, 5 Jan. 1896, the Papers of Andrew Funkhouser, Duke University Library, Durham, N.C.; *Fifteenth Annual Report*, Table 11, pp. 66–68.

35. Virginia Education Commission, *Report of the Survey Staff* (Richmond, 1919).

36. William H. Wilkins to the editor, 13 Jan. 1873, *Southern Workman* 2 (Feb. 1873):n.p.; W. A. Thompson to Sydnor, 16 Jan. 1875, Sydnor Papers; W. S. Kennedy to Perry, 8 Feb. 1875, Ashby School Board Papers.

37. P. to the editor, 16 Nov. 1878, *Southern Workman* 8 (Feb. 1879):17; Richard T. McIlwaine, "Some Essentials in the Improvement of Our Public Schools," *Addresses and Papers Bearing Chiefly on Education* (Richmond, 1908), p. 83.

38. Madison School District, Charlotte County, Virginia, Records, 1871–74, University of Virginia Library, Charlottesville; *Nineteenth Annual Report*, Table 11, p. 164; Virginia Education Commission, *Report of the Survey Staff*, p. 137.

39. Bennette W. Bagby to Bennette M. Bagby, 28 Feb. 1878, Papers of Bennette M. Bagby, Duke University Library, Durham, N.C.; Coffman to Perry, 29 Mar. 1878, Ashby School Board Papers; H. to the editor, 10 Nov. 1881, *Southern Workman* 11 (Nov. 1882):110.

40. Degler, *At Odds*, p. 375.

41. "Proceedings of the Triennial Reunion of the Hampton Alumni Association," 28 May 1893, in Louis R. Harlan et al., eds., *The Booker T. Washington Papers*, 13 vols. (Urbana, 1972–84), 3:329–30.

42. Ruffner, "Teachers," undated lecture, Papers of William Henry Ruffner, Historical Foundation of the Presbyterian and Reformed Churches, Montreat, N.C.; S. to the editor, 17 Feb. 1883, *Southern Workman* 12 (Dec. 1883):124.

43. "Proceedings of the Triennial Reunion," p. 330; T. to the editor, 30 Mar. 1876, *Southern Workman* 5 (June 1876):46; B. to the editor, 15 Dec. 1882, ibid. 12 (Apr. 1883):42.

44. Alice V. Goodman to Robert C. Mabry, 6 Sept. 1886, Papers of Robert C. Mabry, Duke University Library, Durham, N.C.

45. B. to the editor, Jan. 1879, *Southern Workman* 8 (Feb. 1879):30; S. to the

editor, ibid. 9 (Apr. 1880):42; Coffman to Perry, 30 Oct. 1878, Ashby School Board Papers.

46. D. to the editor, n.d., *Southern Workman* 8 (Oct. 1879):100; George T. Taylor to the editor, 15 Mar. 1875, ibid. 4 (May 1875):39.

47. Gainesville School Board Minutebook, 7 Jan. 1882. Despite the disapproval of state officials, the practice of providing salary incentives to increase attendance persisted in this community until the 1890s. See ibid., 1 Feb. 1879; State Superintendent John E. Massey to George C. Round, undated, Records of the Manassas District School Board, Prince William County School Board Records, Prince William County School Board Records Center, Manassas, Va.

48. D. to the editor, 28 Oct. 1878, *Southern Workman* 7 (Dec. 1878):92; R. to the editor, 24 Dec. 1879, ibid. 9 (Feb. 1880):18.

49. Gainesville School Board Minutebook, 22 Sept. 1877. For a similar example, see ibid., 28 Apr. 1908.

50. For a description of this process, see George E. Caskie, "Needful School Legislation," *Virginia School Journal* 1 (Jan. 1892):10–11.

51. Alfred S. Pryor to W. C. Tate, 1 July 1879, Papers of W. C. Tate, University of Virginia Library, Charlottesville; George S. Funkhouser, teacher's contract, 30 Sept. 1896, Funkhouser Papers; M. to the editor, 23 Mar. 1884, *Southern Workman* 13 (July 1884):82; W. to the editor, 23 Sept. 1875, ibid. 4 (Nov. 1875):87; *Virginia School Journal* 1 (June 1892):174; see also "A Teacher" to the editor, ibid. 2 (Feb. 1893):43.

52. Alexander Truatt, "Reports from Virginia Colored Teachers," *Southern Workman* 10 (Aug. 1881):86; H.J.A. Bryant to the Haytokah District School Board (Nottoway County, Virginia), 4 Oct. 1875, Sydnor Papers; S. to the editor, 19 Apr. 1879, *Southern Workman* 7 (Aug. 1878):60; M. to the editor, 21 Mar. 1879, ibid. 8 (June 1879):66.

53. J. G. Johnson, "A History of Textbook Selection and Use with Particular Reference to the Schools of Charlottesville," *McGuffey Reader* (Charlottesville) 6 (1936):29; *Sixteenth Annual Report of the Superintendent of Public Instruction of Virginia* (Richmond, 1886), p. 19.

54. *First Annual Report of the Superintendent of Public Instruction of Virginia* (Richmond, 1871), p. 195; *Second Annual Report*, pp. 32, 37; *Sixteenth Annual Report*, pp. 16–17, 18.

55. For accounts of the textbook industry, see Henry Hobart Vail, *A History of the McGuffey Reader* (Cleveland, 1910), pp. 39–41, 50–54, 57–62; Johnson, "History of Textbook Selection," pp. 31, 49.

56. Beverly A. Hancock, speech, 20 Nov. 1901, *Report of the Proceedings and Debates of the Constitutional Convention of the State of Virginia Held in the City of Richmond June 12, 1901 to June 26, 1902*, 2 vols. (Richmond, 1906), 1:1161.

57. Ruffner, circular, 24 June 1877, in Johnson, "History of Textbook Selection," p. 47.

58. John A. Nietz, "Why the Longevity of the McGuffey Reader?" *History of Education Quarterly* 4 (1964):120, 121; Vail, *History of the McGuffey Reader*, p. 70.

59. For comprehensive accounts of the history of schoolbooks, see Charles T. Carpenter, *History of American Schoolbooks* (Philadelphia, 1963); Richard D.

Mosier, *Making the American Mind: Social and Moral Ideas in the McGuffey Readers* (New York, 1947); John A. Nietz, *Old Textbooks: Spelling, Grammar, Reading, Arithmetic, Geography, American History, Civil Government, Physiology, Penmanship, Art, Music—As Taught in the Common Schools from Colonial Days to 1900* (Pittsburgh, 1961); and Ruth M. Elson, *Guardians of Tradition: American Schoolbooks of the Nineteenth Century* (Lincoln, Neb., 1964).

60. See *First Annual Report*, p. 195; *Fifteenth Annual Report*, Table 12, pp. 73–75; William A. Link, "Public Schools and Social Change in Rural Virginia, 1870–1920" (Ph.D. dissertation, University of Virginia, 1981), Table 4.9, pp. 124–26; Nietz, "Why the Longevity of the McGuffey Reader?" p. 119; Vail, *History of the McGuffey Reader*, pp. 4, 39–41.

61. George Frederick Holmes, *An Elementary Grammar of the English Language* (New York, 1871), pp. 16, 21, 23, 29, 66; and Matthew Fontaine Maury, *Elementary Geography* (New York, 1882), pp. 4–6. Maury prefaced his book by stating that geography was exposure to "the world and the different kinds of people and animals that live in it. . . . We shall learn a great deal that is new and strange," he warned (ibid., p. 3).

62. Elson, *Guardians of Tradition*, pp. 25–35; William Holmes McGuffey, *McGuffey's Third Eclectic Reader* (Cincinnati, 1879), p. 111; J. Merton England, "The Democratic Faith in American Schoolbooks," *American Quarterly* 15 (1963):197; Holmes, *Elementary Grammar*, p. 18.

63. "Man proposes, but God disposes," readers were reminded (Holmes, *Elementary Grammar*, p. 35).

64. George Frederick Holmes, *Holmes' Third Reader* (New York, 1870), pp. 101–4, 115–18.

65. England, "Democratic Faith in American Schoolbooks"; Nietz, "Why the Longevity of the McGuffey Reader?" p. 123. "Education meant indoctrination," writes England, "indoctrination in the familiar catalogue of moral virtues of Protestant, agrarian-commercial America: industry, thrift, practicality, temperance, honesty, plain living, patriotism, and piety" (pp. 194, 199). As one verse ran in *The McGuffey Reader*,

"I'm a very friendly clock
  For this truth to all I tell,
  Life is short, improve it well."
(*McGuffey's Second Eclectic Reader* [Cincinnati, 1879], p. 80).

66. *Holmes' Third Reader*, p. 111; see also William Holmes McGuffey, *McGuffey's Fifth Eclectic Reader* (Cincinnati, 1879), pp. 162–63; *McGuffey's Third Eclectic Reader*, pp. 72, 158.

67. *Holmes' Third Reader*, pp. 36–37, 129, 152. In another story, a boy was scolded for deception, which was, the author emphasized, "as sinful" as lying (ibid., pp. 122–25).

68. Maury, *Elementary Geography*, p. 21; Maury, *First Lessons in Geography* (New York, 1876), pp. 27, 38; see also England, "Democratic Faith in American Schoolbooks," p. 199; Guyot, quoted in Elson, *Guardians of Tradition*, p. 67.

69. Mary Tucker Magill, *History of Virginia for the Use of the Schools* (Baltimore, 1876), pp. 7, 71.

70. George Frederick Holmes, *A School History of the United States of America* (New York, 1871), p. 3; Ruffner, circular, 24 June 1877, p. 48.

71. Kibler, "Autobiography."

72. Virginia Education Commission, *Report of the Survey Staff*, pp. 86, 88.

73. Johnson, "Autobiography"; Ruffner, circular, 24 June 1877, p. 48; *Holmes' Third Reader*, p. 3.

74. Mrs. Malinda Chance Sumpter, quoted in "Sketches of Early Teachers of Lee County, Virginia," MS in the Library of Congress, Washington, D.C.; *Holmes' First Reader*, p. 4; Nietz, *Old Textbooks*, p. 43.

75. Ruffner to his daughters, 2 Mar. 1873, Ruffner Papers.

76. Edward S. Joynes, quoted in Cornelius T. Heatwole, *A History of Education in Virginia* (New York, 1916), pp. 111–12.

77. Edward Eggleston, *The Hoosier School-Master* (New York, 1928), p. 34.

78. Joynes, quoted in Heatwole, *History of Education in Virginia*, pp. 111–12.

79. Kibler, "Autobiography."

Chapter 4

1. Andrew Jackson Fiedler, "A History of the Educational Journals of Virginia" (M.A. thesis, University of Virginia, 1942), pp. 147–48, 155.

2. "New School Officers—Department of Education," *Virginia Journal of Education* 11 (1918):292–93; William L. Bowden, "History of the Cooperative Education Association of Virginia: An Analysis of a Community Development Agency" (Ph.D. dissertation, University of Chicago, 1958), Appendix A, pp. 512, 531.

3. "Report of the Committee of Twelve on Rural Schools," *Journal of the Proceedings and Addresses of the National Education Association, 1897* (Chicago, 1897), pp. 398–99 (hereinafter cited as *NEA Proceedings*); Wayne Fuller, *The Old Country School: The Story of Rural Education in the Middle West* (Chicago, 1982), pp. 101–2.

4. Henry Sabin, "Horace Mann's Country School," *NEA Proceedings, 1894*, pp. 206, 208; "Report of the Committee of Twelve."

5. David B. Tyack, *The One Best System: A History of Urban Education* (Cambridge, Mass., 1974), pp. 137–47, 182–98. For case studies of the impact of these administrative progressives, see Sol Cohen, *Progressive and Urban School Reform: The Public Education Association of New York City, 1895–1954* (New York, 1964); William H. Issel, "Modernization in Philadelphia School Reform, 1882–1905," *Pennsylvania Magazine of History and Biography* 94 (1970):358–83; Elinor M. Gersman, "Progressive Reform of the St. Louis School Board, 1897," *History of Education Quarterly* 10 (1970):3–21.

6. *Richmond Times*, 16 Mar. 1902. On the origins and composition of the REA, see *Virginia School Journal* 9 (May 1900):132, Louis R. Harlan, *Separate and Unequal: Public School Campaigns and Racism in Southern Seaboard States, 1901–1915* (Chapel Hill, 1958), p. 149.

7. Walter Russell Bowie, *Sunrise in the South: The Life of Mary-Cooke Branch Munford* (Richmond, 1942); Sarah McCulloh Lemmon, entry in Edward T. James et al., eds., *Notable American Women: A Biographical Dictionary*, 3 vols. (Cambridge, Mass., 1971), 2:600–601; Lloyd C. Taylor, Jr., "Lila Meade Valentine: The FFV as Reformer," *Virginia Magazine of History and Biography* 70 (1962):471–87.

8. Mary Munford, "Woman's Part in the Educational Progress of the South," in Samuel C. Mitchell, ed., *The South in the Building of the Nation*, 13 vols. (Richmond, 1909–13), 10:643–44.

9. *Seventh Annual Report of the Richmond Education Association, 1906–1907* (Richmond, 1907), p. 9; *Ninth Annual Report of the Richmond Education Association, 1908–1909* (Richmond, 1909), p. 9.

10. James M. McPherson, *The Abolitionist Legacy: From Reconstruction to the NAACP* (Princeton, 1975).

11. J.L.M. Curry, *Education of Negroes since 1860* (Baltimore, 1894); Ullin W. Leavell, *Philanthropy in Negro Education* (Nashville, 1930); and Harvey Wish, "Negro Education and the Progressive Movement," *Journal of Negro History* 49 (1964):184–200.

12. J.L.M. Curry, *A Brief Sketch of George Peabody, and a History of the Peabody Education Fund through Thirty Years* (Cambridge, Mass., 1898); Hoy Taylor, *An Interpretation of the Early Administration of the Peabody Education Fund* (Nashville, 1933); and Joseph Walter Broujlette, *The Third Phase of the Peabody Education Fund* (Nashville, 1940).

13. Alvah Holvey, *Barnas Sears: A Christian Educator* (New York, 1902); A. D. Mayo, *A Ministry of Education in the South* (Boston, 1889), pp. 3–7.

14. Edith Armstrong Talbot, *Samuel Chapman Armstrong* (New York, 1904); Samuel Chapman Armstrong, *Twenty-two Years of Work at Hampton Institute* (Hampton, Va., 1893).

15. A. D. Mayo, "Services of Dr. Curry in Connection with the Peabody Fund," *Report of the United States Commissioner of Education, 1903*, 2 vols. (Washington, D.C., 1905), 1:524–47; Jessie Pearl Rice, *J.L.M. Curry* (New York, 1949).

16. Dumas Malone, *Edwin Anderson Alderman* (New York, 1940); Rose Holder, *McIver of North Carolina* (Chapel Hill, 1957); John Milton Cooper, Jr., *Walter Hines Page: The Southerner as American, 1855–1918* (Chapel Hill, 1977).

17. Walter Hines Page, *The Rebuilding of Old Commonwealths* (New York, 1902), pp. 120–22; Edwin A. Alderman, "The University and the State in the South," *NEA Proceedings, 1896*, pp. 278–79.

18. Samuel C. Mitchell, "Our Educational Opportunity," letter to the editor, 16 Apr. 1902, *Richmond Times*, 20 Apr. 1902.

19. J.L.M. Curry, "Education in the South," *Proceedings of the Second Capon Springs Conference for Education in the South, 1899* (Raleigh, N.C., 1899), pp. 37–38 (hereinafter cited as *CES Proceedings*, followed by date).

20. Hollis B. Frissell to Julius D. Dreher, 27 Mar. 1899, letterpress book, Papers of Hollis Burke Frissell, Hampton University Archives, Hampton, Va.; Edgar G. Murphy, "The Task of the Leader: A Discussion of Some of the Conditions of Public Leadership in Our Southern States," *Sewanee Review* 15 (1907):21; Edwin A. Alderman, quoted in *Richmond Times-Dispatch*, 23 Mar. 1908.

21. Frissell to Dreher, 27 Mar. 1899; Robert Frazer, "Conditions Relating to Public Education in Virginia," MS report, 24 Mar. 1903, Frissell Papers.

22. Page, *Rebuilding of Old Commonwealths*, pp. 145–46, 150–51.

23. Samuel C. Mitchell, "An Aftermath of Appomattox," MS memoir in the Rare Book Collection, University of Virginia Library, Charlottesville; Wickliffe Rose, "The Educational Movement in the South," *Report of the United States Commissioner of Education, 1903*, 2 vols. (Washington, D.C., 1905), 1:390; Robert C. Ogden, memorandum to the Southern Education Board, 1902, Papers of Robert Curtis Ogden, Library of Congress, Washington, D.C.

24. William E. Garnett, "Training the Future Country Dwellers," *Virginia Journal of Education* 6 (Oct. 1912):15. For other examples, see Booker T. Washington, "Educational Engineers," *Southern Workman* 39 (July 1910):405; and Samuel C. Mitchell, "Some Characteristics of the Southern Renaissance," *Virginia Journal of Education* 3 (Feb. 1910):311.

25. *Biennial Report of the Superintendent of Public Instruction... 1899–1900 and 1900–1901* (Richmond, 1901), pp. xxvi, xxvii.

26. Frissell to Alderman, 10 Jan. 1902, letterpress book, Frissell Papers; J. P. McConnell, "Opportunity of the School Trustee," *Virginia Journal of Education* 11 (Feb. 1918):270; Charles W. Dabney, "The Public School Problem in the South," *CES Proceedings, 1901*, p. 51; Robert Frazer, "Virginia's Educational Outlook," *CES Proceedings, 1902*, p. 36.

27. Frederick T. Gates, "The Country School of To-Morrow," in General Education Board, *Occasional Papers*, no. 1 (New York, 1914), p. 9.

28. Samuel C. Mitchell, "The Task of the Neighborhood," *Southern Workman* 36 (May 1907):266.

29. Charles W. Dabney, "The Rural School as a Center of Country Life," *CES Proceedings, 1912*, p. 149.

30. Joseph D. Eggleston, "Possibilities of Extension Work in Virginia," *Proceedings of the Rural Life Conference Held at the University of Virginia July 13th to 16th 1909* (Charlottesville, 1909), pp. 12–13.

31. Hervin U. Roop, "Some Elements of Model Rural Schools," *Annual Proceedings of the Virginia State Teachers' Association, 1909–1910* (Richmond, 1910), p. 74.

32. Edwin A. Alderman, "The Child and the State," *CES Proceedings, 1902*, p. 58; Alderman, "Northern Aid to Southern Education," *The Independent* 53 (10 Oct. 1901):2411; R. C. Stearnes, "Entering on a Broader Field," *Virginia Journal of Education* 6 (Feb. 1913):223.

33. Samuel C. Mitchell, "The Challenge of the South for a Better Nation," MS in Papers of Samuel C. Mitchell, Library of Congress, Washington, D.C.; Mitchell, "The Ethics of Democracy," MS speech, 30 Dec. 1908, ibid.

34. Edwin A. Alderman, "Sectionalism and Nationality," MS speech, 22 Dec. 1906, Papers of Edwin Anderson Alderman, University of Virginia Library, Charlottesville.

35. Charles W. Dabney, "The Rural School as a Center of Country Life," p. 151.

36. Joseph D. Eggleston, "The Spiritual Basis of Co-operation," *Virginia Journal of Education* 4 (Mar. 1911):377.

37. Murphy, "The Task of the Leader," p. 3; Page, *Rebuilding of Old Commonwealths*, p. 103.

38. J. B. Ely, "The School's Duty to the Community," *Virginia Journal of Education* 1 (Dec. 1907):3; *Richmond Times*, 12 Nov. 1901.

39. Joseph D. Eggleston, "Consolidation and Transportation in Virginia," *Proceedings of the Rural Life Conference Held at the University of Virginia Summer School July 13th to 15, 1910* (Charlottesville, 1910), pp. 254–55.

40. Samuel C. Mitchell, "Some Characteristics of the Southern Renaissance," *Virginia Journal of Education* 3 (Feb. 1910):311.

41. Bruce R. Payne, "Social Service of the Public High School in the South," MS speech, 30 Dec. 1905, Papers of the General Education Board, Rockefeller Archive Center, North Tarrytown, N.Y.

42. W. L. Pickard, "Address of Welcome," *CEA Proceedings, 1906*, pp. 11–12.

43. V. O. Key, *Southern Politics in State and Nation* (New York, 1949), p. 19.

44. Allen W. Moger, "The Origin of the Democratic Machine in Virginia," *Journal of Southern History* 7 (1942):183–209; Charles Wynes, *Race Relations in Virginia, 1871–1902* (Charlottesville, 1966), pp. 51–55; William E. Larsen, *Montague of Virginia: The Making of a Southern Progressive* (Baton Rouge, 1965), pp. 70–88; Henry C. Ferrell, Jr., "Claude A. Swanson of Virginia" (Ph.D. dissertation, University of Virginia, 1964), pp. 103–6.

45. On the Virginia constitutional convention, see Ralph C. McDanel, *The Virginia Constitutional Convention of 1901–1902* (Baltimore, 1928); Raymond Pulley, *Old Virginia Restored: An Interpretation of the Progressive Impulse* (Charlottesville, 1968), pp. 66–68; and, especially, Wythe W. Holt, Jr., "Virginia's Constitutional Convention of 1901–1902" (Ph.D. dissertation, University of Virginia, 1979).

46. William E. Larsen, "Governor Andrew Jackson Montague: Spokesman for the New Virginia" (Masters' thesis, University of Virginia, 1958), pp. 141–43; Ferrell, "Swanson," pp. 164–65.

47. *Richmond Times-Dispatch*, 10 May 1905.

48. Larsen, "Governor Montague," pp. 151–62.

49. Ferrell, "Swanson," pp. 192–97, 199–205; Swanson, address in Richmond, Nov. 1906, printed copy, Papers of James Gibson Johnson, University of Virginia Library, Charlottesville.

50. J. Morgan Kousser, *The Shaping of Southern Politics: Suffrage Restriction and the Establishment of the One-Party South* (New Haven, 1974).

Chapter 5

1. Paul Brandon Barringer to Lila Meade Valentine, 12 May 1902, Papers of Lila Meade Valentine, Virginia Historical Society, Richmond.

2. Wallace Buttrick, quoted in "The Awakening of Caroline County," editorial, *Southern Workman* 43 (June 1914):335.

3. Wickliffe Rose, "The Educational Movement in the South," *Report of the United States Commissioner of Education, 1903*, 2 vols. (Washington, D.C.,

1905), 1:360–61; Charles William Dabney, *Universal Education in the South*, 2 vols. (Chapel Hill, 1936), 2:3–6.

4. Dabney, *Universal Education*, 2:7–8; Robert C. Ogden to Charles D. McIver, 3 Sept. 1904, Papers of Charles Duncan McIver, University of North Carolina at Greensboro Library. See also George Foster Peabody to George S. Dickerman, 27 Aug. 1900, Papers of George S. Dickerman, Southern Education Board Papers, Southern Historical Collection, University of North Carolina, Chapel Hill.

5. McIver to Edwin A. Alderman, 13 Jan. 1902, Papers of Edwin A. Alderman, University of Virginia Library, Charlottesville.

6. Dabney, *Universal Education*, 2:23–24.

7. Ogden to George S. Dickerman, 11 Mar. 1901, Dickerman Papers.

8. William T. Harris to Charles W. Dabney, 29 Nov. 1901, Records of the United States Bureau of Education, outgoing correspondence, Record Group 12, National Archives, Washington, D.C.

9. The Reverend James Cannon, "General Education Board: Our Attitude," letter to the editor, 15 Apr. 1902, *Richmond Times*, 20 Apr. 1902; Barringer to Valentine, 12 May 1902.

10. Page to McIver, 8 Apr. 1902, McIver Papers; Ogden to McIver, 28 Oct. 1904, ibid. See also Ogden to Hollis B. Frissell, 8 Apr. 1902, Papers of Hollis Burke Frissell, Hampton University Archives, Hampton, Va.

11. J.L.M. Curry, "Education in the Southern States," *Proceedings of the Second Capon Springs Conference for Education in the South, 1899* (Raleigh, N.C., 1899), pp. 37–38 (hereinafter cited as *CES Proceedings*, followed by date). For an example of the accommodating attitudes on the part of northerners, see Ogden to Valentine, 13 Apr. 1903, Papers of the Richmond Education Association, Virginia Historical Society, Richmond.

12. Louis R. Harlan, *Separate and Unequal: Public School Campaigns and Racism in the Southern Seaboard States, 1901–1915* (Chapel Hill, 1958); E. C. Branson to Valentine, 27 Oct. 1902, Valentine Papers.

13. See Alderman to Frissell, 23 Nov. 1901, Frissell Papers; Dabney to McIver, 29 Nov. 1901, McIver Papers.

14. Harlan, *Separate and Unequal*, p. 78, n. 14; Murphy to McIver, 4 Apr. 1903, McIver Papers.

15. Frissell, circular letter to public officials of Virginia, undated [ca. 1903], Frissell Papers; Frissell to Henry St. George Tucker, 8 Jan. 1902, Papers of the Tucker Family, Southern Historical Collection, University of North Carolina, Chapel Hill. For other examples, see Frissell to McIver, 31 Dec. 1904; Tucker, MS report, 1904, McIver Papers.

16. Dabney, *Universal Education*, 2:32. Although the towns of Winston and Salem were not united until 1913, I will refer to them as "Winston-Salem."

17. Dabney, "Memoir," MS in Papers of Charles William Dabney, Southern Historical Collection, University of North Carolina, Chapel Hill. For a description of the route of Ogden's train, see "Proposed Itinerary of Hampton-Winston-Tuskegee Excursion," 11 Mar. 1901, Dickerman Papers.

18. Mitchell to Dabney, Dec. 1942, quoted in Dabney, "Memoir"; Alderman to Marcus C. S. Noble, 25 Mar. 1929, Dumas Malone Collection, University of Virginia Library, Charlottesville.

19. "Results of an Informal Conference, Greensboro, N.C., 13 Sept. 1901, of Dr. Frissell, Dr. McIver and Dr. Dabney, with regard to the organization and work of the Executive Board of the Conference for Southern Education," Dabney Papers; Frissell to Dabney, 4 Oct. 1901, letterpress copy, Frissell Papers.

20. Dabney, "The Work of the Bureau," *CES Proceedings, 1902*, pp. 38–39; "Results of an Informal Conference, 13 Sept. 1901," Dabney Papers; "Results of an Informal Conference with regard to the organization and work of the Executive Board of the Winston-Salem conference for Southern Education, held at Asheville, N.C., 14th of September, 1901," Frissell Papers; Minutes of the Southern Education Board, 6 Nov. 1901, Papers of the Southern Education Board, Southern Historical Collection, University of North Carolina, Chapel Hill.

21. "The Southern Education Board: Its Origins, Organization, and Proposed Work," Dec. 1901, Dabney Papers.

22. Curry to McIver, 4 Dec. 1901, McIver Papers. On the SEB's organization, see Ogden to Dickerman, 7 Oct. 1901, Dickerman Papers.

23. McIver to Murphy, 18 Mar. 1903, letterpress copy, McIver Papers; "Report of Robert Frazer," Dec. 1904, Frissell Papers.

24. William L. Bowden, "History of the Cooperative Education Association of Virginia: An Analysis of a Community Development Agency" (Ph.D. dissertation, University of Chicago, 1958), Appendix A, pp. 524–28. For descriptions of the proposed roles of the two agents, see Frissell to Tucker, 31 Dec. 1901, Tucker Family Papers; Frazer to Ogden, 29 Nov. 1901, Papers of George Foster Peabody, Library of Congress, Washington, D.C.

25. Joseph D. Eggleston to Frissell, 19 Feb. 1902, Frissell Papers. I am indebted to Tucker's granddaughter, Mrs. Forrest Fletcher of Lexington, Virginia, for her recollections of Tucker's role in the SEB.

26. Frissell to William H. Baldwin, 19 Nov. 1901, letterpress copy, Frissell Papers. For other accounts of the early campaign in Virginia, see "Report of Robert Frazer," Dec. 1904; Frazer to Frissell, 30 Nov. 1901; and Frissell to Alderman, 10 Jan. 1902, letterpress copy, ibid.

27. Tucker, MS report, in Frissell, MS report to the SEB, 1903, McIver Papers.

28. McIver to Curry, 17 Jan. 1902, letterpress copy, ibid.

29. Frazer to Frissell, 29, 30 Jan. 1902; Eggleston to Frissell, 19 Feb. 1902; Frazer, "Conditions Relating to Public Education in Virginia," MS report, 24 Mar. 1903, all in Frissell Papers.

30. Frazer to Tucker, 17 June 1902, Tucker Family Papers; also Frazer to Frissell, 1 Aug. 1903, and "Report of Robert Frazer, Field Agent of the Southern Educational Board for Virginia," 31 July 1903, both in Frissell Papers; Frazer, MS report, 30 Nov. 1903, McIver Papers.

31. Tucker, MS report, 1904, McIver Papers.

32. "Report of Robert Frazer," Dec. 1904.

33. *Richmond Times*, 13, 14, 16 Feb. 1902; Harlan, *Separate and Unequal*, pp. 147–48.

34. Eggleston to Frissell, 19 Feb. 1902, Frissell Papers.

35. McIver to Frazer, 15 Mar. 1902, letterpress copy, McIver Papers.

36. Frazer to Frissell, 12 July 1902, Frissell Papers; Frazer, MS report, 30 Nov. 1903, McIver Papers.

37. The thrust of the attack is found in Edward Ingle, *The Ogden Movement: An Educational Monopoly in the Making* (Baltimore, 1908).

38. "Report of Robert Frazer," Dec. 1904.

39. Dabney to Murphy, 7 Dec. 1903, copy enclosed in Dabney to McIver, 14 Dec. 1903, McIver Papers.

40. SEB minutes, 12 Jan. 1903, and 10 Aug. 1904. On the change in SEB strategy, see Ogden to McIver, 16, 22 Mar., 25 Apr. 1906, McIver Papers; Ogden to W. E. Gonzales, 28 Mar. 1905, Dickerman Papers.

41. Ogden to Valentine, 8 May 1903, Valentine Papers; Frazer to Tucker, 17 June 1902, Tucker Family Papers.

42. Tucker to Alderman, 9 Jan. 1902, Alderman Papers; Tucker to Frissell, 12 Feb. 1902, Frissell Papers; McIver, speech, 1 Mar. 1902, in *Richmond Times*, 2 Mar. 1902; McIver to Ogden, 28 Feb. 1902, letterpress copy, McIver Papers; *Annual Report of the Richmond Education Association, 1902* (Richmond, 1902), p. 7. For examples of contacts between the Richmond women and groups from provincial towns, see Francis Carter Scott to Valentine, 13 June 1902; Ethel Hall to Valentine, 17 June 1902; and Edwin Christian Glass to Valentine, 10 Mar. 1903, all in Valentine Papers.

43. Frazer to Frissell, 11 Mar. 1904, Frissell Papers; Frissell to McIver, 4 Feb. 1904; Ogden to Mitchell, 10 Mar. 1904, McIver Papers. On the founding of the CEA, see Bowden, "Cooperative Education Association of Virginia," pp. 134–35, 137, 144, 149–50, 174. See also McIver to Frissell, 12 Mar. 1904, letterpress copy; Mitchell to McIver, 28 Mar. 1904, Frissell to McIver, 27 Dec. 1904, all in McIver Papers; Mitchell to Frissell, 14 Mar. 1904, and "Report of Robert Frazer," Dec. 1904, both in the Frissell Papers; *Richmond Times-Dispatch*, 25 Mar. 1904.

44. Walter Russell Bowie, *Sunrise in the South: The Life of Mary-Cooke Branch Munford* (Richmond, 1942), p. 75. On the May Campaign and its consequences, see Dabney, *Universal Education*, 2:325–28; Harlan, *Separate and Unequal*, pp. 150–57; Marjorie F. Underhill, "The Virginia Phase of the Ogden Movement: A Campaign for Universal Education" (Master's thesis, University of Virginia, 1952); Cornelius J. Heatwole, *A History of Education in Virginia* (New York, 1916), pp. 314–16.

45. Quoted in Bowden, "Cooperative Education Association of Virginia," p. 225; *Richmond Times-Dispatch*, 25 Nov. 1909.

46. Joseph D. Eggleston, "Claude A. Swanson—A Sketch," *Virginia Journal of Education* 1 (Oct. 1907):5.

47. Bowden, "Cooperative Education Association of Virginia," pp. 214, 247, 250.

48. Ogden to McIver, 18 Mar. 1904, and McIver's reply, 23 Mar. 1904, letterpress copy, McIver Papers. For an expression of the same change in approach, see Alderman to Wallace Buttrick, 20 Oct. 1904, Papers of the General Education Board, Rockefeller Archive Center, North Tarrytown, N.Y.

49. Raymond Fosdick, *Adventure in Giving: The Story of the General Education Board, a Foundation Established by John D. Rockefeller* (New York, 1962), pp. 5–9.

50. Harlan, *Separate and Unequal*, pp. 85–86.

51. Wallace Buttrick, "The Beginning and Aims of the General Education

Board," *Journal and Proceedings of the NEA, 1903*, p. 121.

52. John D. Rockefeller, *Random Reminiscences of Men and Events* (New York, 1909), pp. 192–93; Fosdick, *Adventure in Giving*, p. 9; William H. Baldwin, "The Present Problem of Negro Education," *Journal of Social Science* 37 (1899):61. For one example of the tendency to confuse the GEB and SEB, see Donald Spivey, *Schooling for the New Slavery: Black Industrial Education, 1868–1915* (Westport, Conn., 1978), pp. 90–94.

53. When the GEB was disbanded in 1960, it had spent almost \$325 million (Fosdick, *Adventure in Giving*, p. 1).

54. Allan Nevins, *Study in Power: John D. Rockefeller, Industrialist and Philanthropist*, 2 vols. (New York, 1953), 2:301; Raymond Fosdick, *The Story of the Rockefeller Foundation* (New York, 1952), pp. 4–6. A revealing analysis of the roots and objectives of Rockefeller philanthropy is provided in John Ettling, *The Germ of Laziness: Rockefeller Philanthropy and Public Health in the New South* (Cambridge, Mass., 1981), pp. 49–72.

55. General Education Board, *The General Education Board: An Account of Its Activities, 1902–1914* (New York, 1914), p. 83; GEB minutes, 28 Mar. 1905; Buttrick to Alderman, carbon copy, 1 Apr. 1905; Bruce R. Payne to Buttrick, 30 May 1905; Buttrick to Payne, 14 Dec. 1905, all in Papers of the General Education Board.

56. Bruce R. Payne, "Report of Secondary Education in Virginia for the Month of February, 1906"; Payne, "Report of Secondary Education in Virginia for the Month of March, 1906," Papers of the General Education Board.

57. Payne to T. O. Sandy, 9 Feb. 1908, enclosed in Payne to Mitchell, 10 Feb. 1908, and Payne to Frissell, 10 Feb. 1908, Papers of Samuel Chiles Mitchell, Library of Congress, Washington, D.C.

58. "Secondary Education in Virginia, Report of Bruce R. Payne for the Month of October, 1906," Papers of the General Education Board.

59. Dumas Malone, *Edwin Anderson Alderman* (New York, 1940), pp. 203–4; Buttrick to Payne, 31 May 1905, Papers of the General Education Board.

60. Payne to Buttrick, 6 July 1907; J. M. Page to Buttrick, 14 May 1914, Papers of the General Education Board.

61. It was significant that Maphis was Eggleston's candidate and that Alderman opposed him. See Alderman to Buttrick, 14, 15 Apr. 1911; Eggleston to Alderman, Feb. 1911; and Buttrick to Alderman, 13 Apr. 1911, ibid.

62. Alderman to Abraham Flexner, 2 Sept. 1919; Harris Hart to Flexner, 17 Dec. 1919; Flexner to Hart, 23 Dec. 1919, ibid.

63. Report of the SEB to the Russell Sage Foundation, 1912, Papers of Albert J. Bourland, Southern Education Board Papers, Southern Historical Collection, University of North Carolina, Chapel Hill; Jesse H. Binford, "The League as a Factor in the Life of the Community," *Annual Report of the Co-Operative Education Association of Virginia, 1912* (Richmond, 1912), p. 10.

64. For descriptions of the role of women in the CEA, see Mary Munford, "Southern Woman's Work in Education," *Southern Workman* 38 (May 1909):266; L. R. Dashiell, "Report of the Organization of Citizens' Leagues in the State of Virginia," *CES Proceedings, 1910*, pp. 286–87; "Co-Operative Education Association of Virginia, Report of J. H. Binford, Executive Secretary for the Quarter End-

ing March 31, 1902," MS in Frissell Papers. On the leagues, see Mercer Weldon Kay, "The History and Significance of the Student Cooperative Association of Virginia" (M.Ed. thesis, University of Richmond, 1957), pp. 6–9.

65. Binford, "Report," *CES Proceedings, 1912*, pp. 325–26.

66. Binford, report of the CEA for the quarter ending 30 Sept. 1912, Bourland Papers; "Minutes of the Executive Committee of the Co-Operative Education Association of Virginia," 29 Dec. 1913, Frissell Papers.

67. Samuel C. Mitchell, "The Task of the Neighborhood," *Southern Workman* 36 (May 1907):266; John P. McConnell to Mitchell, 4 Feb. 1908, Mitchell Papers. See also McConnell to Mitchell, 27 Mar. 1908, ibid.

68. Bruce R. Payne, report for Jan. and Feb. 1909, Papers of the General Education Board.

69. SEB minutes, 2 Feb. 1910; L. R. Dashiell to Frissell, 31 Jan. 1910; Munford to Frissell, 6 Jan. 1911, Frissell Papers; Binford to Stearnes, 4 Aug. 1910, Papers of Reamur Coleman Stearnes, University of Virginia Library, Charlottesville; Jackson Davis, "Education in the South," *Nation* 98 (23 Apr. 1914):458.

70. CEA, memorandum, 1912; Bourland to Binford, 28 Oct. 1913, Bourland Papers; Bourland to Frissell, 21 Nov. 1913, Frissell Papers.

71. The GEB had previously successfully sponsored rural school supervision at the Harrisonburg normal school. See Julian A. Burruss to Wickliffe Rose, 18 Apr. 1910; Rose to Burruss, 26 Apr. 1910; Bourland to Burruss, 31 Oct. 1912, Bourland Papers.

72. Munford to E. C. Sage, 5 Aug. 1914; Munford to Buttrick, 14 July 1914, Papers of the General Education Board.

73. Flexner to Stearnes, 1 July 1914, Stearnes Papers.

Chapter 6

1. These studies have often been referred to as "revisionist." For one example, see Michael B. Katz, *The Irony of Early School Reform: Educational Innovation in Mid-Nineteenth Century Massachusetts* (Cambridge, Mass., 1968). These conclusions have been substantially or in part accepted by Stanley Schultz, *The Culture Factory: Boston Schools, 1789–1860* (New York, 1973); Carl F. Kaestle, *The Evolution of an Urban School System: New York City, 1750–1850* (Cambridge, Mass., 1973); Selwyn K. Troen, *The Public and the Schools: Shaping the St. Louis System, 1838–1920* (Columbia, Mo., 1975); and David B. Tyack, *The One Best System: A History of American Urban Education* (Cambridge, Mass., 1974). A recent study, David John Hogan, *Class and Reform: School and Society in Chicago, 1880–1930* (Philadelphia, 1985), modifies the revisionist view by arguing that a "market revolution" and processes of class formation were instrumental in the coming of reform and modernization. For examples of this approach to the study of rural schools, see William L. Bowers, *The Country Life Movement in America, 1900–1920* (Port Washington, N.Y., 1974), and especially David B. Danbom, *The Resisted Revolution: Urban America and the Industrialization of Agriculture, 1900–1920* (Ames, Iowa, 1979).

2. Michael B. Katz, *Class, Bureaucracy, and Schools: The Illusion of Educational Change in America* (New York, 1971).

3. David L. Carlton, *Mill and Town in South Carolina, 1880–1920* (Baton Rouge, 1982).

4. Edward F. Overton, "A Study of the Life and Work of Joseph DuPuy Eggleston, Junior" (Ph.D. dissertation, University of Virginia, 1943), pp. 275–79; Frank A. Magruder, *Recent Administration in Virginia* (Baltimore, 1912), p. 32.

5. *Twentieth Annual Report of the Superintendent of Public Instruction of Virginia* (Richmond, 1890), Tables 2 and 9, pp. 8–10, 42–44; *Biennial Report of the Superintendent of Public Instruction . . . 1909–1910 and 1910–1911* (Richmond, 1913), Table 7, pp. 237–56; *Annual Report of the Superintendent of Public Instruction of Virginia . . . 1920–21* (Richmond, 1922), pp. 132–34. By 1920, the regional differential in these categories, however, persisted, ranging between 168 days Tidewater counties employed county superintendents to the 300 days urban counties employed theirs. In contrast, most of the state's regions were similar in another respect: the proportion of time county superintendents spent in inspecting schools. Here the only important difference was between urban counties, where superintendents spent less than half their time as compared with the rest of the state in inspecting schools—a figure explained by the growing tendency of superintendents to develop bureaucratic staffs that did the inspecting and which they administered. See Appendix 3.0.

6. *Annual Report, 1920–21*, pp. 132–35.

7. Bruce R. Payne, "Distribution of the High School Fund," in MS report, Mar. 1906, Papers of the General Education Board, Rockfeller Archive Center, North Tarrytown, N.Y.; Overton, "Eggleston," pp. 275–79, 330–34, 366–68; James L. B. Buck, *The Development of Public Schools in Virginia, 1607–1952* (Richmond, 1952), pp. 165–66.

8. Overton, "Eggleston," p. 194.

9. See Appendix 3.1. The Pearson correlation coefficients for wealth and population density and school term show strong correlations between these variables. These correlations are strong and significant at the state level. See Appendix 6.4.

10. White attendance grew from 37 percent in 1900 to 58 percent in 1920; black attendance increased from 25 percent in 1900 to 42 percent in 1920. Appendix 1.5 provides one measure of school availability—schoolrooms per square mile, which increased by 64 percent between 1870 and 1900 and by 32 percent between 1900 and 1920. See Appendixes 1.3, 1.5, 3.2, 3.3, and 3.4.

11. For a breakdown by region and race of percentage of one-room schools in 1920, see Appendix 3.5. For the statistical associations between poverty and sparse population and one-room schools for both races, see Appendixes 6.6 and 6.7. Statistically, the presence and activity of school officials also associated with a lower proportion of one-room schools, although these factors were less consistently important than economic variables. Thus visits from inspectors from the county superintendent's office in 1920 correlated with black one-room schools statewide at $-.29$ (N = 78, p = .01), and a lower level of school inspections associated statewide with a greater number of black one-room schools (r = .31, N = 46, p = .03). The relationship between modernizing

school officials and the disappearance of small schools becomes much clearer in a regional analysis. In Appalachia, for example, the coefficient for days employed of the county superintendent and white one-room schools was −.54 (N = 13, p = .06) and −.42 for state inspections and white one-room schools (N = 21, p = .06); in the northern Piedmont, the coefficient for the number of days county superintendents were employed and white one-room schools was −.68 (N = 13, p = .01).

12. Dumas Malone, *Edwin Anderson Alderman* (New York, 1940), pp. 203–4; Overton, "Eggleston," pp. 261–63, 373; Elizabeth H. Kepner, "Education under Joseph W. Southall, 1898–1906" (M.A. thesis, University of Virginia, 1939), pp. 39, 42; Charles G. Maphis, "State Board of Examiners," *Virginia Journal of Education* 4 (Oct. 1910):13.

13. State Board of Examiners, printed circular, 10 May 1906, Papers of James Gibson Johnson, University of Virginia Library, Charlottesville; E. H. Russell to Mitchell, 11 Feb. 1908, Papers of Samuel Chiles Mitchell, Library of Congress, Washington, D.C.

14. Charles G. Maphis, 1 Sept. 1909, quoted in Overton, "Eggleston," p. 375; *Annual Report of the Superintendent of Public Instruction... 1912–1913* (Richmond, 1915), pp. 19–20; Cox, "The Office of the Virginia Department of Education," p. 119.

15. *Annual Report of the Superintendent of Public Instruction... 1915–16* (Richmond, 1916), ninth summary, p. 82; *Annual Report of the Superintendent of Public Instruction... 1917–18* (Richmond, 1919), pp. 30–37. See also A. B. Chandler, Jr., "Certification of Teachers—New Legislation," *Virginia Journal of Education* 4 (Mar. 1911):398–400; "Kinds of Supervisors," ibid., pp. 349–50.

16. On the origins of these organizations, see R. C. Stearnes to Francis S. Chase, 14 Feb. 1942, quoted in Overton, "Eggleston," pp. 387–89; Rupert Picott, *History of the Virginia Teachers' Association* (Washington, D.C., 1975).

17. *Biennial Report of the Superintendent of Public Instruction... 1907–1908 and 1908–1909* (Richmond, 1910), p. 22.

18. R. C. Stearnes, "Work of the Virginia State Teachers' Association," *Third Annual Bulletin of the Virginia State Teachers' Association* (N.p., 1905), p. 24. Data about membership in teachers' associations are scattered and probably inflated. According to the *Annual Report, 1920–21*, slightly more than two-thirds of the teachers of rural Virginia belonged to professional teachers' associations. These figures were not broken down by gender or race; data were not reported for fourteen counties. Regionally, there was some difference in membership in professional organizations; the highest proportion of membership existed in Appalachia (82 percent) and the urbanized counties (93 percent) and the lowest in the northern Piedmont (58 percent) and Southside (65 percent). See Appendix 3.8.

19. J. R. Hunter, "The Extra-Mural Duties of the Teacher," *Virginia State Teachers' Association, Annual Proceedings, 1911–1912, 1912–1913* (Richmond, 1913), pp. 97–98.

20. Eggleston to A. J. Bourland, 13 Feb. 1911, Papers of Albert J. Bourland, Southern Historical Collection, University of North Carolina, Chapel Hill.

21. S. C. Carrington to Stearnes, 2 Apr. 1906, Papers of Reamur Coleman

Stearnes, University of Virginia Library, Charlottesville; J. F. Britton to the editor, 4 Feb. 1907, *Manassas Democrat*, clipping in Minutebook of the Manassas District School Board, Prince William County School Board Records, Prince William County School Board Records Center, Manassas, Va.

22. J.M.H. Randolph to Stearnes, 10 July 1916, Stearnes Papers. See also Thomas J. Bates to W. G. Rennolds, 1 Dec. [1914?], Papers of William Gregory Rennolds, Virginia State Library, Richmond.

23. Statewide, population density correlated with the number of schools never inspected at − .27 (N = 55, p = .05), but agricultural wealth did not associate. Farm ownership, however, correlated with a lesser degree of involvement in school leagues and membership in teachers' associations.

24. R. Randolph Jones to Sallie Jones, 7, 9 July 1909, Papers of R. Randolph Jones, Duke University Library, Durham, N.C.

25. J. H. Binford, "Rural School Problems," *Virginia Journal of Education* 5 (Nov. 1911):56.

26. *Annual Report, 1915–16*, pp. 32, 82.

27. Mrs. Mary G. Atkins to Rennolds, 11 Aug. 1915, Rennolds Papers.

28. Bush Wilkins, introduction to Stearnes speech, 1916, Stearnes Papers.

29. Virginia Education Commission, *Report of the Survey Staff* (Richmond, 1919), p. 137; J. H. Binford, "What Would I Do?" *Virginia Journal of Education* 9 (Oct. 1915):63.

30. Minnie C. Auderton to Rennolds, 26 Aug. 1915, Rennolds Papers. For another example of such conflict, see Minutebook of the Brentsville District School Board, 10 Mar. 1913, Prince William County School Board Records, Prince William County School Board Records Center, Manassas, Va. For statistics on school session and attendance, see Appendixes 3.1 and 3.2.

31. Overton, "Eggleston," pp. 281, 282; Payne, "Distribution of the High School Fund," MS report, Mar. 1906, Papers of the General Education Board.

32. Charles G. Maphis to W. W. Brierly, 11 Mar. 1916; Maphis, "Educational Progress in Virginia," June 1914–June 1915; Maphis to E. C. Sage, 11 Dec. 1912; Maphis to Buttrick, 15 May 1914, Papers of the General Education Board; A. C. Cooper to Stearnes, 19 Feb. 1917, Stearnes Papers. For an example of the establishment of a district high school, see Brentsville School Board Minutebook, 31 July 1908 and 25 May 1914. A regional breakdown of high school enrollment for both races shows interregional differences by 1920. Among whites, the highest enrollment tended to be in eastern Virginia, especially in counties with a higher percentage of blacks, suggesting that high school expansion diverted significant amounts of funds toward white students and away from black students. The conclusion that early high school development was locally directed and influenced by race is also borne out by statistical correlations, which showed that statewide factors such as black farm ownership and percentage black correspond with higher white school enrollments. See Appendixes 3.6 and 6.8.

33. *Annual Report of the Superintendent of Public Instruction...1914–15* (Richmond, 1917), p. 20; *Annual Report of the Superintendent of Public Instruction...1916–17* (Richmond, 1918), pp. 147, 152; *Annual Report of the Superintendent of Public Instruction...1920–21* (Richmond, 1922), pp. 113–15, 117–19.

34. Joseph D. Eggleston and Robert W. Bruère, *The Work of the Rural School* (New York, 1913), p. 176; Eggleston, "Consolidation and Transportation in Virginia," *Rural Life Conference Held at the University of Virginia Summer School July 13th to 15, 1910* (Charlottesville, 1910), p. 258; L. C. Brogden, G. M. Lynch, and T. S. Settle, "Consolidation of Rural Schools and Public Transportation of Pupils," *Proceedings of the Fifteenth Conference for Education in the South, Nashville, Tennessee April 3d, 4th, and 5th, 1912* (Washington, D.C., 1912), pp. 237–38 (hereinafter cited as *CES Proceedings*, followed by date). See also Otis E. Hall, "How Consolidation Is Effected," Bourland Papers (Bourland sent about one hundred copies of this report to school officials across the South), and A. C. Monahan, *Consolidation of Rural Schools and Transportation of Pupils at Public Expense*, U.S. Bureau of Education, Bulletin 30 (Washington, D.C., 1914).

35. *Biennial Report of the Superintendent of Public Instruction . . . 1899–1900 and 1900–1901* (Richmond, 1901), p. xxxi.

36. Logan W. Page, "Good Roads Mean Better Schools," *Virginia Journal of Education* 4 (Jan. 1911):254–55; *Biennial Report, 1899–1900 and 1900–1901*, p. xxxiii; Eggleston, "Consolidation and Transportation," p. 259.

37. Minutebook of the Ashby District School Board, 4 June 1907, University of Virginia Library, Charlottesville.

38. Hollis B. Frissell, "Report to the Southern Education Board," 1 Oct. 1904, Papers of Hollis B. Frissell, Hampton University Archives, Hampton, Va.; Walter M. Acree to Rennolds, 10 June 1914, Rennolds Papers.

39. *Biennial Report of the Superintendent of Public Instruction . . . 1905–1906 and 1906–1907* (Richmond, 1908), pp. 62, 48.

40. T. S. Settle, report on rural schools in Virginia, 1 Oct. 1911, Bourland Papers.

41. A survey conducted by the Country Life Commission, although unscientific, suggests the prevalence of discontent among rural Americans. See Olaf F. Larson and Thomas B. Jones, "The Unpublished Data from Roosevelt's Commission on Country Life," *Agricultural History* 50 (1976):583–99. On opposition to rural school reform, see Bowers, *Country Life Movement*, pp. 108–9; Danbom, *Resisted Revolution*, pp. 79–81; Clayton S. Ellsworth, "The Coming of Rural Consolidated Schools to the Ohio Valley, 1892–1912," *Agricultural History* 30 (1950): 119–28.

42. George Herbert Betts and Otis Earle Hall, *Better Rural Schools* (Indianapolis, 1914), p. 291. On the legal provisions for school consolidation, see Monahan, *Consolidation of Rural Schools*, pp. 34–43.

43. Ashby School Board Minutebook, 10 May 1910; Jeffries to Rennolds, 28 Sept. 1916, Rennolds Papers.

44. James S. Thomas, "Consolidation of Schools and Transportation of Pupils in Virginia," *Biennial Report, 1905–1906 and 1906–1907*, p. 551. Mrs. J. R. Haile to Rennolds, 8 Sept. 1913, Rennolds Papers.

45. George Hulvey, "The Consolidation of Schools," *CES Proceedings 1903*, p. 87; Manassas School Board Minutebook, 1 Jan. 1900; *Biennial Report of the Superintendent of Public Instruction . . . 1897–1898 and 1898–1899* (Richmond, 1899), pp. xxvii, xxix.

46. "Annual Report of Robert Frazer," MS report, 1905, Bourland Papers; J. H. Binford to Rennolds, 16 Mar. 1916, Rennolds Papers.

47. Frazer, MS report to the SEB, 30 Nov. 1903, in Frissell, MS report, 1904, Papers of Charles Duncan McIver, University of North Carolina at Greensboro Library; MS report of T. S. Settle, 1911, Bourland Papers; Eggleston and Bruère, *Work of the Rural School*, p. 187. See also *Biennial Report, 1905–1906 and 1906–1907*, p. 57.

48. Manassas School Board Minutebook, 26 Aug. 1906, 26 Jan. 1907.

49. Minutebook of the Gainesville District School Board, 27 June 1908, Prince William County School Board Records, Prince William County School Board Records Center, Manassas, Va.

50. Ashby School Board Minutebook, 19 July 1900; Frazer, MS report to the SEB, 14 Apr. 1903, McIver Papers.

51. Brentsville School Board Minutebook, 9 Sept. 1909; Manassas School Board Minutebook, 1 Mar., 22 May, 21, 22 June 1915, 6 May 1916.

52. Virginia Education Commission, *Report of the Survey Staff*, p. 222.

Chapter 7

1. Allen W. Freeman, "The Rural School—An Essential Factor in Sanitary Progress," *Proceedings of the Fourteenth Conference for Education in the South, Jacksonville, Florida April 19th, 20th, and 21st, 1911* (Knoxville, 1911), pp. 203–4, 211 (hereinafter cited as *CES Proceedings*, followed by date).

2. John Ettling, *The Germ of Laziness: Rockefeller Philanthropy and Public Health in the New South* (Cambridge, Mass., 1981), pp. 107–21, 164–66. For further analysis of health conditions, see D. Clayton Brown, "Health of Farm Children in the South, 1900–1950," *Agricultural History* 54 (1979):170–87.

3. Ettling, *Germ of Laziness*, p. 108.

4. Wickliffe Rose to Allen W. Freeman, 26 Nov. 1910, Records of the Rockefeller Sanitary Commission for the Eradication of the Hookworm Disease in the Southern States, Rockefeller Archive Center, North Tarrytown, N.Y. (hereinafter cited as RSC).

5. John A. Ferrell, *The Rural School and Hookworm Disease*, U.S. Bureau of Education Bulletin 20 (Washington, D.C., 1914), pp. 10, 12.

6. Wickliffe Rose to Frederick T. Gates, 25 Oct. 1911; Allen W. Freeman to Rose, 24 Nov. 1911, RSC. For other examples, see "Statistical Report," 1910, and W. A. Plecker to Freeman, 10 Jan. 1911, ibid.

7. Freeman to Rose, 24 Nov. 1911, ibid.

8. Ettling, *Germ of Laziness*, pp. 209–11.

9. W. A. Plecker, "An Appeal to the Teachers—Particularly of Southside and Tidewater Virginia," *Virginia Journal of Education* 5 (Oct. 1911):21. See also "Hygienic Education to Fight the Hookworm," *Review of Reviews* 48 (1913):100.

10. State Board of Education of Virginia to County Teachers, ca. 1911, RSC.

11. Freeman, "Rural School," p. 207.

12. Roy K. Flannagan, *Sanitary Survey of the Schools of Orange County, Va.*, U.S. Bureau of Education Bulletin 17 (Washington, D.C., 1914), pp. 21, 25.

13. Freeman, "Rural School," p. 210.

14. Rockefeller Sanitary Commission for the Eradication of Hookworm Disease, *First Annual Report of the Scientific Secretary for Year Ending January 25, 1911* (Washington, D.C., 1911), p. 27; Freeman to Rose, 25, 30, Nov. 1910, RSC. On the need for the hookworm campaign to improve sanitary facilities in schools, see Rose to Freeman, 8 Sept. 1914; Freeman to Rose, 4 Sept. 1914, RSC. For an overview of the broad effect of the Rockefeller Commission, see Charles V. Chapin, *A Report on State Public Health Work* (Chicago, 1916), p. 185. In 1900, about a third of Virginia rural schools had outhouses. But this average varied regionally, from a high of 72 percent in the Valley to a low of 24 percent in the Southside. See Appendix 1.8.

15. Ferrell, *Rural School and Hookworm Disease*, 41. The state also specified that outhouses had to follow state-mandated guidelines: they had to be at least 4 × 6 feet in size, be made of tongue-and-grooved dressed lumber with galvanized steel roof and blinds, and have two coats of paint. See Minutebook of the Manassas District School Board, 7 Feb. 1913; Minutebook of the Brentsville District School Board, 16 Jan. 1914, both in Prince William County School Board Records, Prince William County Records Center, Manassas, Va.

16. *Bulletin of the North Carolina Board of Health* 27 (June 1912):104.

17. For a discussion of the growing popularity of medical inspection in the South, see Joseph D. Eggleston and Robert W. Bruère, *The Work of the Rural School* (New York, 1913), pp. 31, 33; Dorothy Orr, *History of Education in Georgia* (Chapel Hill, 1950), p. 271; and Chapin, *Report on State Public Health Work*, p. 155.

18. J. G. Johnson, "A History of Textbook Selection and Use with Particular Reference to the Schools of Charlottesville," *McGuffey Reader* (Charlottesville) 6 (1936); J. G. Johnson, "A History of Textbook Selection and Use in Virginia with Particular Reference to the Schools of Charlottesville [and] Books of a High School Grade," *McGuffey Reader* (Charlottesville) 6 (1937); "Course of Study for the Primary and Grammar Grades of the Public Schools of Virginia," 1907, Papers of James Gibson Johnson, University of Virginia Library, Charlottesville.

19. Johnson, "History of Textbook Selection" (1936), p. 68; Daniel T. Rodgers, *The Work Ethic in Industrializing America, 1850–1920* (Chicago, 1978), pp. 125–52; Margaret W. Haliburton, *Playmates: A Primer* (Richmond, 1906).

20. Logan Douglass Howell, *The Howell Second Reader* (New York, 1910), pp. 49–54, 57.

21. Ibid., pp. 57, 117.

22. Philip Alexander Bruce, *A School History of the United States* (New York, 1912), pp. 12, 326–27; J.L.M. Curry, *The Southern States of the American Union Considered in Their Relation to the Constitution of the United States and the Resulting Union* (Richmond, 1895), pp. 3–4, 183; Royall B. Smithey, *History of Virginia: A Brief Text Book for Schools* (New York, 1915), pp. 15–18.

23. Curry, *Southern States*, pp. 230–32.

24. Thomas Jackson Woofter, *Teaching in Rural Schools* (New York, 1917), p.

228; Howard L. McBain, *How We Are Governed in Virginia and the Nation* (Richmond, 1908), p. 4; William E. Fox, *Civil Government of Virginia* (New York, 1904), p. 5.

25. Ferrell, *Rural School and Hookworm Disease*, p. 23; Freeman to Rose, 17 Feb. 1912, RSC.

26. John W. Ritchie, *Primer on Sanitation: Being a Simple Textbook on Disease Germs and How to Fight Them*, rev. ed. (New York, 1919), pp. 170–73; Solomon Weir Newmayer and Edwin L. Broone, *Health Habits* (New York, 1928), pp. 188–91.

27. Rodgers, *Work Ethic*, pp. 24–124; Dominick Cavallo, *Muscles and Morals: Organized Playgrounds and Urban Reform, 1880–1920* (Philadelphia, 1981).

28. Junius L. Merriam, *Child Life and the Curriculum* (New York, 1920), pp. v–vi.

29. Columbus N. Millard, *The Building and Care of the Body* (New York, 1910), p. 210; William O. Krohn, *Graded Lessons in Hygiene* (New York, 1907), pp. 233–35.

30. For a general account, see Alfred Charles True, *A History of Agricultural Education in the United States, 1785–1925* (Washington, D.C., 1929).

31. Quoted in Lex Renda, "The Advent of Agricultural Progressivism, 1900–1916" (seminar paper, University of Virginia, 1984), p. 23.

32. Quoted in ibid., p. 24.

33. F. W. Howe, "School Agriculture in Its Relation to the Community," *Proceedings of the Rural Life Conference Held at the University of Virginia July 13th to 16th 1909* (Charlottesville, 1909), pp. 66, 67, 69; Joseph D. Eggleston, "Public High Schools," *CES Proceedings 1908*, p. 54.

34. Lindsay Crawley, "Sixteen Reasons Why [the] State Should Aid Our Agricultural High Schools," 1916, Papers of Joseph DuPuy Eggleston, Special Collections Division, Virginia Polytechnic Institute and State University Library, Blacksburg.

35. Ibid.; John R. Hutcheson to editor, *Southern Planter* 71 (Oct. 1910):1022. For an example of the founding of an agricultural high school, see Manassas School Board Minutebook, 27 May 1908.

36. Renda, "Advent of Agricultural Progressivism," pp. 26–27; J. S. Cooley to editor, *Southern Planter* 73 (July 1912):782; George C. Round to Eggleston, 10 Apr. 1908, Records of the Manassas District School Board, Prince William County School Board Records, Prince William County School Board Records Center, Manassas, Va.

37. Joseph D. Eggleston, "Extension Work in Virginia," *Virginia Journal of Education* 3 (Oct. 1909):18; Duncan Lyle Kinnear, "A History of Agricultural Education in Virginia with Special Emphasis on the Secondary School Level" (Ph.D. dissertation, Ohio State University, 1952), pp. 301–4.

38. Renda, "Advent of Agricultural Progressivism"; J. S. Cooley to editor, *Southern Planter* 73 (July 1912):782; Lindsay Crawley to Eggleston, 18 Apr. 1917, Eggleston Papers.

39. Kinnear, "History of Agricultural Education," pp. 287, 290–91, 313; L. Crawley, "Agricultural High Schools in Virginia," *Virginia Journal of Education* 10

(1915–16):77; Flournoy McGehee to Eggleston, 6 Apr. 1916; R. R. Tolbert to Eggleston, 10 July 1916; Crawley to Eggleston, 8 Apr. 1917, Eggleston Papers.

40. Eggleston to Crawley, 8 Feb. 1916, 11 Feb. 1917, Eggleston Papers; see also Eggleston to W. G. Wyson, 8 Oct. 1916, ibid.

41. Crawley, "Agricultural High Schools in Virginia," p. 78; O. A. Thomas, "The Functions of an Agricultural High School," *Virginia Journal of Education* 9 (Dec. 1915):177. On the failure of agricultural education, see David B. Danbom, *The Resisted Revolution: Urban America and the Industrialization of Agriculture, 1900–1920* (Ames, Iowa, 1979), pp. 77–79, and Wayne Fuller, *The Old Country School: The Story of Rural Education in the Middle West* (Chicago, 1982), pp. 224–26.

42. R. R. Tolbert to Eggleston, 10 July 1916, Eggleston Papers.

43. W. S. Hale to Stearnes, 6 Feb. 1917, Papers of Reamur Coleman Stearnes, University of Virginia Library, Charlottesville; John R. Hutcheson (state supervisor of agricultural high schools), quoted in Kinnear, "History of Agricultural Education," 321–22.

44. Minutes of the Prince William County School Board, 21 Apr. 1908, Prince William County School Board Records Center, Manassas, Va.; *Manassas Democrat*, Oct. 1911, clipping in Manassas School Board Minutebook; Herbert F. Button, "Agricultural High School at Manassas," *Virginia Journal of Education* 4 (Oct. 1910):29–30.

45. George C. Round to R. C. Stearnes, 6 Aug. 1911, Manassas District Records; Manassas School Board Minutebook, 10, 31 Jan. 1912. For an account of the episode, see R. Worth Peters, "Secondary Education in Manassas, Virginia, 1890–1925" (M.A. thesis, University of Virginia, 1939), pp. 115–17.

46. Crawley, "Agricultural High Schools in Virginia," p. 78.

47. McGehee to Eggleston, 6 Apr. 1916, Eggleston Papers.

48. Charles P. Graham to Eggleston, 17 June 1916; F. Scott Hale to Eggleston, 9 June 1916, ibid.

49. Eggleston to Graham, 11 July 1916, ibid.

50. Crawley, "Sixteen Reasons Why."

51. Renda, "Advent of Agricultural Progressivism," p. 25; Crawley to Eggleston, 6 Mar. 1917, Eggleston Papers.

52. Charles William Dabney, *Universal Education in the South*, 2 vols. (Chapel Hill, 1936), 2:205–6; True, *History of Agricultural Education*; Virginia State Board of Education, *Plan of the State Board for Vocational Education*, Bulletin 1, No. 1, Supplement 2 (Richmond, 1918); U.S. Federal Board for Vocational Education, *Federal Board for Vocational Education, Statement of Policies* (Washington, D.C., 1917); Kinnear, "History of Agricultural Education," p. 369.

53. Seaman A. Knapp, "Farmers' Cooperative Demonstration Work in the Southern States," in Samuel C. Mitchell, ed., *The South in the Building of the Nation*, 13 vols. (Richmond, 1909–13), 10:605–7, 612.

54. Dabney, *Universal Education*, 2:172–204; W. B. Mercier, *Status and Results of Extension Work in the Southern States, 1903–1921* (Washington, D.C., 1921); Grant McConnell, *Decline of Agrarian Democracy* (Berkeley, 1953), pp. 44–46; Joseph C. Bailey, *Seaman A. Knapp, Schoolmaster of American Agriculture* (New

York, 1945); Roy V. Scott, *The Reluctant Farmer: The Rise of Agricultural Extension to 1914* (Urbana, 1970).

55. Danbom, *Resisted Revolution*, pp. 86–96.

56. Knapp, "Farmers' Cooperative Demonstration Work," p. 612; Report of L. Marsh Walker, Albemarle County, Virginia, 20 Oct. 1910, Records of the County Extension Service, U.S. Department of Agriculture, National Archives, Washington, D.C.; see also General Education Board, *The General Education Board: An Account of Its Activities, 1902–1914* (New York, 1914), p. 27; T. O. Sandy, "Farmers' Co-Operative Demonstration Work in Virginia," *Southern Workman* 38 (Feb. 1909):110; J. D. Eggleston, "Historical Statement," 3 Feb. 1916, County Extension Service Records.

57. Jack Temple Kirby, *Westmoreland Davis: Virginia Planter-Politician, 1859–1942* (Charlottesville, 1968), pp. 31–32; Joseph D. Eggleston, *Extension Work in Virginia, 1907–1940* (Blacksburg, 1941).

58. Reports of L. Marsh Walker, Albemarle County, Virginia, 20 Oct. 1910, 1916, County Extension Service Records.

59. E. O. Reynolds, letter to editor, *Stuart* (Va.) *Enterprise*, 4 Feb. 1915, clipping in Eggleston Papers.

60. Report of annual county agents' meeting, Blacksburg, 24–25 Feb. 1913, ibid.

61. "Report of Committee on How to Extend the Club Work and Make It Effective in Counties Where No Agents Are Employed," ca. 1915, ibid.

62. Report of annual county agents' meeting, Blacksburg, Va., 26–30 Jan. 1914, ibid; Jesse M. Jones, "Boys' Club Work in Virginia: Review of This Important Branch of the State's Agricultural Work," *Virginia Journal of Education* 11 (Nov. 1917):109–10.

63. Hollis B. Frissell to Eggleston, 4 Jan. 1915, Eggleston Papers.

64. J. B. Pierce to Eggleston, 20 Feb. 1915; I. W. Hill to Eggleston, 2 Apr. 1915, enclosing "A Plan for the Organization of the Farm Makers' Clubs among Negro Boys in the Southern States"; Pierce, annual report, 1914, ibid. For other discussions of black county agents, see Earl W. Crosby, "Limited Success against Long Odds: The Black County Agent," *Agricultural History* 57 (1983):277–88; and Crosby, "The Roots of Black Agricultural Extension Work," *Historian* 39 (1977): 28–47.

65. Report of county agents' meeting, 1914; "Summary of Home Demonstration Work Done in Virginia for the Year Ending 1915," Eggleston Papers.

66. Report of county agents' meeting, 1914; Report of the Home Demonstration Work, 1915, County Extension Service Records.

67. Rhea C. Scott, "Demonstration Work for Girls," *Virginia Journal of Education* 10 (1915–16):74. See also Ella G. Agnew, "The Story of the First Decade of Home Demonstration Work in Virginia, July 1, 1910–January 1, 1920," MS in author's possession. I am grateful to Harriet S. Tynes and Blackwell P. Robinson of Greensboro, N.C., for bringing this document to my attention.

68. "Report of Rhea C. Scott, Harrisonburg, Va.," 1915, County Extension Service Records.

69. Ella Agnew, weekly reports, 27 Mar., 30 Oct. 1915; "Summary of Home

Demonstration Work," 1915, Eggleston Papers; Report of the Home Demonstration Work, 1915, County Extension Service Records.

70. "Summary of Home Demonstration Work," 1915, Eggleston Papers.

71. Report of county agents' meeting, 1914; Agnew, weekly report, 30 Oct. 1915; "Summary of Home Demonstration Work," 1915, Eggleston Papers.

72. Rhea C. Scott, monthly report, Jan. 1916; Agnew to Eggleston, 8 Feb. 1916; Agnew to Scott, 8 Feb. 1916, ibid. A subsequent investigation of Scott on charges of insubordination was initiated by Agnew, but she was eventually forced to retract the charges. See Charles T. Lassiter to Eggleston, 16 Sept. 1916; Eggleston to Lassiter, 19 Oct. 1916; Agnew to Jesse M. Jones, 23 Oct. 1916; Agnew to Eggleston, 7 Nov. 1916; Lassiter to Jones, 4 Dec. 1916, ibid.

73. Mrs. Maggie King, Alleghany Co., and Mrs. Juliet Gish, in "Report of the Annual Meeting of the County Workers of the Home Demonstration Work in Virginia," 3–8 May 1915; Agnew, weekly reports, 22 Jan., 5 Feb. 1916, all in ibid.

74. Jackson Davis, "Continuation Schools in Virginia," 1914, clipping in ibid. For a discussion of the supervising industrial education, or Jeanes, teachers, see Chapter 8.

75. "Annual Report of L. A. Jenkins, Assistant District Agent for 1915," Eggleston Papers.

76. Ibid.

77. Davis, "Continuation Schools."

Chapter 8

1. C. Vann Woodward, *Origins of the New South, 1877–1913* (Baton Rouge, 1951), pp. 369–95; J. Morgan Kousser, *The Shaping of Southern Politics: Suffrage Restriction and the Establishment of the One-Party South* (New Haven, 1974); and Louis R. Harlan, *Separate and Unequal: Public School Campaigns and Racism in the Southern Seaboard States, 1901–1915* (Chapel Hill, 1958), provide the best descriptions of the relationship between reform and Jim Crow. For more specific studies of progressives and black education, see Judy Mohraz, *The Separate Problem: Case Studies of Black Education in the North, 1900–1930* (Westport, Conn., 1979); Robert G. Sherer, *Subordination or Liberation? The Development and Conflicting Theories of Black Education in Nineteenth Century Alabama* (University, Ala., 1977); James D. Anderson, "Education for Servitude: The Social Purposes of Schooling in the Black South, 1870–1930" (Ph.D. dissertation, University of Illinois, Champaign-Urbana, 1973); and Donald Spivey, *Schooling for the New Slavery: Black Industrial Education, 1868–1915* (Westport, Conn., 1978).

2. Booker T. Washington to James Hardy Dillard, 30 July 1909, in Louis R. Harlan et al., eds., *The Booker T. Washington Papers*, 13 vols. (Urbana, 1972–84), 10:153.

3. Quoted in James D. Anderson, "Northern Philanthropists and the Shaping of Southern Black Rural Education, 1902–1935," *History of Education Quarterly* 18 (1978):392; Jackson Davis, "Practical Training in Negro Rural Schools," *Journal*

of *Proceedings of the Southern Educational Association, 1913* (Birmingham, Ala., 1913), p. 168.

4. Ulrich Bonnell Phillips, *American Negro Slavery: A Survey of the Supply, Employment and Control of Negro Labor as Determined by the Plantation Regime* (New York, 1918), p. 343. On Phillips and southern reform, see Daniel Joseph Singal, *The War Within: From Victorian to Modernist Thought in the South, 1919–1945* (Chapel Hill, 1982), pp. 37–57; and John Herbert Roper, *U. B. Phillips: A Southern Mind* (Macon, Ga., 1984).

5. Samuel C. Mitchell, "My Neighbor, the Negro," address at Hampton, Va., 29 Jan. 1911, *Southern Workman* 40 (Mar. 1911):141.

6. Edwin A. Alderman, "The Child and the State," *Proceedings of the Fifth Conference for Education in the South Held at Athens, Georgia April 24, 25, and 26, 1902* (Knoxville, 1902), p. 60 (hereinafter cited as *CES Proceedings*, followed by date); Charles W. Dabney, "The Public School Problem," ibid., *1901*, p. 62. For general discussions of Victorian attitudes toward race, see Ronald T. Takaki, *Iron Cages: Race and Culture in Nineteenth Century America* (New York, 1979); Reginald Horsman, *Manifest Destiny: The Origins of American Racial Anglo-Saxonism* (Cambridge, Mass., 1981); George M. Fredrickson, *The Black Image in the White Mind: The Debate on Afro-American Character and Destiny* (New York, 1971); and Joel Williamson, *The Crucible of Race: Black-White Relations in the American South since Emancipation* (New York, 1984).

7. George T. Winston, "Industrial Training in Relation to the Negro Problem," *CES Proceedings, 1901*, p. 106; Amory Dwight Mayo, *The Duty of the White American towards His Colored Fellow Citizen* (Washington, D.C., n.d.), pp. 14–15; Mayo, *The Negro American in the New American Life* (N.p., 1889), pp. 3, 7; Hollis B. Frissell, "Negro Education," MS speech, 4 May 1907, Papers of Hollis B. Frissell, Hampton University Archives, Hampton, Va.

8. Booker T. Washington, "Industrial Training for the Negro," 27 Jan. 1898, Harlan, et al., eds., *Booker T. Washington Papers*, 4:367–68; Frissell, letter to the editor, 23 Feb. 1904, *Richmond Times-Dispatch*, typed MS, Frissell Papers; William H. Baldwin, "The Present Problem of Negro Education," *CES Proceedings 1899*, p. 94.

9. "Twenty-Second Annual Report of the Principal for the School and Fiscal Year Ending June 30, 1890," *Southern Workman* 19 (June 1890):63.

10. Samuel C. Mitchell, "The Task of the Neighborhood," *Southern Workman* 36 (May 1907):270; William H. Baldwin, "The Present Problem of Negro Education," *Journal of Social Science* 37 (1899):53.

11. Edwin A. Alderman, "Education for Black and White," *The Independent* 53 (7 Nov. 1901):2648; Alderman, "The Negro," clipping of speech, *New Orleans Times-Democrat*, 20 Jan. 1904, Papers of Edwin Anderson Alderman, University of Virginia Library, Charlottesville. For more on Alderman's racial views, see Alderman, notes for a speech, 7 Nov. 1901, and Alderman to Hamilton W. Mabie, 24 Sept. 1901, ibid.

12. Edgar Gardner Murphy, *Problems of the Present South* (New York, 1904), p. 75.

13. See Charles William Dabney, *Universal Education in the South*, 2 vols. (Chapel Hill, 1936), 1:486–88; Elizabeth Jacoway, *Yankee Missionaries in the*

South: the Penn School Experiment (Baton Rouge, 1980); "Manassas Industrial Institute," undated MS in Papers of the General Education Board, Rockefeller Archive Center, North Tarrytown, N.Y. For discussions of the curriculum of the industrial institutes, see Louis R. Harlan, *Booker T. Washington: The Making of a Black Leader, 1856–1901* (New York, 1972), pp. 52–77, and Harlan, *Booker T. Washington: The Wizard of Tuskegee, 1901–1915* (New York, 1983); James D. Anderson, "The Hampton Model of Normal School Industrial Education, 1868–1900," in Vincent P. Franklin and James D. Anderson, eds., *New Perspectives on Black Educational History* (Boston, 1978), pp. 71–78; and Spivey, *Schooling for the New Slavery*, pp. 16–44.

14. Murphy, *Problems of the Present South*, p. 80; Booker T. Washington, "Some Results of the Armstrong Idea," *Southern Workman* 28 (March 1909):174–75; Hollis B. Frissell, "Negro Education," MS speech, 4 May 1907, Frissell Papers. See also Frissell to Edwin M. Bulkey, 3 July 1906, Papers of George Foster Peabody, Library of Congress, Washington, D.C.; Washington, "Industrial Education," speech before Alabama Teachers' Association, 7 Apr. 1887, Harlan, et al., eds., *Booker T. Washington Papers*, 2:193.

15. Washington, "The Educational Outlook in the South," *Journal and Proceedings of the National Educational Association, 1884* (Madison, Wisc., 1884), p. 126; James Hugo Johnston to S. C. Mitchell, 22 Feb. 1908, Papers of Samuel Chiles Mitchell, Library of Congress, Washington, D.C.

16. William H. Baldwin, "The Present Problem of Negro Education," *CES Proceedings, 1899*, pp. 98–100, 106–7; Ogden quoted in Anderson, "Northern Philanthropists," p. 374; John L. Campbell to James H. Dillard, 9 Feb. 1909, Papers of James Hardy Dillard, University of Virginia Library, Charlottesville. See also Orra Langhorne to Walter Hines Page, 13 Mar. 1902, Papers of the General Education Board, and S. E. Breed, "Industrial Training as a Factor in the Development of the Negro Woman," *CES Proceedings, 1899*, p. 84.

17. *Richmond Times*, 25 Dec. 1901; Hollis B. Frissell, "The Progress of Negro Education," *South Atlantic Quarterly* 6 (1907):43–44; Murphy, *Problems of the Present South*, pp. 63–64.

18. For examples of such opposition or indifference, see Fannie Brown to Rennolds, 1 Mar. 1920, Papers of William Gregory Rennolds, Virginia State Library, Richmond, and William H. Johnson, "The Public School System of Virginia," speech, ca. 1915, Papers of William H. Johnson, Virginia State University Library, Petersburg.

19. Harlan, *Washington: The Wizard of Tuskegee*, esp. pp. 247–51.

20. W.E.B. Du Bois, *The Souls of Black Folk* (1903; reprint, Greenwich, Conn., 1961), pp. 42–54; Du Bois, "The Hampton Idea," in Herbert Aptheker, ed., *The Education of Black People: Ten Critiques, 1906–1930* (Amherst, Mass., 1973), pp. 5–15.

21. Quoted in Anderson, "Hampton Model," pp. 78–84.

22. Ibid., p. 78.

23. For accounts of the strike, see W.E.B. Du Bois, "The Hampton Strike," *Nation* 125 (1927):471–72; "Hampton Tweaks the Reins," *Survey* 59 (1927–28):206; *Southern Workman* 56 (Dec. 1927):544–45, 569–72.

24. Frissell to Morris K. Jessup, 23 Dec. 1898, typed copy, Papers of the South-

ern Education Board, Southern Historical Collection, University of North Carolina, Chapel Hill.

25. On Dillard and the origins of the Jeanes Fund, see Lance George Edward Jones, *The Jeanes Teacher in the United States, 1908–1933: An Account of Twenty-Five Years' Experience in the Supervision of Negro Rural Schools* (Chapel Hill, 1933), pp. 17–19, 20–21; Arthur D. Wright, *The Rural School Fund, Inc. (Anna T. Jeanes Foundation), 1907–1933* (Washington, D.C., 1933); Kara Vaughn Jackson, et al., *The Jeanes Story: A Chapter in the History of American Education, 1908–1968* (Atlanta, 1979); and Harlan, *Washington: The Wizard of Tuskegee*, pp. 194–96.

26. Mitchell to Frissell, 9 Feb. 1906, Frissell Papers. The efforts of the teacher-organizers from Petersburg are discussed in James T. Phillips, "League Work in Negro Schools," *Virginia Journal of Education* 4 (Mar. 1911):409; and Phillips and John M. Gandy, "The Negro Teachers' and School Improvement League of Virginia," ibid., pp. 409–10; James Hugo Johnston to S. C. Mitchell, 26 Feb., 6 Mar. 1908; Dillard to Mitchell, 27 May 1908; John M. Gandy to Mitchell, 27 May 1908, Mitchell Papers; Dillard, "Negro Rural School Fund, Anna T. Jeanes Foundation, Statement I," 3 June 1908, Dillard Papers. On the Hampton effort, see W.T.B. Williams, "Hampton Institute's Extension Work," *Southern Workman* 39 (Jan. 1910):54.

27. Thomas C. Walker, "How to Arouse the Interest of the Community in Schools," *Twelfth Annual Report of the Hampton Negro Conference* (Hampton, Va., 1908), p. 67; see also Dillard, "Negro Rural School Fund, Statement I," 3 June 1908.

28. W.T.B. Williams, "Negro Schools and Educational Progress in the South," *Twelfth Annual Report of the Hampton Negro Conference*, p. 63; "Use of Hampton's Rural School Fund," *Southern Workman* 38 (Feb. 1909):71–72.

29. "Extract from Report of President [Dillard] at meeting held Dec. 16, 1909," MS in Dillard Papers; Jones, *Jeanes Teacher*, pp. 40–45.

30. Jones, *The Jeanes Teacher*, pp. 15–16, 23–25, 26, 28, 29–30, 33; Jackson Davis, "Supervision of Rural Schools for Negroes," 1913, Papers of the General Education Board; Davis to Dillard, 21 May 1908, in Jones, *Jeanes Teacher*, pp. 41–42; Dillard, MS memoir, Dillard Papers.

31. Jones, *Jeanes Teacher*, pp. 47–48.

32. Benjamin Brawley, *Doctor Dillard of the Jeanes Fund* (New York, 1930), p. 62.

33. Dillard to Frissell, 4 Jan. 1912, Frissell Papers; Anderson, "Northern Philanthropists," pp. 382–83.

34. Brawley, *Doctor Dillard*, p. 62.

35. Ibid., p. 60.

36. Virginia E. Randolph, "A Brief Report of the Manual Training Work Done in the Colored Schools of Henrico County, Va. for Session 1908–1909," in Jones, *Jeanes Teacher*, p. 127. See also Dillard, memorandum to the Jeanes board, 20 Sept. 1909, Peabody Papers; Dillard, "Negro Rural School Fund, Statement V," 10 June 1909, Dillard Papers.

37. Davis, "Practical Training," pp. 161–62; "Report of Jackson Davis," 1912,

Papers of Albert J. Bourland, Southern Education Board Papers, Southern Historical Collection, University of North Carolina, Chapel Hill.

38. Samuel L. Smith, *Builders of Goodwill: The Story of the State Agents of Negro Education in the South, 1910 to 1950* (Nashville, 1950), pp. 64–68.

39. Ibid., pp. 52–53; Edwin R. Embree, *Julius Rosenwald Fund: Review of Two Decades, 1917–1936* (Chicago, 1936), p. 23; Edwin R. Embree and Julia Waxman, *Investment in People: The Story of the Julius Rosenwald Fund* (New York, 1949), pp. 37–59.

40. Thomas Jesse Jones, *Educational Adaptations: Report of Ten Years' Work of the Phelps-Stokes Fund, 1910–1920* (New York, 1920), pp. 63–64, 67, 68.

41. Dabney, *Universal Education*, 2:457.

42. Thomas Jesse Jones, *Negro Education in the United States* (Washington, D.C., 1917). On the impact of *Negro Education*, see George B. Tindall, *The Emergence of the New South, 1913–1945* (Baton Rouge, 1967), pp. 268–69.

43. *Annual Report of the Superintendent of Public Instruction . . . 1920–21* (Richmond, 1922), pp. 122–23.

44. For more explicit elaborations of the racial politics of educational reform, see Harlan, *Separate and Unequal*, and Lester Lamon, *Black Tennesseans, 1900–1930* (Knoxville, 1977), pp. 59–87.

45. Jackson Davis to Buttrick, 20 Feb. 1914, Papers of the General Education Board.

46. Dillard, "A Happy Development: Story of County Training Schools," in *Selected Writings of James Hardy Dillard* (Washington, D.C., 1932), p. 17.

47. Dillard, introduction to "Courses of Study for County Training Schools for Negroes in the South," Mar. 1917, MS in Papers of the General Education Board.

48. Davis, memorandum, "Policies Concerning the County Training Schools," 17 May 1919, ibid.

49. Charles K. Graham to Davis, 17 June 1915; Flexner to Davis, carbon copy, 23 June 1915, ibid.; Davis, "Practical Training," p. 165.

50. Henry A. Bullock, *A History of Negro Education from 1619 to the Present* (Cambridge, Mass., 1967), pp. 158–59; James H. Dillard, "County Machinery for Colored Schools in the South," *School and Society* 6 (8 Sept. 1917):293–95; Davis, "County Training Schools," MS, enclosed in Buttrick to Davis, 29 June 1918; Leo Favrot to E. C. Sage, 2 Apr. 1917, Papers of the General Education Board.

51. MS report, 1917–18, Papers of the General Education Board; Leo M. Favrot, *A Study of County Training Schools for Negroes in the South* (Charlottesville, 1923).

52. E. C. Sage, confidential memorandum, "County Training Schools for Negroes," 15 Nov. 1915, Papers of the General Education Board.

53. Robert R. Moton, "Signs of Growing Co-Operation," *Southern Workman* 43 (Oct. 1914):555; Davis, "Practical Training," pp. 162–63.

54. "Introduction," *Fourteenth Annual Report of the Hampton Negro Conference* (Hampton, Va., 1910), pp. 13–14.

55. W.T.B. Williams, "The Negro Organization Society," *Fifteenth Annual Report of the Hampton Negro Conference* (Hampton, Va., 1911), p. 68; Allen W. Washington, "Teaching Men to Live: Work of the Negro Organization Society of Vir-

ginia," speech at Hampton, 26 Apr. 1917, *Southern Workman* 46 (July 1917):402. On the NOS and its extensive impact in the twentieth century, consult Elizabeth Cobb Jordan, "The Impact of the Negro Organization Society on Public Support for Education in Virginia, 1912–1950" (Ed.D. dissertation, University of Virginia, 1978).

56. "Virginia's Negro Teachers' Association," *Southern Workman* 46 (May 1917):264.

57. Williams, "Negro Organization Society," p. 67; "The Negro Organization Society," *Southern Workman* 40 (May 1911):262.

58. The Reverend A. A. Graham, "Negro Progress and Self-Help," *Hampton Negro Conference, 1911*, p. 75; Booker T. Washington, "What Co-Operation Can Accomplish," speech before the NOS, 12 Nov. 1914, *Southern Workman* 48 (Dec. 1914):660.

59. On the Commission on Interracial Cooperation and interracialism, see Ann Wells Ellis, "A Crusade against 'Wretched Attitudes': The Commission on Interracial Cooperation's Activities in Atlanta," *Atlanta Historical Journal* 23 (1979):21–44, and Morton Sosna, *In Search of the Silent South: Southern Liberals and the Race Issue* (New York, 1977), pp. 20–41, 105–20.

Afterword

1. U.S. Department of Commerce, Bureau of the Census, *1980 Census of Population* (Washington, D.C., 1983), vol. 48, Table 8, p. 23; ibid., Table 3, pp. 34–35.

2. These per capita income statistics, as I noted earlier, are at least partly a reflection of the suburbanization of northern Virginia. See ibid., vol. 48, Table 203, pp. 46–57; W. Vance Grant and Thomas D. Snyder, *Digest of Education Statistics* (Washington, D.C., 1984), Table 11, p. 16.

3. Nationally, per capita expenditures for public education in 1981 were $643.51; in Virginia they were $627.55 (Grant and Snyder, *Digest*, Table 11, p. 16).

4. Ibid, Table 51, p. 62.

5. Diane Ravitch, *The Troubled Crusade: American Education, 1945–1980* (New York, 1983).

6. Nationally, median rural black family income was $10,747 and that for whites was $18,520; in Virginia, the same figures were $12,705 and $17,962 (*1980 Census of Population*, vol. 1, Table 297, pp. 489–90; ibid., vol. 48, Table 238, pp. 872–73).

Index

Adult education, 91; and county extension, 166–69; and home demonstration, 169–72
Africa: racial development of, 175
Agnew, Ella, 169
Agricultural high schools: purposes of, 161–62; creation of, 162; curriculum in, 162–63; problems in, 163–66
Agricultural wealth: in northern Piedmont, 12; in Shenandoah Valley, 12; in Southside, 12; and enrollments, 21; and school expenditures, 22, 230 (n. 51); and attendance, 55–57; and teachers' salaries, 58, 238 (n. 30); and modernization, 130–31, 135; and school session, 230 (n. 51), 250 (n. 9); and school inspection, 252 (n. 23)
Alderman, Edwin Anderson, 84, 92, 107; and GEB, 118–19, 122, 150
Alexandria County, Va., 22
Amelia County, Va., 58
American Missionary Association, 82
Appalachia (Va.), 10, 12; economic change in, 129
Appomattox Agricultural High School, 163
Arabs, 67
Arkansas: school consolidation in, 143
Armstrong, Samuel Chapman, 82, 101, 176, 177
Asia: racial development of, 175
Attendance: in American rural schools, 6; and child labor, 6, 54–57; impact of sparse population on, 37; state requirements for, 37, 46–

49, 235 (n. 1); of blacks, 41, 55; factors behind truancy, 53–57; and poverty, 56; in Northeast and Middle West, 56-57; reformers advocate changes in, 90; growth in after 1900, 129, 131, 137; expansion of, 228 (n. 41), 236 (n. 15), 250 (n. 10); and race, 237 (n. 23)

Bailey, Liberty Hyde, 161
Baldwin, William Henry, Jr., 176
Baptists, 34, 116
Barbour, John S., 95
Barren Ground (1925), 13
Barringer, Paul Brandon, 162
Better Farming Day, 122
Better Health Day, 122
Binford, Jesse H., 121, 135
Black education: and fears of slave literacy, 8; and missionary schools, 8, 81–82, 101; incorporation of into southern public school system, 8–9; adopted in postbellum Virginia, 17–18; white opposition to, 18–20; and school administration, 39–40; and school finance, 40–41; and autonomy, 41–43; and black teachers, 42, 58; overcrowding in black schools, 51–52; role of black teachers, 61; and higher education, 82; and abandonment by northerners, 103–4; and reform, 173–74; and industrial education, 177–82; and Jeanes teachers, 183–89; and county training schools, 189–91; and NOS, 191–93

265